ROYAL AGRIC

International Business Culture

third edition

Terry Garrison is Professor of International Business
at Henley Management College and
Leader of the Strategy Faculty

DEDICATION

For Judith Ann

Ne ingrati videamur

International Business Culture

third edition

Professor Terry Garrison

ELM Publications

This third edition of **International Business Culture** is published July 2001 by ELM Publications/Training, Seaton House, Kings Ripton, Huntingdon, Cambridgeshire PE28 2NJ.

Telephone: 01487 773254 (orders)
or 01487 773238 (tutors/editorial)
Fax: 01487 773359
email elm@elm-training.co.uk
www.elm-training.co.uk

Printed by St Edmundsbury Press, Newmarket Industrial Estate, Minden Road, Bury St Edmunds, Suffolk, England.

ISBN 1 85450 290 5

British Library Cataloguing-in-Publication Data. A catalogue record for this publication is available from The British Library.

CONTENTS

Part One – Text

v

Part Two – Case Studies

LIST OF EXHIBITS, FIGURES AND TABLES
Chapters 1 – 8

PREFACE

This book represents an unusual and ambitious attempt to meet a substantial need in an increasingly important management field: cross-cultural management. It is a novel contribution in two ways. Firstly, its focus is not just on the popular aspects of different behaviours, typically exhibited in teamwork involving people from different nations, but on the rationales for those behavioural stances. Thus, the book throws some light on the question *what*? but seeks to more strongly illuminate the question *why*? In so doing it distinguishes between the superstructure of a nation's business culture and the *bedrock*.

The first is relatively easy to assimilate because it is immediately visible. It concerns how individuals communicate with, and behave towards, one another in business contexts. It involves such issues as whether a country's trains run on time and whether its workers strike rarely or frequently. It reflects the relative status of parts of the nation's business life, like financial services and manufacturing, and how business people tend to view the activities they involve. There are many books which offer detailed advice on how to deal with super-structural matters.

The bedrock is a more difficult proposition to pin down. It deals with what we commonly call the issue of *where these people are coming from*. It focuses on key factors, often invisible and always difficult for a foreigner to make out, which shape and predetermine the visible super-structure of someone else's country. Factors like that of a nation's politics, or its economics, or even its religions. Perhaps the key drivers stem from the country's current circumstances. Maybe they are the product of important episodes in that nation's history which have left an indelible mark. Almost certainly they involve deeply-ingrained values.

Either way, the bedrock factors of many nations' business culture tend to be, at one and the same time, strategic and heavily under-researched and under-publicised. Yet they are, as this book seeks to indicate, of vital importance for all those involved in international management activity. They need to be understood if only because they indicate whether the major trading countries of the world are all competing on the same basis. As the book's discussion of *corporatism* and *individualism* shows, we are far from doing so.

The second area of contribution is in the extent to which the book covers the interplay between national business cultures and the cultures of companies. Whilst this book is not intended to be a breakthrough contribution to theory in this field, it does contain a modicum of theoretical perspective. Its main aim, however, is to show why an understanding of a nation's business culture bedrock is vital to the business analyst, to indicate which factors are of major importance in cross-cultural work and, lastly but not least, to provide contemporaneous case examples that illustrate clearly how bedrock factors impact. It is a book for the practitioner who needs to raise his or her cross-cultural awareness by a substantial amount. In this way, a particular feature that will be found of value is the Triangle Test©, a methodology for use by members of international teams to help pose questions with their partners about important, but often undisclosed, differences of attitude, viewpoint and values. The Triangle Test © will be found of great value as a business culture audit tool for use in joint venture situations.

Another novel feature of the book is the fact that its analytical toolkit deals less with the common currency of inter-cultural analysis (sociology and anthropology) than with economics and political science. In so doing, it will be found of value to those concerned with the *hard* differences between national cultures, as opposed to the *soft*. Of the need for this treatment of the subject the author has little doubt. Over the entire world companies are focusing more and more on their ability to forge joint ventures and alliances – to build business federations. They need to be aware of more than just the phenomena of actual and potential business partners' behaviours and sociological explanations for them. They want to know about the economic and political *whys*? This is what the book is predominantly about. It is hoped it will provide much that is of value to those who wish, and increasingly need, to learn. As the German proverb has it, *andere Länder, andere Sitten* – other countries, other customs – a trust we all need to relearn over and over again in these challenging multicultural times.

Terry Garrison,
Henley Management College,
June 2001

CHAPTER 1

An Introduction to International Business Culture

■ The Need to Know: a strategic perspective

Imagine for a moment that you work for Krauss-Maffei Wegmann, the builders of Germany's world-famous Leopard tank. Or for Alvis, the British defence specialist which makes Britain's war-tested Warrior armoured personnel carrier, having acquired GKN's tank division in 1999. You are a professional engineer-manager with a track record of high-level technical success behind you, but you have never worked outside your own country nor in any cross-border collaborative venture. Now, for the first time in your career, you are faced with a somewhat worrying and novel test of your competence: working within an embryonic Anglo-German joint venture to develop a shared product, the so-called European Battlefield Taxi. It is scheduled to enter service in 2006.

It is a time of some anxiety for you, but not because you doubt your abilities as an engineer. Of these there is no question. Dealing with strangers from another country, even highly qualified engineers like yourself, is quite another matter. What will they be like? Where, as we say, will they be coming from? What priorities will they have? Will they actually seek to share in the creative endeavour or simply want to frustrate what you want? Will they try to take the project over? How will they behave? Do they communicate as you do? What's their chain of command like? Are they paid on the same basis as you are? Does their company value their services as engineers? The questions come thick and fast.

And they all relate to the central issue of business culture: the often _implicit_ and _internalised_ codes of thinking and behaviour which govern our approach to business and which can differ from those of other nations' codes.

1

Many questions have to do with the most serious matter of all: your (and your cross-border partner's) perception of who might win and who might lose in the relationship, if, in fact, it turns out not to be the positive sum game you are hoping for. Whatever else, Table 1.1 below alone may lead you to suspect that some very basic differences between Germany and Britain could affect attitudes towards project leadership within a joint venture.

Element	Nation		
	Germany	France	UK
Area (Sq km, k)	357	552	244
GDP ($ bn)	2260	1465	1433
GDP/head ($ k)	27.3	24.9	23.9
Population (million)	81.9	58.3	58.1
Stock market capitalisation ($ bn – end 1997)	825.2	674.3	1996.2
Unemployment (% - end 1998)	9.1	11.3	6.3

TABLE 1.1: A THREE-NATION COMPARISON

Source: *The Economist*, The World in 2000, L'Etat du Monde, *La Decouverte*, 2000 and William Mercer, *The Sunday Times* 2/7/2000

Of course, you may very well already be a seasoned international traveller, or even have experience of working as an expatriate manager in an overseas division of your company. Indeed, you might have carried out many negotiations, either as an export manager or as a member of just such a cross-border team as will be involved with the Battlefield Taxi. If you have such experience, you will know that we can always limit our business risks and enhance our successes by knowing more about those with whom we deal. The inexperienced have much to learn since ignorance in matters inter-cultural can never amount to bliss.

Here, so far as the Battlefield Taxi project is concerned, a basic knowledge of European politics and economics is needed as a background to understanding differences between the business culture approaches of both sides.

■ Business Culture and the case of the Battlefield Taxi

The Battlefield Taxi case results from the facts that, at the Farnborough Air Show in 1998, France, Germany, Britain and Italy signed a treaty to create an embryonic European arms procurement agency (Occar, based in Bonn). Wegmann and GKN, the then-leading project sponsors, were delighted that Occar was committed to purchasing a common fighting vehicle for use by the first three countries and were enthusiastic about the prospects for collaboration among European arms makers. Giat was the French partner in the £3 billion collaborative programme until, in 1999, the French government decided to withdraw, having decided that it wanted a more heavily-armoured vehicle than was reportedly being planned. This pull-out was widely regarded as a major blow to efforts at European defence collaboration.

As can be easily appreciated, the Occar move promised to reduce the amount of competition in the European defence industry and lessen the business risks involved for survivors. It would also serve, it was hoped, to strengthen European producers against their American rivals. Thus, it was envisaged that central purchasing would bring about

- a necessary and desirable transformation in the ownership and alliancing pattern of European firms which furthered the possibility of collaboration; and
- a framework for containing the potential acrimony and possible dog-eat-dog rivalry that might have erupted among European producers (and their governments) had there been no agreement to manage defence procurement on a supranational basis.

The principal reasons for Occar were firstly, that the cost of armaments was so high that each country in Europe needed a supplier with the lowest possible prices (i.e., the biggest economies of scale). Secondly, Occar was designed to cope with the problems that countries were typically disposed to giving preference to their own domestic producers, even when their comparatively small production volumes prevented them from setting attractive prices, and to insist in any international collaboration on the principle of *juste retour.* Under this principle you insist on getting a work share which is in direct proportion to your national financial contribution. Such factors are of great importance because they often influence salient aspects of a nation's thinking about how commerce should be handled, in other words, its business culture.

In the past, any European country's reliance on its own domestic arms makers was, of course, habitual and ingrained in its culture – its normal way of managing its own affairs. Placing business with domestic suppliers was done both as a matter of national interest and pride, and for reasons of keeping up employment in what was, for most countries, one of the highest value-adding industrial sectors. Problematically in the late 1990s, the result often was defence firms which were too small to survive in a more open business world and which needed friends – either domestic or cross-border – to keep them company. At this time, a protectionist approach like this could no longer be justified, even by the richest European countries, because of economic pressures and a falling demand for defence products.

A third reason for Occar was that the defence industry in the USA had become concentrated as never before, with mergers and take-overs increasingly common. Whilst this change was no more than a logical response to the inevitable consequences of a decline in the amount of arms money being spent by the Pentagon, its effect on the world trading picture was staggering. The minute an enlarged US arms supplier became more competitive in its domestic market through better scale economies and a reduced volume of competition, it became, *ipso facto*, more capable of winning a bigger share of the shrinking world trade in arms. Under such circumstances, the American gain would inevitably be the European loss, unless, that is, its arms makers could somehow begin to work together defensively for their common good

Hence, these three reasons combined to oblige European countries to join a collaborative purchasing system and to push their producers into joint ventures and alliances. Depending on whether they viewed the outcome as positive or negative, individual countries put a different slant on what was really *force majeure*. All members would lose some national sovereignty merely from the fact of pooling control over arms supply. Some would even lose some of their more famous factories, once they were shown to be uncompetitive, since they could no longer shelter behind a domestic monopoly. Some might even, unless they were covered by an European equivalent of the sort of anti-acquisition poison pill defence used by some major companies in the USA, themselves become take-over targets for foreign buyers. Whichever outcome occurred, their individual business cultures would be significantly affected by the fact of having to work together for mutual benefit.

Those companies who, like Krauss-Maffei Wegmann, had much to gain from collaboration (and much to lose from its absence) revealed a highly positive attitude. Others were pleased that decisions about their competitors were to be taken out of the hands of national governments, which had traditionally protected their own defence suppliers. Some politicians might have been delighted that unpleasant decisions (say, about plant closures in their region) were in future to be taken at a supra-national, and not national, level. They could avoid blame. France, as we have seen in the Battlefield Taxi context, took a radically different view of its defence needs and seemed to place a higher *value* on its national interest than on the *value* of European co-operation.

Why is it important to know of the political and economic background to Occar and the Battlefield Taxi situation and of what nations value? Simply because the study of business culture does not only involve analysing people's physical behaviour in a social context – as driven by anthropological, sociological and even psychological factors – but also developing insights into the drivers which pre-determine and shape it. These can be political. They can be economic. They may even be religious.

Whatever the macro picture, in our example you are now involved as a professional engineer in a joint trans-national venture of high technical complexity. The contract has been a long time coming but is now agreed. The German and British governments pledged in November 1999 to buy 2000 Battlefield Taxis at a price of £2 billion for delivery in 2006. The design phase alone is worth £70m.

From now on as a team member, unless there are very tight culture specifications governing the way of working across the borders, you may find yourself asking increasingly searching questions, such as "Who is in charge?" "Whose rules apply?" "Whose design is best?" "Where will everything be made?" "Who will be the dominant partner if there is no absolute leader?" "How will my partners view my qualifications and technical expertise as against theirs?"

Additionally, remember that this is a project which is driven by the politics of international defence procurement and one to which there is no realistic alternative. *You may, therefore, be involved in a marriage of business convenience with substantial political ramifications.* Under such circumstances, knowing more of your future collaborators and what makes them speak and act as they do is mere common sense.

Of course, the example given so far is not an isolated instance of the need for managers to be increasingly more aware of how people abroad manage their affairs. All over the world mergers, take-overs, alliances and joint ventures are coming into existence at an unparalleled rate for the soundest of economic reasons – pooling technology cost, achieving scale economies, accessing partners' markets and so on. The more it becomes a matter, as in this case, of strategic necessity, the less choice you have about whether you need to learn more of the business culture of the corporate foreigner.

■ Whose Rules Rule?

The export manager has always had this need to know as much as possible about the business culture of customers. Without his or her knowledge of the habits and customs of clients abroad and, of course, insights into the political and economic context in which they work, export sales are well-nigh impossible. For multinational companies operating around the globe, a detailed central awareness of the differing mind-sets and approaches to managing money or human resources or time that exist at the company's periphery, i.e., in the company's decentralised country divisions, is indispensable. Or so you would think.

In the heyday of Britain's global empire there was, however, comparatively little concern for the preoccupations and mind-sets of the global multitude that was governed. It was simply a case of *Rule Britannia*. The balance of power between the centre and the colonial periphery – London and Kingston, Jamaica, for instance – meant that the commercial behaviour norms decided upon by the British government and city of London became standard practice throughout. Britain's business culture framework was imposed, in fact, firstly, by force and, secondly, by civilising politics.

Implicit and explicit political and commercial rules can mean standardisation of activities, approaches and thought processes which, in their turn, develop into cultural habits. The USSR of Stalin, Kruschev, Andropov and Brezhnev had a consistent culture pattern, as did the German civil service regime instituted in Bismarck's Germany and observable today. In the New Economy world of money-minded American multi-nationals there is a requirement for standardised rules on, say, employing people or managing assets for shareholder value. These rules create a pattern of homogeneous business culture.

If you are the dominant partner in a political (or business) relationship and control the resources and all the motivational carrots and sticks, such as Britain was in colonial times, then you may not want to share the power but simply to give the orders. Your partners may obey, willingly or grudgingly or not at all. At all events, you might tend to under-estimate the feelings of those on whom you seek to impose your version of the truth or, more popularly your culture. A dangerous set of circumstances.

Country	Country allows TV pictures of		General Regulatory Climate		
	Nudity	Hard Pornography	Lenient	Moderate	Severe
France	Y	Y	Y		
Germany	Y	Y	Y		
Ireland	N	N			Y
UK	Y	N		Y	

TABLE 1.2: DIFFERENT ATTITUDES TO ON-SCREEN PORNOGRAPHY
Source: *The European* 9-15/11/95. Legend: Y=Yes N=No

In the past, *ethnocentrism*, the feeling that your approach is naturally and inevitably superior to anyone else's, triumphed under many authoritarian regimes, like Hitler's, and is an ever-present danger in any partnerships among unequals. *Xenophobia* thrives in conditions of ignorance and inequality, also. This is a distaste, even a contempt or hatred, of foreigners based simply on the fact that they are different or, more importantly in a particular space-time context, inferior. This is the way in which the Romans viewed barbarians, for example, or the manner in which Spanish conquistadors treated the indigenous inhabitants of Central America. Of course, in our enlightened world, there is no place for the bigotry that accompanies both of these negative features of culture. Or, at least, judging by Table 1.2 page 7, we might hope so.

The European business world has been much influenced in the last three decades by the industrial and commercial rule-making paradigms or models provided by the USA, Japan and Korea. Reasons of profitability and cost-effective management have dictated new working practices often originating in the success of (say) *kaizen* (total quality thinking), *just-in-time* logistics and *shareholder value* in these countries' domestic systems. Naturally enough, if we are wise, we copy aspects of the business culture of others in order, by analogy, to try to share in their success.

So different is the commercial context today from what it was in the eighteenth and nineteenth centuries, and even for that matter in the 1980s, that no company or nation, however mighty, can afford the arrogance of not knowing or caring what others think or do. As never before, as Table 1.3 page 9 indicates, we are part of an interdependent global trading system. Unless we have the might of America, we cannot arbitrarily aspire to set the rules for others' commercial behaviour, even if we want to, however hard we might try. But we possibly can try to figure out common rules to which we can all subscribe.

Moreover, it takes little ingenuity to figure out the main consequence of this commercial togetherness: the internationalisation of business. By this is meant not only rising cross-border trade but also the increase in cross-border mergers, take-overs, alliances and joint ventures between erstwhile competitors who intend somehow to curb the negative consequences for their companies of an unchecked rise in global competition. Either way, more knowledge of foreign business cultures is needed by all those playing the trans-national business game.

For firms to have cross-border alliances in marketing and manufacturing is easier said than done. Clear though the logic of co-operation is, the risks involved in working with foreigners, who may have different rules on how business should be done, raise the stakes considerably. It is no easy matter to arrange the mechanics and finance of a joint venture or alliance and then try to approximate the underlying, perhaps divergent, business cultures to fit the *togetherness* equation.

(1)	The increasing cost of (i) research and development into advanced technology products or services like genetic engineering, aerospace and multimedia and (ii) capital investment in technology-intensive industries and (iii) technological isolation (and consequent business failure) of the marginal competitor who cannot spend enough to stay in the high technology race.
(2)	The increasing difficulty of recouping high fixed cost levels unless mass sales are achieved. Since mass sales are clearly problematic in any one country, or even trade bloc, an international presence is necessary for any company that wants to remain in business as a leader. The alternative, of course, is to become a supplier or sub-supplier to such leaders. Or to become a high-margin niche player, if that can be done.
(3)	The need to manufacture in the most cost-effective parts of the world and sell in the richest, bearing in mind the transportation and distribution costs.
(4)	The increasing difficulty of penetrating trade blocs (EU, NAFTA, Asia Pacific) outside your own, on grounds of marketing cost, transportation difficulty and/or residual protectionism.
(5)	The increasing commoditisation of products, i.e. the loss of status of individual brands and the consequent rise in price competition. If everyone manufactures to the same exacting standards as required by international consumers who think alike, then price can become the key variable even in the knowledge-intensive service sector.
(6)	The increasing applicability/exportability/mobility of high-grade, once even arcane, technology. It is now possible to move technology quite easily from high-cost developed nations to low-cost developing nations without any loss of production quality.
(7)	The increasing openness of the global market-place as a result of the GATT & WTO trade deals. It is now more difficult than ever for individual countries to protect their domestic markets without inviting reciprocal trade sanctions.
(8)	Increases in (i) the footloose nature of international capital, investors having the opportunity as never before of investing their capital in bonds and equity shares world-wide wherever and whenever they choose and (ii) the volume of hot international money available for instantaneous international investment and, equally possible, dis-investment. This amounts to a sort of game of *Instant International Monopoly*.

TABLE 1.3: EIGHT KEY DRIVERS IN INTERNATIONAL BUSINESS

Naturally, if an Italian clothing maker is thinking of a joint venture with an Indian textile producer, there are many technical issues to deal with. For instance, there is the extent to which the resulting business may have adequate size (to achieve scale economies in manufacture and/or increase marketing penetration, for instance) or enough financial dynamism or security. But, on top of this, come such thorny issues as the manner of management direction and control, potential Italian-Indian value differences in respect, for instance, of pay rates, working conditions and bribery. "Who is in charge?" and "How is the relationship to be managed?" are also questions of critical political, and not just management, importance in such an economically-nationalistic country as India.

The USA
The USA avoided a trade battle with the European Union by agreeing to change a controversial law that required Italian and French designers to put a "Made in China" label on many of their expensive silk goods. The USA made the concession in talks at the World Trade Organization ... thus defusing a potentially explosive trans-Atlantic dispute. The source of the tension was a USA law requiring any cloth woven in one country to identify that nation on the finished product's label.

European manufacturers
Had been outraged by the law, which they said threatened to disrupt more than $145 million in annual exports of luxury silk scarves, ties and other products to the USA. Some of Europe's best-known brands, such as Giorgio Armani and Gucci, fell under the law; they profit handsomely from their "Made in Europe" labels, but import nearly all of their silk from China.

EXHIBIT 1.1: WHO MAKES WHAT AND WHY IT MATTERS

Source: US & EU sew up row over silk labels,
Brian Coleman, *The Wall St Journal, Europe* 8-9/8/97

As a consequence few managers are, therefore, likely to be able to contemplate a safe and successful career if they have little understanding of what happens economically and politically outside their own country. Indeed, for the British, it is a matter of supreme good fortune that the international commercial *lingua franca* in the early twenty-first century will be English. If it were not, this country, with its poor record of speaking other tongues (one legacy of empire, incidentally), might be in serious international trading difficulty. Of course, if European history had been different, the inhabitants of this offshore island might have had to become polyglots, like the Dutch.

Whichever the position you find yourself in as a manager working for a domestic company, a multinational or within a business federation – there is clearly an inescapable need to know more of the workings of the world abroad.

■ The Need to Explore

Mathematics is a precise science. So is chemistry. Each deals with facts and with the ever-present need to determine cause and effect relationships. Engineering similarly seeks to establish objective if-then linkages, which allow specific conclusions to be drawn from gathered data. Each is a field where theories have been, and are, constructed to allow predictions to be made about the behaviour of things (properties of chemicals, for example) under certain conditions and/or change agents. They are not "hard" sciences if data cannot be measured, relationships factually and objectively determined, tests validated, functions proven.

Measuring human behaviours is the task of professional sociologists, psychologists and anthropologists. They consider themselves quite naturally to be scientists since the tools they use – the experiment, the survey, the test, statistical analysis – originate in hard science. So also do the tools of economists and political scientists, although here the analysis methodology (with the exception of econometrics) is less rooted in scientific objectivity. As Table 1.4 page 12 illustrates, the fields they seek to cover are extensive.

It is of value to note the view of the anthropologists F. Kluckhohn and F.L. Strodtbeck (1961) that mankind's major concerns are with problems of a universal nature arising from relationships with, or more properly orientations towards, nature (climate, geography etc.), time and people. Such orientations naturally fall into the study domains outlined in Table 1.4 below.

So, out of this possible range of issues, what can be measured that would be of value to members of a joint venture management team such as that of Krauss-Maffei Wegmann and Alvis?

Firstly, information about the *value systems* of the groups involved. The groups themselves can typically range in size from individual organisations (the German civil service) to entire nations (the British). Naturally, their values are best imputed from systematically-gathered data taken from what is regarded as a statistically viable sample. This enables the analyst to state with some confidence the value set of the group studied (the things or concepts that people value) and the rank order in the value set (the priority they place upon them). Table 1.5 page 14, gives an interesting picture of some other peoples' value sets.

Social Science	Definition
Anthropology	The zoological study of mankind. Deals specially with its evolution, history and physiological aspects of behaviour such as communication, behavioural ritual, strength of sex-based or other pecking orders, acceptance of myths and religious beliefs.
Sociology	The study of man as a social animal, i.e., how an individual society as a whole is made up. The focus is on patterns of societal behaviour and group structures which are influenced or constrained by inter-dependence and power relationships, inherited or acquired.
Psychology	The study of the human mind and the nature of how mental processes affect individual behaviour in terms, say, of logical/emotional reactions.
Economics	The study of features of systems involving the production, distribution and exchange of wealth within society. Economists study the patterns of behaviour shown by individuals, groups and nations as revealed in the ways they seek to take advantage of scarce physical resources.
Politics	Political scientists examine the distribution and use of legitimate authority and power within society. Rule structures, decision-making systems and ideologies (belief systems espoused by political actors as a basis for action programmes) are key issues.

TABLE 1.4: KEY FIELDS OF STUDY IN THE SOCIAL SCIENCES

Secondly, the *risk-return orientation* of the groups in question. This is a measure of what risks their members are prepared to run for a given return and dictates in part the stance that people adopt in their behaviours – passive/active, aggressive/defensive and so on.

Thirdly, the extent of *group co-operation*. Some groups naturally bond together, with all members working together for the common good, whilst others seem to be almost accidental communities made up of individuals who attend predominantly to their own self-interests. The management implications of this groupism/individualism distinction are, of course, massive in so far as the *glue* that binds an organisation together is concerned. Do you, as a matter of interest, sing a company song with your colleagues before starting the day's work? Do you indulge in time-honoured salaryman-type rituals, such as drinking together after working hours with your boss, for social bonding, rather than enjoyment purposes? Do you systematically find employment for the relatives of your employees?

Other subordinate features of group cooperation are whether

- people seem to be capable of planning over the long term or are more concerned with short-term pay-offs;

- group members are used to working in hierarchies where the leaders are clearly visible and obedience is commonplace or where there is a greater sense of egalitarianism;

- people are direct and down-to-earth in how they communicate or whether they are keen to erect a sort of shell around themselves which prevents them from being exposed.

Note that, in making such a selection, the inter-cultural analyst could be accused of acting in a *culture-bound* fashion, i.e., listing the things that he or she, from his/her individual national culture perspective, considers important. Indeed, in some rather more *politically-correct* cultures it might be considered inappropriate to draw up a list at all. At all times we have to remember that different groups have value sets which may be wholly congruent but can be totally incongruent with, even antagonistic to, our own.

Country	Bribe Payers Index (the lower the score out of 10, the more corrupt the nation) as computed by Transparency International and Goettingen University.
China	3.1
S. Korea	3.4
Taiwan	3.5
Italy	3.7
Malaysia	3.9
Japan	5.1
France	5.2
Spain	5.3
Singapore	5.7
United States	6.2
Germany	6.2
Belgium	6.8

TABLE 1.5: THE GLOBAL DIRTY DOZEN?
Source: *The Guardian,* 25/10/99

The Guardian-Inbucon survey of British boardroom rewards published in August 2000 indicated that salaries of directors of the FTSE top 100 companies were rising four times faster than the average increase for other employees. The average pay gap between chief executives and workers in Britain, according to remuneration experts Towers Perrin, was already 24 times (as compared with 15 times in Germany and 13 times in egalitarian Sweden).

However, US-style pay packets were certainly becoming more common in continental Europe as companies, obliged to stop relying on friendly banks and forced to tap global equity markets for cash, became exposed to pressures from shareholders to perform better. The Institute of Director's head of policy, Ruth Lea, admitted that the CEO pay spiral was "a bit mad" but that was how markets worked. "Markets are not moral things" she declared "It's like what's happening in football. It's the way international markets work these days".

EXHIBIT 1.2: TELLING IT THE WAY IT IS
Source: Lea defends pay "madness", *The Guardian,* 23/8/2000

The dividing line between the physical and the social sciences is, of course, not the calibre or expertise of the researchers nor the validity of their studies, but the raw material under investigation and the methodology applied. Any study in the social sciences must take account of not just the individual and the group (ranging from company to entire nation, for example) but also of the specific context in which the behaviours under review are taking place, given the assumptions that

- behaviours can differ according to the purely physical circumstances that individuals or groups are in, for example, in terms of wealth/poverty or geographical location or health or age profile; and
- behaviours can/may alter over time as some physical circumstances change. These last could include, for instance, unemployment, the price of raw materials like oil, or the climate;
- behaviours do alter as a function of the ageing of individuals and the maturity and/or maturation of a society.

Moreover, talking about national culture as if it had an independent existence may in itself be misleading. After all, we can identify various types of culture – youth culture, drug culture, fashion culture – which, in some cases, transcend national boundaries by creating shared-interest groups, sometimes pejoratively called sub-cultures. European football culture, as an aggregate, may be another case in point, with international copy-cat behaviour being the cultural norm as when, for instance, Italian soccer fans run amok because English fans have already done so.

Not only that, we must also bear in mind that measuring cultural differences between groups is made more difficult by the fact of changing technology. To what extent, say, might the collective mindset of Chinese managers change over time because of the Internet? How are people's innate views of the rightness of corporate hierarchy altered by their experience of redundancy resulting from the installation of labour-saving technology?

This degree of definition is not semantic. It is necessary because we must beware of drawing over-elaborate and generalist conclusions from any study of individuals or groups which purports to establish behavioural predictability. All French businessmen do not behave the same. They do not have the same attitudes, opinions

and beliefs. They do not act in the same way. And they don't persist with the same approaches and stances over time. It may be that many French businessmen do – but not all. As far as possible, we must avoid stereotyping.

There are indeed concepts to be elaborated, for example, typologies of the components of culture such as those we shall examine in the next section). Cultural tendencies can be observed and monitored (members of a group at a given point in time having similar behaviours) and from which valid conclusions can be drawn. But, there are no deterministic laws of human culture, which can be said to hold under all circumstances. At least, at present. This last caveat needs to be said since the vast bulk of culture studies have been carried out in single cultures (so-called *emic* studies). What is needed before proper inter-cultural models can start to be established is a substantial increase in *etic* or cross-border studies. (Pike, 1954) These are analyses of behaviours which cover more than one nation, whatever the unit of research (club, company or even the nation itself), and which allow comparative cross-cultural findings to be produced.

Some of the generic difficulties that can arise in international team-working are evidenced in Table 1.6 page 17. In spite of this, we have no alternative but to measure all pertinent aspects of individual and group business behaviour and draw appropriate, if limited, conclusions. The alternative, ignorance, is intolerable if you are sharing a decision as a senior executive in a cross-border management team like Krauss-Maffei Wegmann-Alvis. You do not want, to use Berry's terminology (Table 1.6 page 17), to be *assimilated* (at least without good reason) and especially not *decultured*.

In this particular team management situation you would be concerned with information gathered from all angles – and not just those of social science. Thus, you need to know such things as:

- what is the attitude of the UK and German governments to what you are doing in strategic product-development terms?

- how important, relatively speaking, are the short-term and long-term team goals to you and your partners and how far ahead do your respective strategic visions reach?

16

- which interventionist role, if any, is played in the company's management decisions by the government (at state/federal level) or by the country's banking system?

- what are the partners' terms and conditions of work (minimum wage, participative management system, maximum working time etc.) and how heavily unionised are they?

- what are the comparative approaches to hiring and firing?

- does each partner sees itself as purely "shareholder-driven" or operating in an arena where the general satisfaction of stakeholders is paramount?

Form of Acculturation (i.e. the adjustment that occurs when two groups come together)	Features
Integration	A allows B to retain many of the practices to which B is wedded. Over time cultural adaptation by both takes place and a common A+B culture emerges.
Assimilation	B willingly gives up its culture in exchange for A's. B ceases to exist as a separate cultural identity and is assimilated into A's culture.
Separation	B wishes to remain culturally independent of A and resists all tries at persuasion or coercion. A and B remain separate cultures.
De-culturation	B does not value the culture of A, the dominant partner, very highly. But it is not so enamoured of its own to seek to preserve it. B, thus, becomes alienated and loses cultural identity.
Imposition	A imposes its culture on B. It forces B to accept its ways of thinking and working.

TABLE 1.6: BERRY'S MODES OF ACCULTURATION (Berry 1983)

It is self-evident that team members also need to know as much as possible about the potential behaviours of national and European purchasers of the product – the Battlefield Taxi – and about the manner in which the demand may be handled and whether that can be profitably managed.

Who might lead in the collaborative relationship – and who might follow – is of prime concern, so that also needs to be carefully studied as a strategic issue in its own right. No company in today's circumstances will find it easy in any joint venture to impose its will on any partner. Indeed, to try to do so would be a negation of the idea of partnership. It follows from this that the worst sin that can possibly be committed by the team player is to imagine that the other foreign members of the team automatically embrace the same value set as he/she does and that they seek exactly the same aims. The second sin is to imagine that the other members are *caricatures* or even *stereotypes* of a foreign culture and automatically embrace a value set which is different. Partnership in culture means a patient voyage of enquiry and discovery. The need to understand, like the need to know, cannot be dealt with at a superficial level.

CHAPTER 2

Inter-Cultural Analysis – Theoretical Perspectives

■ The Iceberg Model

Nothing is more difficult to define, given the amorphous, shifting nature of the subject, than culture. Literally every cross-cultural theorist of note has contributed to the great game of writing a definition of it. Here, for the sake of brevity and clarity, we will content ourselves with the definition that has greatest currency at present; Geert Hofstede's assertion that culture is a *software of the mind* which dictates patterns of group behaviour and communication, especially at the national level. (1991)

It is interesting to note that the word *culture* derives from the root of the same Latin verb that gives us the words *cult* and *cultivation*. The first carries the connotations of a system of religious belief or worship and the rites and ritauls associated with it. The second relates to the degree of educational, social or aesthetic refinement possessed by the members of a group. It is arguable that culture has more to do with the values that bind a group together – the gods they worship – than it has to do with refinement.

As we shall see, Hofstede's research led him to believe that such behaviour and communication can be codified at the level of how particular nations go about their business and the values they hold dear. A more simplistic version of this, as we have already seen, would be that cohesive groups (at club, company and nation level) may tend towards a *collective mindset* on key issues. This is the shorthand we will be using to consider aspects of culture at the national level. Exhibit 2.1 page 20 presents a more formal view of Hofstede's key ideas about the components of culture.

To achieve clarity in our discussion on the make-up of a nation's culture we shall be using a straightforward model: that of an iceberg divided into two sections. These are the visible, tangible **super-structure** and the difficult-to-make-out, below-the-water-line **bedrock**. This concept is presented in Figure 2.1 page 20.

Hofstede uses the example of an onion to show how culture is manifested. Values lie at the heart of the onion and deal with the ideas and things that we desire, esteem, dislike or hate. Groups can codify values into societal norms or standards for behaviours. Norms and rituals, are forms of action or activity which bind a group together. Ways of greeting and other forms of social intercourse which are highly standardised are involved. These make patterns of behaviour predictable and, therefore, dependable. Norms and Rituals are the part of the onion nearest to its heart.

The penultimate layer of the onion is made up of the way in which we pattern aspects of our behaviours on societal heroes who, in the process, can become role models.

The outer skin of the Hofstede culture onion comprises the symbols the group holds dear. These range from flags and national anthems (visible manifestations of the existence of the nation) to national celebrations and festivities. They can even include institutions, like the monarchy.

EXHIBIT 2.1: THE HOFSTEDE CULTURE ONION (1991)

Beginning with the super-structural elements, we can create a checklist of salient factors the international team will have to address. This must cover those elements in the national culture of a foreign country which can become known quickly through personal experience by any team member. These include:

- patterns of physical behaviour and communication (how people behave and talk to each other at work, in the street etc.). The physical environment (clean/dirty, modern/antiquated etc.). The workings of the transport system (trains running on time) and industry (trade union activity etc.). The mood of the nation, as expressed on the street or in the media (optimistic/pessimistic, dynamic/static).

- those systems which partly shape the visible elements of the nation's business culture and are easily noted during a visit. Managing work (hiring, firing, paying, contracting, participation, representation), for example. Questions arise as to whether the systems in use are permissive and tolerant or authoritarian and economically neo-liberal (i.e., boss-driven and demanding strict value for money). The French instance, has a large civil service which enjoys under the state, for *acquis sociaux* system a degree of privilege (job security, pension rights etc.) that is very difficult to reduce.

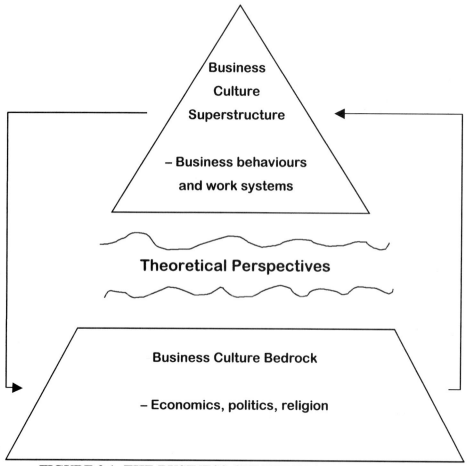

FIGURE 2.1: THE BUSINESS CULTURE ICEBERG MODEL
© Terry Garrison, 1996

NOTES: (1) Theoretical frameworks drawn from sociology, psychology and anthropology are used to analyse behaviour and work systems. The arrows signify patterns of influence.
(2) The culture bedrock is investigated using tools from the historical, political, economic and religious sciences.

The typical British firm is less prepared, by contrast, to give the same treatment pro-rata to its part-time work-force as to its full-timers and has little interest in either a maximum working week or in a minimum wage. Nor for that matter are Britain's business leaders overly interested in the model of participative management used in continental Europe.

To be more precise, when a French businessman visits, say, the USA for the first time these, then, are the things he sees, hears and may tend to internalise as the key features of the nation's culture. This is, for him, *how things are done around here.* He compares and contrasts his personal vision of America with his own version of French domestic business culture and his preconceptions of what he thought America might be like and makes a positive or negative judgement as the case may be. Certainly, whatever else, it is different!

Clearly, the physical features of how the nation operates and the systems creating the work output cannot be isolated from either the natures of institutions employing the workforces or from their economic and political systems. To a comparative stranger in a new country, these artefacts – institutions and politico-economic systems – are sometimes by no means easy to either understand or to factor into the business-handling equation. Consider Exhibit 2.2 page 23 as an example.

Is it likely, for example, that a politically-correct and scrupulously-moral USA businesswoman visiting China for the first time would understand that the Chinese do not value human life as the West claims to do and do not recognise that they are doing anything wrong by employing prisoners in factories? Maybe she would, but what might the *culture shock* do to her preconceptions?

Hence, we need to add to our listing four further bedrock elements which allow us to probe the culture of the country we are interested in more deeply. They are:

- the basic nature of the employing institutions. These can be divided into civil service, public sector industry and private sector industry and commerce. This last can be further divided by size (large-scale, SME), activity (manufacturing, assembly, services), resources (labour-intensive or knowledge-intensive) and level of technological advancement;

In America, this is what they call a no-brainer. Since 1985, a provision in German law known as the Employment Protection Act has allowed companies to offer certain types of jobs on a fixed term, rather than permanent, basis for a period up to two years. No big deal, you might say, except that in a country where the words Sie sind gefeuert ("you are fired") are all but verboten, and in which labour costs remain the highest in the world, such a law can be a very big deal indeed.

The law will expire later this year unless the Chancellor chooses to renew it… with safeguards against employer abuse. But his government partners, the Greens, are against and so too are many trade unions who view such contracts as a threat to their stranglehold on labour markets. They are a threat to their institutional interests, of course, but to most other people they are a blessing. Indeed Mr Schroeder should get busy figuring out other ways to further liberalise the labour market… Like changing the German law which requires employers to give six months paid maternity leave and guarantee the mother's job for up to three years…

EXHIBIT 2.2 HOW THEY DO THINGS IN GERMANY
Based on "Schroeder's No Brainer", editorial in
The Wall Street Journal, 18-19/8/2000

- The country's political and economic systems. These can range in theory from a totalitarian polity (i.e., political system) and a command-administrative economy to a high-level democracy and a market economy. The German-type *Sozialmarktwirstschaft* or social market economy is the recognisable continental European model. As we shall see later, each *policonomy* permutation (i.e., combination of type of polity and type of economy) may result in different pay-offs for citizens in terms of freedom/order, consumption/investment, guns/butter and risk/security;

- The resource profile of the country in terms of its economic and demographic make-up. The economist calls the first of these *factor endowments* and lists such elements as the location of the country, its terrain, climate and natural resources (oil, agriculture etc.), wealth (e.g., from international trade, entrepôt activity etc.) and demographic structure.

- The country's history. We need to seek to establish any special patterns of past experience which have conditioned the nation's thinking and/or its institutions. War, revolution and colonial experiences are the influences which seem to be most significant. Sudden changes in the value of a nation's currency are of great importance, too. For example, the collapse of the German economy in 1923 through hyper-inflation dominated the thinking of the Bundesbank about stability of currency, interest rates and money supply well into the 1990s. By virtue of the degree of German influence on the modus operandi and success criteria of the European Monetary Institute (the forerunner of the European Central Bank), this cataclysmic event has, also, shaped the workings of economic and monetary union in Europe.

Although we may deal separately with these six bedrock elements in our Iceberg Model as drivers and shapers of behaviours, the fact is that all are inter-dependent and constantly influence and are influenced by all the others. A powerful understanding of a nation's business culture can only be gained by asking pertinent questions at each level.

Ease of understanding is, thus, greatly increased if we use the model of the iceberg presented in Figure 2.1 page 21 to capture the easily-visible, superstructural behavioural elements and the harder-to-process, bedrock drivers. The next section of this chapter contains a review of the most significant of these perspectives.

■ **Perspectives on the Superstructure**

Although not a physical science, few other topics studied by mankind can be said to be studied with more scientific diligence – or more enthusiasm – than culture. Furthermore, it has been, and still is, the happy hunting ground for a myriad of analysts concerned with, at one extreme, researching the minutiae of group behaviours and, at the other, with speculative *armchair theorising* seeking to capture the essential elements of the cultural dimension. The Holy Grail in this field of enquiry is, of course, a grand universalist theory which explains key features of just why different nations differ in their orientations to basic behavioural bases, like the management of money, power and people. Our concern, however, is with more useful perspectives.

By common consent, the most important present-day theoretician in the inter-cultural analysis field is Geert Hofstede, elements of whose work we have already mentioned. His seminal books – *Cultures and Organisations* (1991) and *Culture's Consequences* (1980) – are rooted in a major piece of social anthropology research carried out in the 1960s. This involved a survey of the opinions, attitudes and beliefs of a large-scale sample of IBM employees in the same kinds of management positions in 50 countries. The nature of his empirical *Dimensions of National Culture* study and the manner of its execution conferred a level of validity on the results to the point where it is widely respected as a fundamental guide to key orientational differences among the nations studied. An instance of such differences is given in Exhibit 2.3 below.

A monosodium glutamate flavour enhancer made by the Japanese food company Ajinomoto Co has long been as common as salt or sugar in many Indonesian kitchens. It is said to improve the taste of everything. But last week an influential organisation of Muslim clerics proclaimed that Ajinomoto's MSG contains enzymes grown on pork fat despite labelling on its packages that says that the products conform to Islamic food laws.

Pig products are a culinary no-go for Muslims... The announcement has caused a colossal case of national indigestion and stores have pulled tons of Ajinomoto's products off the shelves and the plant in East Java has been shut. Muslims make up 85 percent of Indonesia's 203m people. "It's like growing plants on filth" said Amidhan, the chairman of the clerics' organisation, who, like many Indonesians, uses only one name.

EXHIBIT 2.3: A CASE OF ORIENTATIONAL DIFFERENCE
MSG enhances Indonesian tension, Rajiv Chandrasekaran,
The International Herald Tribune, 12/1/2001

Hofstede's focus was values (the importance people place on the positive features of life, like truth, morality, beauty, cleanliness, wealth etc.) and the variation between nations in value sets, especially in terms of what people want to strive for. The study sought to adopt a scientifically-correct posture of *cultural relativism*, i.e., never assuming that the culture of one country can be used to bench-mark another country's culture in any way. Different countries, after all, do worship different gods.

The questions posed to the IBM respondents were aimed not at elucidating the discrete differentiations of regional, ethnic, gender, generation and social class which naturally occur as influences upon national culture. They were targeted on issues of hierarchy, independence, gender stereotyping and risk management. An explanation of these variables is given in Table 2.1 below.

(1) **Power Distance**	The manner in which different countries deal with the existence of inequalities which are socially or economically determined. Hofstede sought to determine how any such inequalities were handled in managerial systems by probing authority and power relationships between superior and subordinate. The theoretical construct used to measure this feature was called *power distance*, the range for which was *small – large*.
(2) **Collectivism and Individualism**	The intensity of the relationship between the individual and the group. In some countries being a "loner" and pursuing your own individual self-interest is seen as perfectly natural. In others a group ethos – a need for bonding and tight co-operation among members – is regarded by many as the optimal way for society to run. The tendency that nations have to act in this was measured by means of the *Individualism – Collectivism* scale.
(3) **Masculinity and Femininity**	The orientation that a country has towards gender issues. Hofstede's distinction here was between *masculine* and *feminine* countries according to the accent placed on aggressive/passive behaviours and the sexual allocation of work roles.
(4) **Uncertainty Avoidance**	Handling uncertainty. This relates to the willingness of businessmen within a country (on the basis of the evidence he gathered) to take risks or to act in such a way as to protect, say, possessions and operational systems. *Uncertainty avoidance –* or, more commonly, risk aversion – was the name of this construct.

TABLE 2.1: THE FOUR FOCUSES OF HOFSTEDE'S IBM STUDY

Figure 2.2 page 28 and 2.3 page 29 present Hofstede's findings for the major groups of countries he investigated in the form of outline maps.

So far as the trade-off between collectivism and power distance is concerned, Figure 2.2 page 28 shows that European countries differ markedly from South American countries in that the former are strongly oriented to individualism and egalitarianism whilst the latter tend to score highly in terms of collectivism and authoritarianism. A further important feature of both maps is that Anglo-Saxon and Romance countries differ greatly in their positions on power distance (low v high) and uncertainty avoidance (low v high). German sphere and Anglo-Saxon countries also show position dissimilarities on collectivism (higher-lower) and uncertainty avoidance (higher-lower). The relationship between collectivism and uncertainty avoidance is shown in Figure 2.3 page 29 where:

(a) South American and Romance countries are distinguished by their comparatively high levels of risk aversion; and

(b) Asia Pacific and South American countries score highly in the extent of their collectivism.

We need to include in our discussion of Hofstede's contribution to the study of national cultures yet another dimension: how a particular country handles the important business culture element of time. Why is it that some countries (Japan and Germany, for example) seem to be able to handle their business affairs comfortably on a long-term basis, planning strategically over a time horizon as long as 30 years, whereas, for others, short-termism is the natural order of things (Britain and USA, for example).

Country Grouping	Aggregate Long-term Orientation Score in points (i.e., the extent to which decision makers tend to take a long-term view is reflected by the comparative number of points scored)
Asia Pacific countries (China, Hong Kong, Taiwan, Japan, S. Korea)	456
Anglo Saxon countries (GB, USA, Australia, N. Zealand, Canada)	138

TABLE 2.2: COMPARATIVE LONG-TERM ORIENTATIONS
(Hofstede, 1991)

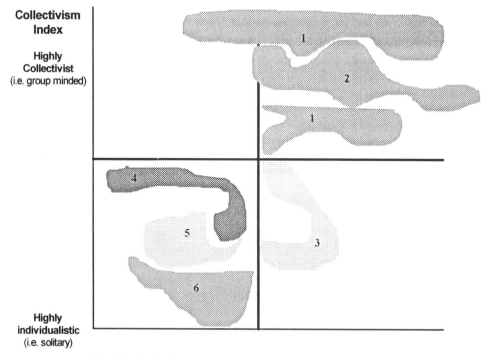

FIGURE 2.2: MAPPING COLLECTIVISM AND POWER DISTANCE
(Hofstede, 1991)

NOTES

(i) The numbers indicate the position of (1) S. American countries (2) Asia Pacific countries, (3) Romance European countries (4) German Sphere countries (5) Northern European countries and (6) Anglo Saxon countries. These groups are made up as follows:

  (1) Southern American countries are Costa Rica, Colombia, Peru, Ecuador, Venezuela, Guatemala, Panama, Mexico, Brazil, Uruguay, Argentina, Chile.

  (2) Asia Pacific countries are Korea, Taiwan, Hong Kong, Singapore, Indonesia, Malaysia, Philippines.

  (3) Romance European countries are Spain, Italy, France, Belgium.

  (4) German Sphere countries are Austria, Germany, Switzerland.

  (5) North European countries are Denmark, Norway, Finland, Sweden.

  (6) Anglo Saxon Countries are Great Britain, USA, Canada, Australia, New Zealand, Netherlands.

(ii) The map shapes are approximations only and loosely based on Hofstede's ranking system. They are used for expository reasons only.

(iii) Explanation: Countries in Group 3 are highly individualistic and freedom-loving. They are also intolerant of authoritarian behaviour.

28

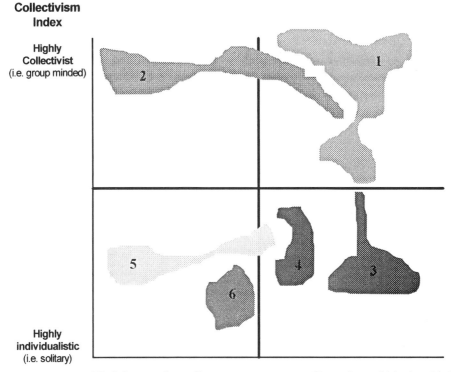

Collectivism Index

Highly Collectivist (i.e. group minded)

Highly individualistic (i.e. solitary)

Weak (i.e. sure of oneself)   **Strong** (i.e. can't tolerate ambiguity)

Uncertainty Avoidance Index

FIGURE 2.3: MAPPING COLLECTIVISM – UNCERTAINTY AVOIDANCE (Hofstede, 1991)

NOTES

(i)   The numbers indicate the position of (1) S. American countries (2) Asia Pacific countries, (3) Romance European countries (4) German Sphere countries (5) Northern European countries and (6) Anglo Saxon countries. They are as follows:

    (1) Southern American countries are Costa Rica, Colombia, Peru, Ecuador, Venezuela, Guatemala, Panama, Mexico, Brazil, Uruguay, Argentina, Chile.

    (2) Asia Pacific countries are Korea, Taiwan, Hong Kong, Singapore, Indonesia, Malaysia, Philippines.

    (3) Romance European countries are Spain, Italy, France, Belgium.

    (4) German Sphere countries are Austria, Germany, Switzerland.

    (5) North European countries are Denmark, Norway, Finland, Sweden.

    (6) Anglo Saxon Countries are Great Britain, USA, Canada, Australia, New Zealand, Netherlands.

(ii) The map shapes are approximations only and loosely based on Hofstede's ranking system. They are used for expository reasons only.

(iii) Explanation: Countries in Group 1 are highly collectivist and have a strong need for rules and regulations to govern how business society works.

The time dimension reference is based on a study by researcher Michael Bond called the Chinese Value Survey. He called it *Confucian dynamism*. On the basis of this study and Hofstede's conclusions drawn from it, country groupings can be ranked in Table 2.2 page 28. Huge differences in attitudes to time (and, therefore, such critical issues as the strategic time horizon for decisions or the requisite speed of payback on investment) are found between Asia Pacific and Anglo Saxon countries.

The second theoretical contribution which is of value here is that outlined by Charles Hampden-Turner and Fons Trompenaars in their book *The Seven Cultures of Capitalism.* (1993) These authors selected, on the basis of research work carried out at the Centre for International Business Studies at Amstelveen, Netherlands, seven macro variables which they regarded as being culturally critical to the creation of wealth. Their book illustrates the extent to which different countries exhibit different patterns of response to each of the variables. As with Hofstede's data, conclusions can be drawn which indicate the extent to which different nations hold different value sets, and hence, have a tendency to approach common problems in different ways.

The variables in which these two authors were interested are different from those addressed by Hofstede and do help to reveal more of what a particular nation is like, on the basis of the evidence presented, at handling its business affairs. From their research perspective, the authors reckoned that the things that mattered were:

- whether the nation's businessfolk were addicted to detail and spent their time factually analysing the challenges presented to them, or whether they were more grandiose, big-picture orientated and driven more by philosophy and principle than practice. This the authors called the *particularism-universalism* dimension.

It is intriguing to speculate in this context on the apparent historical contributions of Europe's two main philosophical schools of thought on this issue. Those principally concerned with logic and rationality, i.e., uncertainty reduction, seem predominantly to come from Germany (Kant and Hegel, for example) and France (Descartes). Philosophers concerned with empiricism and freedom appear to hail in disproportionate numbers from Britain (e.g., Smith and Locke). Note that we shall return to this topic in Chapter 3.

- whether the nation showed itself pre-occupied with internal issues or whether it was outward-looking. This feature could well manifest itself in the degree to which some countries were prepared to *flex and fix* according to external pressures and others felt that resistance to externally-induced change was preferable, even if that might mean breaking under the strain. (*Inner-outer direction*).

- whether the status you enjoy as a business person is ascribed or achieved. Some countries which have a rigid system of socio-economic hierarchy typically accord a degree of positional power and authority on the basis of inheritance. Others, especially the USA, focus on what a person has done or is achieving. That determines the power and influence they have. (*Ascribed v achieved status*).

The third perspective which is critical to our study is that advanced by anthropologist Edward T. Hall. His research led him to believe that particular countries tend to handle two things which are of critical importance to their cultures in different ways. These are time (1983) and inter-personal and group communication (1981).

So far as time is concerned, Hall distinguished between those countries for whom *time is money* and those who take a more relaxed and philosophical view of the pressures it brings, or may bring. In those countries where time is seen as a scarce, indeed finite, resource, communication between business people is done with directness and speed. So, work is planned and execution of work within the time specified is seen as most important. North America and Northern Europe are included in this: *time*, for a good proportion of the business community, tends to be nothing else but *money*. A person's orientation towards time also clearly connotes the economic value he/she places on the other resources used to create wealth and prosperity. Such a linear approach to the use of time he described as *monochronic*.

A *polychronic* approach, by contrast, is one which sees time as not so significant a constraint and, hence, failure to work to deadlines not so earth-shattering. Interestingly, religions such as Hinduism and Buddhism project time as not finite but infinite and life as an endless circular continuum. Their adherents would, therefore, tend to be more oriented to universalism and the eternal verities rather than the nitty-gritty and the daily grind. They would operate, therefore, within a polychronic culture.

31

So far as communication is concerned, Hall is widely esteemed for his work on what he calls *context*.   In his book *Beyond Culture* (1981) he distinguishes between communication situations in differing culture types. The first, labelled *a high context* culture, is one in which both parties involved in the dialogue take much for granted and do not seem to need to spell things out. They understand each other's characters and perspectives, the subtleties of the interplay and the environment in which it is taking place.   Such familiarity allows them to leave much unspoken and yet still be fully understood.   The more collectivist the culture, i.e., the tighter the communitarian relationships that existed among group members, the more *high context* was the culture type.   Japan is still, perhaps, the most prominent example, although, like many other countries, it is undergoing profound change. By contrast, Hall found that an individualist culture typically makes its communication process and content as unambiguous as possible. People speak *fully and frankly*, do not *beat about the bush* and *don't stand on ceremony*.   Such are the hallmarks of the *low context culture*. The USA scores highly on this dimension.

As can be easily imagined, without an understanding of these issues it is extremely difficult for people from a high-context, collectivist culture to do real business with those from a low context, individualist culture with any confidence, unless they re-orientate their attitudes and approaches to suit.

The last theoretical perspective with which we will be concerned as a partial explanation of human behaviours in the visible, superstructural part of the cultural iceberg is that of the concept of a hierarchy of human needs, advanced by Abraham Maslow. (1968)

Maslow conceived of a ladder of motivational human needs stretching from lower (safety, basic physical requirements etc.) to higher (belongingness and self-esteem). As soon as the individual – and, by extension, the group – has satisfied basic needs, there is a tendency to move up the ladder (or hierarchy) to deal with higher-order needs. For Maslow the need that stood at the top was self-actualisation or the ability to fulfil your own destiny. As we shall see later, such a focus is a major business culture force for developing nations, such as Malaysia, which have lived through a long period of colonial subjection and are now anxious to uphold their own independence.

Of course, we need to qualify the use of the word "group" in this context since a group could be:

- a club type, where members associate freely in the pursuit of common interests and goals; or

- an employment association in which members perform paid tasks and in which the relationships are instrumental and contractual. The sociologist Ferninand Tönnies (1957) used the German words *Gemeinschaft* and *Gesellschaft* to distinguish between these two models.

■ Perspectives on the Bedrock

The notion that there are drivers and shapers in the bedrock of a nation's business culture iceberg which affect the visible ways in which its business communities behave is also central to our understanding of cross-cultural issues. So, now we begin the construction of a framework for analysing such bedrock factors – the main theoretical focus of this book – by rehearsing some of the important theoretical and historical elements involved in it. As Exhibit 2.4 below suggests, we can find ourselves dealing with very important issues.

Japan's past ten years have come to be called the "lost decade". The collapse of Sogo encapsulates why. Sogo was an Osaka retailer that collapsed in July 2000 with debts of over £11 billion. It had a Byzantine structure which enabled it to control three subsidiaries publicly and another 24 affiliates less than publicly, through cross-shareholdings, and which allowed the granting of loans to affiliates without the knowledge of shareholders.

This reflects the same cavalier attitude to corporate governance as is shown by Japanese banks who refuse to drive bankrupt clients into bankruptcy. Even the Japanese government initially rejected the notion of Sogo's demise and offered a bailout. The complexity of this array of deeply-entwined vested interests and the support of moribund debtors is the main rason for Japan's decade-long economic sluggishness.

EXHIBIT 2.4: JAPAN STILL IN THE DOLDRUMS
Based on: Housewives' revolt rocks Japan Inc.,
Carl Mortished, *The Times*, 22/7/2000

In terms of theory, the work of Harbison and Myers is a good place to start. (1959) They put forward a striking model of the industrial development of nation states. It has four stages, ranging from the agrarian-feudalistic society (i.e., a master-servant society based on land ownership and exploitation) to that of the industrial democratic state. Their argument is that, in each developmental stage, a nation's culture (C) – as represented by its dominant political and management philosophies and ways of working – is compatible with the nature of its economy, i.e., the processes of production and the products and services created (E). Both C and E move together in a step-wise fashion – and forwards. Sometimes a shift in C causes a movement in E and sometimes vice versa.

Hence, a culture which is orientated towards authoritarianism and based on an agrarian feudalistic economy would tend, as industrial development advanced, to be replaced over time with a democratic society endorsing a participative management philosophy. France can be used as an instance of Harbison and Myers' thesis. It is now an advanced industrial nation, but was once heavily agrarian. As it changed, it replaced the autocracy of its feudal rulers with increasing democracy in both political and industrial management. The break-point came with the French Revolution in 1789 and its slogan of *liberté, egalité, fraternité*.

To an extent, the authoritarian-permissive continuum is also encapsulated by Douglas McGregor's Theory X-Theory Y. (1960) This considers two diametrically-opposed methods of managing people, both practised today in different parts of the world. They are based on different views of the extent to which people

- want to work and are willing to accept responsibility; or

- dislike work and need to be strongly directed as well as on the degree of power and control possessed by the owner of the capital who has hired the workforce in question.

Theory Y is the style reflecting the first set of assumptions whilst Theory X corresponds to the second. As an example, contrast the difference in the harsh way in which indentured labour is exploited in India or Pakistan (c.f. Exhibit 4.2 page 78) with the heavy *Mitbestimmung*, or consensual workforce-participation, approach to management used typically in Germany.

Whilst the case of France backs up other aspects of Harbison and Myers' thinking very well, questions arise as to the extent to which, in general, their C–E theory enables predictions to be made, especially of the tightness of fit between management philosophy and the development stage countries have now reached. In other words, it is debatable whether the theory is deterministic, especially in the light of the *cultural commoditisation* that the globalisation of trade and the diffusion of technology are bringing in their wake.

Take, for example, the situation of turmoil that now exists in China. This is a country in which two development stages co-exist: agrarian-feudalism of a sort and developing/advanced industrialisation. In this contrasting situation, two management approaches are applied. The first is one of tight political control, based on a totalitarian regime model run centrally from Beijing. The second, by contrast, consists of much looser economic management control, based on notions of limited entrepreneurship, that is more decentralised and province-based.

If we then add in the fast economic development of some of China's coastal regions, resulting in many ways from economic liberalisation, and compare it with the low rates of growth of the poorer central provinces, we can see before us an explosive political and economic mix in what is the world's most populous state. The Economic Development Zones of Pudong and Shenzen are where the Chinese action really is. Overall, therefore, China is increasingly less of an anomaly, as seen from the Harbison and Myers' perspective. Certainly, as Exhibit 2.5 page 36 indicates, if its application to join the WTO succeeds, its future as a normal global trade player is more assured.

Nevertheless, the attractiveness of the notion of a tight historical inter-dependence between the economic base of the country and how it manages its commercial affairs is undeniable, at least at a general level. However, in more specific terms, i.e., for particular countries at particular stages in their development, other explanatory variables need to be added to the equation. Here the theoretical contribution of Farmer and Richman (1965) is of value. These researchers conceived of the influences stemming from the bedrock as being the results of the interplay within a country of socio-cultural, legal-political and educational factors, as well as the economic factors outlined by Harbison and Myers.

From their work we conclude that, to fully understand a nation's business behaviours, we need to develop awareness of, and insights into, relevant features of that nation's education system, its social structure and its political machinery at a given point in time. As an example we could cite the extent to which the USA's systems of management and ownership structures were in the 1950s and 1960s still heavily determined by Ivy League membership (i.e., run by graduates from Harvard and Yale, for example) and managed by "old money". Another instance might be the level to which France is still said to be run, even today, by *énarques*, graduates of the country's elitist and prestigious Ecole Nationale d'Administration who have leading roles in the nation's political, civil service and commercial structures. Just compare these cultural phenomena with the nascent culture of the New Economy in America and the rise to economic prominence of its web-surfing generation and its day-traders.

The enthusiasm for globalisation overlooks the disturbing possibility that nationalism, religious hatreds and old-fashioned religional rivalries can disrupt world trade and investment. And geopolitics and global economics are colliding in many ways. Two flash points are oil and electronics, the first depending very heavily on Middle East producers, the second (so far as chips, circuit boards and modems at least are concerned) on Taiwan and China. Globalisation presumes as well that materialism refashions world politics. Countries that trade and invest together accommodate their differences. However, the USA economy is now so intertwined with the global economy that isolationism is unimaginable. And, once a country like China decides to join the world economy, its trade linkages become costlier and costlier to break.

EXHIBIT 2.5: CHINA ON A ONE-WAY STREET
Source: War Scares: Beware, globalisation doesn't have to succeed,
Robert Samuelson, *The International Herald Tribune*, 19/10/2000

Our third bedrock theory focus is organisational. The notion here is that different nations produce, over time and according to their policonomy (i.e., politico-economic) development, institutional frameworks that underpin the workings of the business community in the most beneficial way. William Ouchi's book, *The M-Form Society* (1984), provides an over-view of this by reflecting on the way in which Japan created for itself in the post-war period a powerful base of co-operation among the government, big business, the financial sector and the trade unions. Such a base allowed a powerful form of macro-industrial strategic planning which, in its turn, led to Japanese commercial success in the 1980s and 1990s. But not in the 1990s, when the over-indebtedness of government and banking system on which the model had come to depend, became all too apparent. But it is often hard for countries that have espoused such a system to change, as Exhibit 2.6 below shows.

Asian countries like Malaysia and south Korea are backing away from deregulating their power industries after bungled attempts at reform in California have led to blackouts and pushed the states two largest utilities to the brink of bankruptcy. "Stable supply is our first priority" says Shin Kook Hwan, S. Korea's energy minister."That is more important than market rules". So consumers will have a longer wait for cheaper power.

EXHIBIT 2.6: STABILITY IS WHAT MATTERS
Source: Asia delays deregulatiuon of utilities, Stephen Weisenthal
The International Herald Tribune, 8/2/01

Other theorists, such as Reich and Magaziner (27), long advocated the need for America in particular to study this phenomenon of extensive government-business-labour collaboration – called *corporatism* – and assess whether the planning of aspects of the USA's industrial strategy in such a concerted, collectivist fashion should be adopted. Their thesis was that, in a modern technological age, any national government in consultation with labour and industry must target those strategic industries which are candidates for long-term economic development in the national interest and ensure their forward momentum through government-industry collaboration. The market-place alone is an inadequate guide. Their clarion call, once strong, is becoming increasingly stilled by the onward march of global standardisation in the form of neo-liberal economics, consumer habits and business approaches.

The concepts of corporatism, and its theoretical counterpart individualism, are illustrated in Figure 2.4 page 39. The ring represents the degree of co-operation of all players in the industrial-commercial arena working in a corporatist model: the diagonal lines indicate the situation that typically obtains in an individualistic culture. Here, companies negotiate at arms length the price of labour with the workforces (via their representatives, the trade unions) and they argue over the cost of capital with banks and actual or potential stockholders. The government plays a strictly background role. A corporatist model is one where the government plays, by contrast, a leading role as strategic planner and resource co-ordinator. The state wages not war, but business, in this increasingly dated model.

William Ouchi has a further valuable input to make to this particular debate. (1990) Remarking on the fact that the USA enjoyed, in the immediate post-war period, a massive level of global trade advantage, defence and technological dominance, he finds that the country was guilty of a sort of parallel business culture imperialism. This came about because its theories of capitalistic enterprise and free trade (and their stable companion, democracy), which had seemingly created and maintained the USA's extraordinary capabilities, were accepted, and then sold on, by Americans as universal truths. Equally, they were bought by many of those on the receiving end of Marshall Aid and technology transfer as *the only way to live*. In other words, the American experience during this period tended to encourage the ethnocentric view that all foreign ways of working were necessarily inferior to the American way, a most dangerous cultural bias.

Even today, it remains so. The demise of Soviet Communism in the late 1980s under the quadruple *whammy* of:

- military defeat (Afghanistan);

- economic powerlessness (inability to compete with Reaganite Star Wars spending);

- nuclear management deficiencies (Chernobyl); and

- the unravelling of Comecon and the Warsaw Pact.

has been taken by Russia's opponents as simply underlining once and for all the natural, inevitable and absolute victory of both market economics and democracy. The situation of Russia under President Putin in 2001 does not automatically support this viewpoint.

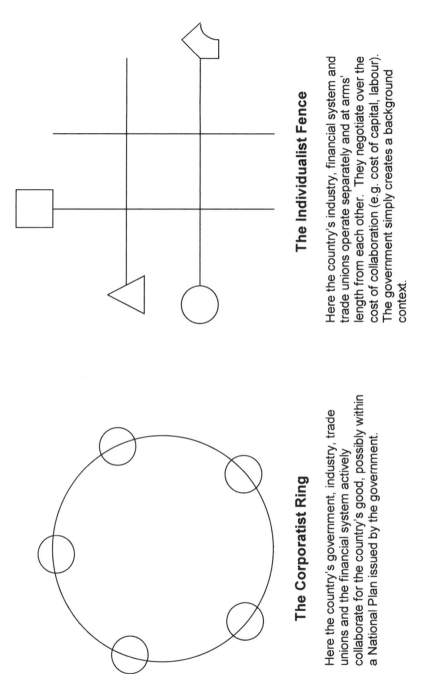

The Individualist Fence

Here the country's industry, financial system and trade unions operate separately and at arms' length from each other. They negotiate over the cost of collaboration (e.g. cost of capital, labour). The government simply creates a background context.

The Corporatist Ring

Here the country's government, industry, trade unions and the financial system actively collaborate for the country's good, possibly within a National Plan issued by the government.

FIGURE 2.4: REPRESENTATION OF THE CORPORATIST AND INDIVIDUALIST BEDROCK CULTURES

Ouchi's counsel in this context is wise: beware of management theories which are culture-bound. Such theories are typically successful best-practice ideas which a national business community has accepted at a given time and under given conditions because they have worked. From this, managers have then come to regard them as imperatives which must be followed by all, as universal panaceas. Business naiveté of this form is a threat. Recent examples in management could include uncritical pursuit of management-by-cliché doctrines such as *stick to the knitting.*

But as we consider the phenomenon of consumerism – based on Exhibit 2.7 page 41 – we might begin to conclude that some of the hyperbole and mass hysteria associated with pop culture and youth culture is, in fact, quasi-universal to the point that theoretical perspectives are no longer culture-bound.

A theoretical framework provided by the celebrated writers Florence Kluckhohn and Fred Strodtbeck (1961) underpins our investigatory toolkit so far as organisational elements are concerned. Called *Culture Orientation Theory* it deals with the following basic human nature factors:

- whether people are basically good or evil, moral or amoral;

- whether people seek to dominate nature and impose their will on circumstances or are relatively fatalistic and accept whatever burdens life places upon them without demur;

- whether the key modality of human activity of the nation appears to be being (e.g., maintaining the status quo) or doing (achieving change), in respect, say, of a critical feature of national life, like religion or government. It is a matter of record that nations tend to move cyclically from one modality to another over time as circumstances change. Perhaps one key to this oscillation is demographic dynamics. A growing proportion of young people in a community at a given point in time might tend to induce change. If coupled with a massive shift in technology (information, automation etc.) and a crumbling of a once-firm social cement as a result of materialistic pressures on the young (i.e., in terms of behavioural norms associated with extended families, respect for one's elders, marriage, morality etc.), change is inevitable;

Fame at last! The five "wannabes", were promoted to instant pop stardom when they won the ITV talent search contest in February 2001. Even though their group had no name, they were overwhelmed by media attention in their first press conference. They had been picked from 3000 applicants after intense auditioning and were over the moon at the prospect of an exclusive picture deal with OK magazine and a contract to record a 12-track album for Polydor. Their first single was already tipped for the No. 1 spot.

One of the group, vivacious Kym Marsh declared "We're not silly and stupid and we're not dummies". Her hair was streaked with red highlights and she wore a T-shirt marked "punk" to emphasise her individuality. Nearly ten million viewers had watched their victory. "I'm looking forward to performing live" continued Kym "and being able to buy my two kids the best of everything and looking after my Mum and Dad". It was clear that they had already had a huge hit of the potent seductive drug they had long been craving: to be known.

EXHIBIT 2.7: AND THE WINNER IS... POP CULTURE
Sources: Winners of fame game get ready for the real thing and We're no dummies, say the instant television popstars, Adam Sherwin, *The Times*, 5/2 and 6/2/01. All you need to be a pop star, Jenny McCartney, *The Sunday Telegraph*, 11/2/2001

- whether people are fixated on the past or focused on the future. The first would typically be the situation in a nation that has experienced past glory (victory in war or leadership of a global empire, for example) whilst the second could be true of a developing nation that has perhaps "thrown off the shackles" of colonialism and is relishing independence and industrialisation. Remaining true to the ideals of the leaders of the past can be a most powerful cultural determinant;
- whether the members of the nation in question like their privacy or tend towards more communal enjoyments, i.e., just how do they conceive of their own territorial and temporal space.

Before we turn our attention to other elements in our practical management toolkit for analysing bedrock culture features, we need to round off the framework we are constructing by considering the meaning of ideology.

Profiles of Management Practices in Three Typical Firms in Singapore Culture			
	American Subsidiary	Japanese Subsidiary	Local Firm
Planning Horizon	Long Range (5 years)	Medium range (3 years)	Short range
Level of Authority Definition	Clear	Unclear	Unclear
Degree of Decentralisation	High	Medium	Low
Leadership Style	Consultative	Autocratic-Participative	Paternalistic-Autocratic
Trust and Confidence in Subordinates	High	Medium	Low
Training Programs	Many	Some, mostly on-the-job training	Few
Motivation	Monetary	Monetary and psychological	Monetary and psychological
Typical Employee Morale	High	High	High

EXHIBIT 2.8: WHAT IT ALL MEANS IN PRACTICE: THE STYLE OF MANAGING IN A MULTICULTURAL SOCIETY – SINGAPORE
Source: Adapted from Joseph Putti, *Management Asian Context*, McGraw Hill, 1991

Individuals are often the creators of the ideas men and women live by. But religious and philosophical concepts sometimes also spring from the conditions in which a nation finds itself at a given time, and vice versa. As such, *the gods they worship* can be home-grown or imported. Where they seem to be created independently of such conditions, they can be the result of individual inspiration or charisma. Sometimes their origins are impossible to track down. Whatever their genesis, it is undeniable that the most powerful ideas can impact heavily on nations, shaping both their characters and their institutions.

Of course, it is not just the ideas that do the shaping. What matters is the extent to which a philosophy – i.e., a set of religious, moral, economic and/or political attitudes, opinions and beliefs – is transformed by its adherents into an ideology. This is a creed that, firstly, you wish non-believers to accept, as it represents the ultimate truth and the optimum way of handling your affairs. Secondly, it is an action programme for winning non-believers over, possibly by force, possibly by persuasion. Thirdly, it is a method for gaining and keeping economic and political power, without which keeping up the belief pattern of the faithful may be difficult. Note that this does not imply that all *believers* actually believe. Note also that millions have died in the process of resisting the ideologies of others, including those of the world's leading religions such as Islam and Christianity.

Leading ideologies also comprise major political doctrines like communism, socialism and capitalism – whether in the form of free enterprise or what Alfred Chandler (1990) called *managerial capitalism*, i.e., the ownership and management of the modern industrial enterprise. Outgrowths from the last-mentioned political doctrines are powerful notions like the welfare state, shareholder value, market fundamentalism, free trade, protectionism and so on.

The danger with all ideologies, as stated before, is that – under certain conditions and at certain times in a nation's life – they can become cultural imperatives which its citizens resist at their peril, irrespective of their rationality.

CHAPTER 3

Lessons From History

■ Introduction

A nation's history shapes its present. Even long-distant effects, based on even more distant causes, can continue to influence a country's business culture into the present because of:

- the ways in which some of its institutions came into existence (e.g., the Bank of England 1694 or the Académie Francaise 1634) and continue to exist even if they mutate with time and impact on today's world (see Exhibit 3.1 page 46);
- the manner in which seminal experiences – war, revolution, colonialism especially – have shaped and still shape public consciousness to such a degree that they dictate long-chain behaviours and attitudes which are hard, if not impossible, to demolish.

On top of these key influences we shall also consider here certain historical aspects of the management of work. Our aim throughout is to show how today's bedrock culture has been influenced by the past. We will focus particularly on European history.

■ The Impact of War

By far and away the greatest impact has been achieved through war. The more exposed a European country was – by virtue of having an indefensible frontier or being incomparably richer and militarily weaker than its neighbours – the more likely it was to be invaded. Not that all countries worked consistently on such a logical basis. Religious schism, for instance, was quite adequate as a cause of international strife, as in the case of the Thirty Years' War (1618-48) which ravaged Germany and prevented its emergence as a unified continental power until 1870. The conflict between Catholic Spain and the Protestant Netherlands, which took place from 1566 to 1609 and which helped create the strategic springboard for the latter's colonial advances, was also rooted in religion.

After two world wars and the dominance of the German language, followed by the repression wrought by decades of Communism during which time people were forced to learn Russian, many Poles are happy that their language now has a chance to thrive and their culture will be protected. This is because of the Polish Language Purity Law which came into effect in August 2000 does not allow the mass use of foreign words like "sex shop", "supermarket" and "plaza".

Such Americanisms have come into Poland in the so-called linguistic invasion that followed the fall of communism in 1989. Passed at the same time was a new Broadcasting Law that stipulates that one-third of the music played on the country's radio stations must be Polish. Both laws result from long-running argument in the Polish parliament between the liberal Freedom Union and the populist Peasants' Party over cultural purity.

The working of the new law is to be monitored by the Polish Language Council who will become a sort of language police patrolling the use of "Polglish".

EXHIBIT 3.1: WORLDS STILL AT WAR
Based on: Poland's language police wage war on "Polglish",
Kate Connolly, *The Guardian*, 4/9/2000

The quarrels of Europe's rulers over inheritances and property have also had their part to play, as Exhibit 3.1 hints. England's long-run fight with France during the Hundred Years' War (1337-1453) and the wide-ranging War of the Spanish Succession (1756-1763) are prominent examples.

What is of primary interest about such European land wars is that they all took place in mainland Europe. They all involved England (later Britain) in one way or another (as combatant or paymaster) but never once was English soil invaded, with the possible exception of 1545 when a small French force landed on the Isle of Wight. The chief reason for this immunity from invasion is, of course, the stretch of water that divides this off-shore island from the mainland. It was found unbridgeable by the Spanish (Armada, 1588), Napoleon (1804) and Hitler (1940). It is a fact that has profoundly shaped the island's sense of inviolability and security, relative, that is, to the exposure of its far-less-fortunate continental neighbours. Thus, all continental countries developed systems for coping with the ever-present threat of intermittent invasion, with which Britain did not need to concern itself.

The second feature of interest about European wars is their frequency and cost. Major wars involving the leading protagonists have taken place in each century since the 14th, with striking regularity, vastly increasing ferocity and considerable switching of alliances. Britain developed in all of their wars an unerring talent for finishing up on the winning side, although, as we know, in the last two wars with Germany, victory could not have been secured without American aid. The ability that Britain had as an off-shore island to change its friends – to alter the pattern of its continental alliances to suit – cannot be over-emphasised. From its enemies it received the sobriquet *Perfidious Albion* or "untrustworthy England", as a result.

The approach was used consistently by Britain's rulers throughout a thousand years of history to divide (and thus rule) its opponents. The sheer frequency of conflict was of less importance to the British than its ability, until now, of preventing any real coalition of continental powers, which would have caused the country real harm. Now, of course, within the context of European Union, Britain is faced with the high probability of an enduring political and economic coalition of its two historic rivals, Germany and France.

The third feature is the extent to which these wars came to demand the mobilisation of the entire resources of nations. The internationalism, extent and savagery of the First and Second World Wars altered the political and social face of Europe. They ultimately consigned to history what we could call an *establishment-driven* model of culture, middle-class security and upper-class social leadership developed in the late 19th century, replacing it with a fresh political power balance resulting from total war and prominently featuring for the first time over the political power of the working classes or, in Marxist terminology, the *proletariat*. The new models of European politics all reflected various forms and degrees of socialism. The post-1945 leaders imposed an all-embracing and highly-welcome model of social assurance, education and health throughout Europe. It is, of course, this very model that all European nations are now finding too expensive to maintain in its existing form.

The historical impact on national cultures is obvious. The more likely your country was to be invaded by a potential enemy – even just out of revenge – the more likely you were to shape your business culture in ways that would quickly and easily respond to that threat. You would place a substantial amount of importance on owning, and maintaining domestic ownership of, industries that had military significance and which created the matériel of war. Even the location of firms would be a matter of political concern. You would focus great attention on the education of engineers and scientists to spearhead your efforts. The rail and road systems would be constructed so as to help with mobilisation and deter the enemy's speedy advance.

To ensure that your strategic industries were well-financed, you might arrange for them to be state-owned or partially-owned by friendly banks, since this would not only provide for capital needs to be met, but would also ensure that the sale of critical national assets to foreigners was not possible. Treating the workforce well would similarly be a priority. You would ensure the maximum degree of commitment to the nation's ideals and obedience to the management hierarchy of the factory in terms of work quality and productivity. Training would be a prime focus so that the supply of skilled labour was dependable. Providing *jobs-for-life* was a standard feature. Japan, in particular, tended to take this approach to extremes. Today, there are still positions in Japanese firms held by employees who do no real work. They are known as *window jobs*.

Those in danger of being invaded would also become very expert in logistics management, having the need to mobilise quickly to repel the invader. This would impose on such countries the need to adopt a sort of *algorithmic* (machine-like) approach on management issues, i.e., a need to find very quickly the key elements in a particular system in order to optimise the results. This approach will later be seen to contrast with other more free-and-easy, experience-driven *heuristic* approaches to problem solving. Government administrators would be drilled in the particulars of their work and in the need for the sort of clockwork precision that military planning requires. Such a systematic, bureaucratic approach to management would tend to become ingrained in the national psyche as being *the only way to work*. A good example is the working of the German civil service in Wilhelmine Germany.

Any country at risk of invasion would put the business of its industry and commerce into a new sphere entirely different from that of countries free from that risk. It would be a sphere in which industry becomes a principal tool of war (and not just a way of making money) and one in which total commitment means economic, as well as military, warfare. It is no exaggeration to say that this was the orientation pursued by Germany under Bismarck in 1870, under Kaiser Wilhelm II and under Hitler. Indeed, under Hitler, Germany was operating under conditions of a war economy from 1935 onwards. The more threatened a country thinks it is, the more likely its political leaders are to view its industry as one of its key weapons and manage it as if it were.

In the course of history most mainland European countries, from Sweden to Italy and from Spain to Russia, have learned and re-learned such lessons from war. Of all of them, France and Germany have been most in the firing line. However, the vast majority have been invaded by foreign troops and systematically ravaged. Britain has never undergone any such experience, and although it has been as much involved in recent wars as our continental neighbours, its people have never been subject to such direct contact with the enemy. The result is that Britain lacks many of the significant features of a corporatist culture which many mainland European states have in the course of their long histories found indispensable.

The consequence of this is that Britain's sense of security (in Hofstede's term, its low level of *uncertainty avoidance*) differs from that of its major European neighbours to a marked degree. So also, its feel for money-making seems to have been much more evident throughout history than its pre-occupation with systematic preparations for waging continental war. Indeed, until the 1914-18 conflict it had never committed itself to anything more than an expeditionary force.

It is worth observing that *jingoism* and a pride in a nation's supposed military superiority often went hand in hand. This word *jingoism* might now be replaced with the word *triumphalism*. In historical terms, it really meant a loud assertion of patriotic values coupled with often bellicose actions. At all events, the tendency was to look upon enemies as inferiors. The British and Germans, with their imperialistic approaches, were especially guilty of this.

Interestingly, this bellicosity and the tribalism on which it is based is now highly visible in the football industry in Europe. For example,

Manchester United's culture is one of mantras (supporters' songs and chants), uniforms (players' kit and supporters' wear) and massive commercialisation pressures (massive transfer fees now subject to new EU systems; Europe-wide competitions; tie-in deals with other sporting groups). All this is aimed at visibility, immediacy and a big presence in the media. This makes for standardisation of football cultures across Europe – even to the extent of ritual clashes among rival fan groups – but accentuates the need for managements to make their individual clubs stand out from others. There is thus the issue of *branding* to consider. Although football fans would perhaps not think in these terms, their brand loyalty (i.e., unquestioning visceral support for their clubs) is an integral part of the clubs' culture.

■ A Question of Political Revolution

Revolution also affected England in a different way and to a different extent from its continental neighbours, even though it, like France and Russia, was guilty of regicide. Perhaps the most interesting dissimilarity is that England's revolution took place in 1649, whilst France's did not occur until 1789, and those of Italy (Benito Mussolini), Spain (Francisco Franco), Russia (Vladimir Illych Lenin) and Germany (Adolf Hitler) took place only in the 20th century. The importance of this fact lies in the way in which autocratic rule – sole rule by a sovereign – was replaced with democratic rule earlier in England than anywhere else in Europe, save perhaps in Scandinavia. This long persistence of top-down rule in many parts of continental Europe inevitably shaped mainland countries' industrial systems and managerial approaches.

The first attack on the king-baron-landowner-serf power distance model so typical of feudalism occurred in England in 1215, when King John was obliged by the military threat of his baronial opponents to sign the Magna Carta, an accord which symbolised political power sharing on the basis of *No Taxation Without Some Representation of the Richest Taxpayers*. The second chamber in Britain's legislature, the un-elected House of Lords, owes its existence to this happening. So also, it could be argued, does much parliamentary government throughout the world. This is because, by the year 1297, the rights of the English parliament to approve taxes and to initiate legislation had been confirmed by the king and the notion of power-sharing had this time expanded to include commoners, i.e., non-aristocrats as well as aristocrats. Only in the city state system of Italy did any such thinking apply at the time in Europe. It, like the England of the period, was effectively ruled by an oligarchy, a set of rich and powerful men. Most other states continued to be managed on the strict top-down feudal absolutism principle (see Table 3.1 page 53).

The revolution carried out against King Charles I by the Puritans in England was as much a religious counter-strike as it was a blow against Charles' tendency to try to re-assert the sort of autocratic government that was still heavily entrenched throughout mainland Europe, except, as has been said, in Italy and in Holland. From this time onward Britain knew of no other form of government but democracy – at first, limited by virtue of a narrow franchise, but later total. Its monarchy and aristocracy developed a flair for co-existence, indeed societal mutation, which was ultimately based on tolerance, flexibility and a strong survival instinct. The fact that middle class ennoblement was possible, especially on grounds of wealth, ensured that the bourgeoisie was not the threat to civil order it became in those parts of the continent where social status and political power were denied to the merchant class because they were merchants and, hence, naturally *socially inferior*. The British business culture was nothing if not adaptable. Wealth connoted formal social status – and still does.

France was the prime example of a system of government that refused to flex and was then broken by bloody revolution. The French king Louis XIV had symbolised the very essence of autocracy, identifying his person with the French state in the phrase *L'état – c'est moi*. His late 17th- early 18th century administration, like those before and after, was driven by those who identified with mercantilism, the doctrine that what matters is the economic power of the state. Jean-Baptiste Colbert, his finance minister, helped his master to extend virtually all aspects of absolutist rule into French life. His bon mot was that every French businessman was *un soldat pour la France*. Colbertisme or state capitalism was managed from the centre via a substantial civil service, staffed predominantly by a professional middle class for many of whom it represented a better form of career advancement than participation in some of the state-run, monopolistic overseas trading companies. Colbert also laid the foundation for state aid to industry, setting up in the process the *manufactures royales* or royal factories. There were even in 1661 French state inspectors checking the quality of goods produced in state factories.

The absence of democracy which such absolutism entailed was visible in France also during the Revolution, where the form of rule was oligarchic and *mob-handed,* and certainly under Emperor Napoleon, where it was dictatorial. He, incidentally, extended the civil service, set up key features of the élitist education system that exists to this day and ran France as a war economy over the period 1804-15. Full-scale democracy was also visibly absent in Russia until 1917, when the Romanov dynasty was eliminated, and also in Germany until 1918 when the last and highly-authoritarian Hohenzollern abdicated from the German throne.

A fascinating aside is the fact that those countries where autocratic absolutism was greatest – Spain and Russia – were those which actually, in the fullness of time, quickly replaced the monarchy with political dictatorships (Franco and Lenin/Stalin) before becoming, in the latter part of the 20th century, democratic. It was as if their populations valued order more than freedom, having experienced the chaos of an excess of freedom.

■ Handling Work

The management of work is yet another area where Britain's historical experiences diverged very early from those of its continental neighbours. The guild system (French *compagnonnage,* German *Zunft*) used to be the way in which consumer products were manufactured in medieval Europe. Forms of agricultural management, involving relative degrees of serfdom, varied also from country to country but mostly obeyed the central principle of obedience to the owner of the land. The more distant you were geographically from the liberalising influence of international trade, i.e., from the coast, the more likely (it seemed) were strict hierarchical land-ownership and -management patterns to apply. Indeed, serfdom was abolished in Russia only in 1861.

The medieval guild system was one of cartels, a limited number of workshops in any given town producing under strict price and quality rules agreed by church and state. Each workshop was owned by a master (Latin *magister,* French *maître,* German *Meister*), who employed journeymen

Britain and Holland: Major Steps towards Democracy		France, Germany, Austria, Spain, Russia: Steps away from Absolutism
King John conceded the Magna Carta after Barons' Revolt. This document formed the basis for trial by jury and sovereignty of parliament.	1215	
Uprising of the Dutch against the absolutism of Philip II of Spain resulted in the establishment in 1588 of the Republic of the United Provinces'.	1566	
	1661	Louis XIV began his reign as the last identifiably absolute monarch of the French.
English Revolution. Execution of Charles I. Oliver Cromwell declared Lord Protector. He ruled until 1660.	1649	
Under Charles II, parliament passed the law of Habeas Corpus - a guarantee of individual liberty and protection against arbitrary arrest in England.	1679	
The Bill of Rights was assented to by William of Orange before he took the throne as a constitutional monarch. It made his rule as king subject to parliamentary democracy.	1689	
	1740	Maria Teresa and Frederick II began their reigns as absolute monarchs in the Austro-Hungarian Empire and Austria and Prussia, respectively.
	1762	Catherine the Great ascended the Russian throne as absolute ruler.
	1789	The French Revolution. It swept away monarchy only to replace it with an emperor, Napoleon I, in 1804. A republic was declared in 1816.
	1871	Reunification of the German Empire under Wilhelm I. He, like the later Romanovs, had strong authoritarian tendencies, but was not an absolute monarch. The defeat of France in 1870 brought the collapse of the Second Empire of Napoleon II.
	1918	The defeat of Germany swept away the monarchy. The monarchy system was replaced by despotism, with Hitler becoming Führer in 1933. Josef Stalin (from 1924) and Benito Mussolini (Il Duce) in power from 1922 were similarly absolute leaders of Italy and USSR, respectively. As was General Franco (the Caudillo) who won the Spanish Civil War in 1939 and died in 1975.
	1945	Defeat of Hitler's Germany brought democracy to Western Europe.
	1989	Dismantling of the Berlin Wall brought democracy to Eastern and Central Europe.

TABLE 3.1: DEMOCRACY VERSUS ABSOLUTISM IN EUROPE

(who worked for daily pay) and apprentices. The latter lived with the master, were fed and clothed by him and received their training at his hands during their seven-year period of tutelage. It was a tightly-prescribed system in which the master had to exercise a duty of care over his workforce. As a consequence, a master of a guild in a town was the leading manufacturer of his type of products and therefore a person of consequence. However, unlike the case in the City of London, where the rank of guild master could result in ennoblement, continental masters were ranked as simply part of the merchant class. For them there was typically no social ladder out of the workshop.

The guild system of manufacture endured in continental Europe much longer than in England, where it was moribund by the 14th century. Its only relic today in Britain is in the activities of the City Livery companies. By contrast, a French eye specialist is still termed *maître* occuliste and a foreman in a German factory is stilled a *Meister.*

Social control was a key preoccupation of church and state throughout medieval Europe. The guild system was an integral part of it as were the top-down rigid management doctrines of the *divine right of kings* and *papal infallibility.* The social control thrust also left its imprint in two important sets of laws. The first were called the sumptuary laws and they carefully laid down what clothing could be worn by different classes. The second related to the inheritance system. Southern Europe was subject to the Salic law in this regard. According to this, the estate of a deceased person had to be divided equally among his heirs. In northern Europe the law specified that, unless otherwise provided for, the eldest son would inherit the estate. Clearly, the implications for land tenure, the size of estates, the career patterns of younger sons etc. were enormous. Overall, the pattern of social life on the continent of Europe was one of a constantly self-reinforcing rigidity and ingrained subservience to those wielding power.

As an aside, it will be recalled that the Enclosure movement in England resulted in the creation of large and extremely productive agricultural holdings. As Swain (1958) points out:

Such enclosures became commonplace after 1760 and reached their greatest frequency during the wars with France 1793-1815, when the high price of grain encouraged speculation in farmland. During the years the great estates of France and Germany were being divided among small peasant proprietors, England became a land of large farms operated by capitalistic methods.

It was precisely such economic divergencies that created fundamentally dissimilar culture bases in different nations. Greece was, and is, a country dominated by small farm holdings.

The manufacturing system in the heart of mainland Europe was itself left undisturbed by some of the innovations which regions closer to the coastline experienced. Indeed, the Catholic church and the feudal state had every reason to preserve the guild system because it fitted very neatly into a structured, systematic and hierarchical cosmos. Britain found very early in its history, however, that the tight stratification involved in the guild system and the price/quality control imposed by Catholic church and state were both incompatible with a realistic merchant or trading ethos. Added to which, as the guilds in England became rich, they became self-seeking, over-expensive and lost their appeal to the public. Nor could you manufacture ships with the sort of tight guild-based system common in continental Europe: you needed to hire workmen when you were building and *fire* them when you were not.

The guild system, by contrast, survived in France and Germany and most especially wherever the aegis of the Catholic church was strong. In a French or South German town an artisan thus needed to have a guild qualification in order to practise, and he needed to abide by the strict codes laid down. The medieval church even had a hand in the issuing of the master's qualification. It certainly helped, along with the civil authorities, to control prices. The German *Handwerkkammer* system exists today in Germany as a major contributor to the country's industrial base by systematically providing for apprentice training. Interestingly, its ethos and origins are those of the medieval guilds. In this it had many analogies with the intensely paternalistic approach followed by Germany's industrialists in the late 19th century. Take, for example, the case of Krupp, the coal-steel-gun conglomerate. So far as this firm was concerned, for example, there was corporate provision of housing, education, health care and even entertainment for all workers. A sort of all-embracing *Krupp-World* was on offer. The other side of the coin, however, was the total obedience to the firm's official rules – the *General*

Directive – that was demanded of each employee. Training was obligatory and job protection mandatory.

Old attitudes die hard and so do some of the systems which are created around them. In mid-1995 there was said to be a massive short-fall in apprenticeship places for trainees in Germany. This was regarded as a major political scandal. By 2001, debate had switched to the issue of Germany's relative shortage of skilled *New Economy* workers, such as software designers, and whether the country should import the competences needed from India in order to create the new economic base. (c.f. Exhibit 3.3 page 61).

■ Controlling Industry

The way industry was managed is also of interest. Trade unionism emerged quite early in Britain as an overtly-recognised political force. The trade unions were established *outside* the companies but could recruit inside them. The major period of their formation started in 1824 with the repeal of the Combination Acts and grew apace after 1851 with the foundation of New Model Unions. By contrast, the creation of similar trade unions in Germany was much hampered by Bismarck's anti-socialist legislation until 1891 and trade unions in Russia were only made legal after 1905. In France, the Confédération Générale de Travail was not founded until 1895.

The continental approach was not to concede political status to organised labour but to try to deal with problems of pay and working conditions inside the industry, and indeed *within* the factory. The individualistic British employers increasingly needed someone with whom to negotiate on the cost of labour, and at arm's length. Naturally enough, the political trade unions in Britain became in time the chief vehicle for the expression of socialist values and helped form today's Labour party. The relationship between Party and trade unions has oscillated over time since the Second World War from warm and friendly to distant and hostile and the unions have never been regarded, as in France and Germany, as players in the social partnership of running the economy.

Wherever industry was state-controlled in continental Europe there was a role for the civil service. In France and Germany the numbers employed in the state administration, in transport and in industry were substantially larger in the 19th century than in Britain. Here, the process of extending the role of the state was very slow as there was a strong historic and nation-wide ethos in favour of private ownership of such elements as health care, education and railways. This resulted in a relative absence from the British scene of the sort of civil service hierarchies which became codified under Bismarck and which in France and Germany constituted a sort of surrogate aristocracy for the upwardly-mobile.

The British could never think of their teachers or railway porters, as did the Germans, as civil servants. Come to that, they have never fully embraced such institutional elements as nation-wide pay rates in industry. Much of the solidity (and stolidity) of public administration in both Germany and France today is due to the traditionalism, self-protection and all-pervasiveness of their administrative services. Exhibit 3.2, below, and Exhibit 3.3 page 61 give a flavour of this monolith.

Francosopie is a comprehensive study of French social trends which is published every two years by its author Gérard Mermet. The Year 2000 edition contains details of the dramatic moving tapestry of French social life in which "les mutants" are contrasted with "les mutins". France, says, the author is a divided two-speed nation with the first group embracing change (they work in private enterprise, drink coca cola, speak English and admire Microsoft).

"Les mutins" ("the rebels"), on the other hand, work on farms or in the public sector, are bewildered by the Internet and shun deodorants. They remain attached to the centralised Jacobin state and remain enamoured of the notion that La France can, in fact, remain wedded to the notion of "l'exception française", i.e., "France is truly different and should remain so" in a globalised world. One of the heroes of the Gallic stereotype that is represented by the "rebels" against change is José Bové, the man who set fire to his home town Macdonald's in Millau.

EXHIBIT 3.2: MUTANTS v REBELS
Based on: Rise of "mutants" leaves France a divided nation,
Adam Sage, *The Times,* 21/11/2000

TOWARDS FREEDOM

ATTACKS ON CATHOLIC CHURCH

- Jean Calvin (1509-64, Martin Luther (1483-1546) for the Church's hierarchy, indulgences etc.
- Francois-Marie Arouet (Voltaire) championed liberty of thought - Candide (1759) - against Catholic dogma.

ATTACKS ON ABSOLUTISM

- John Locke (1623-1704) put forward the major principle of "government with the consent of the governed" in his Two Treatises of Government (1690).
- Baron de Montesquieu's L'Esprit des Lois attacked French absolutism. He lived from 1689-1755.
- Jean-Jacques Rousseau (1712-1778). His Declaration of the Rights of Man spoke of 'man's right of freedom' in a social contract with government. He wrote this on the eve of the French Revolution.
- Jeremy Bentham (1748-1832) created the central argument of Utilitarianism - "the greatest happiness of the greatest number". This was the test for good morals and good government.

LAISSEZ-FAIRE

- Francois Quesney (1694-1774) and Jacques Turgot (1727-1821) were leaders of the Physiocrat School of Economics ('let nature rule'). A direct antithesis to Colbertism (state control) as advocated by Louis XIV's Minister of Finance, Jean Baptiste Colbert (1619-83).
- Adam Smith (1723-90) and David Ricardo (1772-1823) were the major advocates of classical laissez-faire doctrine during Britain's first industrialisation thrust.

TOWARDS CONTROL

DEFENCE OF CATHOLIC CHURCH

- Ignatius de Loyola (1491-1556) founded the Company of Jesus in 1543. Accepted absolute obedience to Pope.
- Bishop Bossuet's Mémoires pour l'instruction du Dauphin (1665) were strictly absolutist and fiercely dogmatic.

DEFENCE OF ABSOLUTISM

- Niccolo Machiavelli (The Prince 1516), Jean Bodin (Republic 1576) and Thomas Hobbes (Leviathan 1651) were all resolute defenders of absolutism. Hobbes argued that man was by nature completely egoistic and, hence, power-driven. The best protection for the individual was an absolute ruler since 'covenants without the sword are but words'. His arguments did not rule out the successful rebellion, however. This took place in England with the Civil War under Oliver Cromwell (1649-60). According to Hobbes, the ruler's will is sovereign only as long as he can enforce it.
- Thomas Hobbes (1588-1679) was the British apologist for absolutism. His views were the very antithesis of those of John Locke.

INTERVENTIONISM

- Karl Marx (1815-1898). Author of the Communist Manifesto (1848) and Das Kapital (1867). In this he saw history as an economic struggle among rival social classes wielding economic and political power with the ultimate victory by working class over the bourgeoisie.
- Otto Von Bismarck (1815-98). Architect, as PM of Prussia of the New Industrial State, highly centralised and heavily administered, with aid to industry and comprehensive social insurance being salient features.

TABLE 3.2: KEY POLITICAL PHILOSOPHIES AFFECTING EUROPEAN BUSINESS CULTURES

This civil service rigidity seems to be yet another example of the difficulty that continental Europe tended to have in living with new forms of more vocal democracy. Here, countries tried alternative ways of managing their public sector workforces, yet none seems to have been able to *flex and fix*, like Britain. In particular, neither France nor Germany has adapted as quickly as Britain has to a rapidly-changing world. Both compared with Britain, still have extremely large civil service bureaucracies. Could it be that political philosophy, as Table 3.2 page 58 indicates, has had a key part to play?

■ Colonialism

The colonisation of parts of America, Africa and Asia by some European countries is yet another area which has left its mark on present-day business culture. Clearly, Britain's current economic strength and world-wide business focus would not have been created, had it not been for the fact that in the nineteenth century it was the world's leading colonial empire. Clearly, also, some part of the Hohenzollern thrust to unify Germany in 1870, was due to the fact that Germany had been eclipsed in the race to acquire colonies by the other continental powers – Britain, France, Spain and Portugal. Failure to grow as a European land power would, it was thought at the time in 1870, consign Germany to second-class status for the conceivable future. Germany's political class did not accept this then as a tolerable prospect. The decision was thus made to seek to gain on land (within Europe) what it had lost at sea (through international colonialism). It was a thrust that was later to re-surface under Hitler as the drive for *Lebensraum* or living space.

For Germany in particular, the pill of having lost out in the race for colonies was particularly bitter. After all, it had led northern Europe commercially in the period from 1100-1400 with the Hanseatic League, the system of German-dominated Baltic trade linked together with main offices (*Kontors*) in London, Cologne, Novgorod and Lübeck. Under this system the merchants of Lübeck and Rostock became politically and economically dominant in the north European region. Then there was also the powerful and advantageous position that Germany had enjoyed in the network of medieval trade fairs that covered the Europe of the day.

At this time this country could have described itself as being in the financial heartland of northern Europe. Certainly, Frankfurt and Leipzig were co-equal in importance with the leading French trade fair centres of Lagny and Bar-sur-Aube at a time when London was, from this perspective, of substantially less commercial significance.

The discovery of the new worlds of America and Asia Pacific changed the status of Germany because:

- at the time it was suffering the economic and political consequences of its dismemberment as a result of the Thirty Years' War (1618-48);

- at the time it had rudimentary access to the Atlantic Ocean through the ports of Hamburg and Bremerhaven, which later became very significant. Most of the ports through which it had achieved its golden Hanse age were in the Baltic.

Such discoveries also changed the status of Italy. Up to the mid-15th century Italy had enjoyed a truly marvellous period of growth under its system of city states such as Genoa, Amalfi and Venice. These were dominated by rich (oligarchic) merchant families and were politically independent of, though often allied with, other feudal states such as Austria, France or Spain. The wealth of such cities was a function of Italy's position at the heart of a trading web that went (by land) to China and (by sea) to India. It thus served, until the silk road was cut by the Turks' seizure of Constantinople in 1453, as the entrepôt centre for the whole of Europe for precious goods such as spices and silk. It had grown rich already as a result of the Crusades from which the Lombards – Italian bankers who were given this collective name – derived much of both their money-changing skills and their capital as bankers. The wealth accumulated by leading families, like the Tolomei (Siena), the Bardi and Medici (Florence) and the Spinola (Genoa) was legendary. The strength of their position was increased by their role as papal tax collectors.

Note that merchant families in other parts of Europe, such as the Holy Roman Empire, also rose to prominence as bankers, e.g., the Fuggers and Welsers.

The new law was blandly called Amendment 2002. Intended to strengthen the 1976 Mitbestimmung Act, which underpins Germany's system of management-worker consultation. It was causing an enormous amount of discord between its principal partisans (the trade union movement) and its key opponents (the German Employers' Federation). The proposal was for a strengthening of Workers' Councils and for an extension of their use to firms with only 51 employees.

Given that the Councils already have broad powers over a range of personnel matters, the new Law means extra costs for the sector it impacts on most – the Mittelstand or large group of medium-sized companies that are said to make up the backbone of German industry – and less flexibility in strategic moves. The Institute for Economic Studies reckons it will cost an extra $1.35 billion. Even within the left-wing government of Gerhard Schroeder, the proposal has caused animosity between the Economics and Labour Ministries.

What is really at stake in the eyes of critics is Germany's commitment to making more moves beyond the government's agreed tax reduction plan to create a more liberal economy. For the trade unions, by contrast, it was a matter of social justice and strengthening the centrepiece of the Rhineland Model of economic management.

EXHIBIT 3.3: AMENDMENT 2002
Based on: Berlin set to approve new workers' rights, John Schmid,
The International Herald Tribune, 14/2/01

As soon as trade with the New Worlds began in earnest, however, Italy's importance started to wane. Its ports were quite simply in the wrong places. There was also the problem that the Turks' seizure of Constantinople in 1453 severed the Silk Road linking Italy and China. Spain and Portugal were not so disadvantaged. Their ports had greater access to the Atlantic and they came to dominate in the early years of the colonial race. Managing the process was relatively simple in the hierarchical Catholic world. Spain was given ownership of all lands west of the Azores by Pope Alexander VI and Portugal and Spain divided up the newly-discovered world between them under the Treaty of Tordesillas in 1494. The approach followed by the two countries was simply to extort wealth (gold and silver) from their colonies.

Mines, such as that at Potosi, were owned by the Spanish crown and business was state-run. There was even an official European agreement to create a government monopoly – called the *Asiento* – covering the importation of slaves from Africa into the New World. As can be imagined, this last was an important commercial property and much disputed. England in fact, won this right as a result of its victory over the French in the War of the Spanish Succession which ended with the Treaty of Utrecht in 1713.

The port that initially gained most from this burgeoning trade was Antwerp: it was Spanish, Catholic and faced the Atlantic. Its bourse was set up in 1485 and its bankers became powerful as financiers of empire. The Netherlands, initially also Spanish-owned, developed in its slipstream. The decline in Spain's power dates in part from its military defeat by the English and the Dutch in 1588 and 1609, respectively. The Dutch particularly rose to prominence at the Spaniards' expense. They rejected any control of the seas, such as had existed under the Treaty of Tordesillas, the Dutch jurist Grotius having put forward the key principle of the *freedom of the seas*. Amsterdam took over from Antwerp as the trading capital of Europe since:

- the government granted monopolies to trading companies like the Dutch East India Company which exploited commercial opportunity to the full;
- the principle of limited liability became widely accepted as the proper basis for business ventures. The previous centuries-old form of the *commenda* or *societas maris* as a collective, merchant-driven enterprise was now superseded by this;
- the availability of capital and trading skills, especially those of the Jews, grew apace;
- Protestantism, the dominant religion, was doctrinally-liberal and economically-friendly as compared with Catholicism;
- the new ships – East Indiamen – built in the Netherlands and Dutch East Indies made long-distance ocean travel feasible.

Undeniably, Spain made a major commercial mistake when, in 1492, it expelled the Sephardic Jews. No doubt it was familiar with the highly exploitive model other European countries, England included, used in respect of the Jews. But, expelling them entirely was different. So welcome were Jewish merchants in Amsterdam that they called it the *New Jerusalem*. Their high-value trading and money skills were much welcomed in London also as an essential ingredient in Britain's later commercial expansion.

It was only when the English put together the same framework strategy as the Dutch – a massive shipbuilding programme, granting monopolies to trading companies and taking advantage of ready capital availability – that her overwhelming competitive advantages came to the fore and she began defeating her trade enemies, the French and the Spanish. After all, Britain also faced the open Atlantic, had iron and coal in abundance and had developed a habit that to continental rulers was as politically strange as it was economically attractive, i.e., that of rewarding profitable trade and licensed piracy alike with ennoblement. In addition Britain was also entirely surrounded by water and necessarily extremely good at ship-building. It was a powerful mixture.

The commercial ascendancy of Britain gathered pace with the exploitation of the assets of colonies in the West Indies. This, as everywhere, was done on the basis of slavery but in a more commercially-viable fashion than an hierarchical France was capable of. The zero-cost work done by the slaves allowed a high level of value added to be gained both by the colonists and by investors in the mother country. Hence, the ending of slavery effectively ruined the British planter class in the West Indies. Their wealth simply vanished as the slaves were liberated.

The theory on which this business came to be based was called *the virtuous circle* since:

- the mother country and the colony were linked together in the enforced exchange of goods – raw materials and food for manufactured goods;
- both parties gained in the exchange, provided, that is, the planters' costs did not include the cost of labour.

But it was the capture of India that provided the take-off point for Britain's greatness. The country's borders were legally sealed; parliament's passing of the Manufacturing Acts forbade Indian domestic manufactures in strategic areas; the Navigation Acts gave Britain the monopoly of trade since only British ships (called *bottoms* at the time) could be legally used; the oligarchic East India Company, and later the British Government, reigned supreme. The virtuous circle model of trade that emerged systematically extracted low value-added food, minerals, commodities and raw materials from India (and, of course, all other colonies and possessions) and sold back high value-added manufactured goods. The profit on the trade from such a rich country stayed in Britain and British manufacturers grew wealthy on a monopoly of industry and trade that was protected, indeed enforced, by British muskets. For as long as Britain's military dominance lasted, that is.

The British belief in free trade stemmed from global trade dominance of this kind. However, what has emerged now from the experience of empire is the City of London's belief that the ability to move capital around the world is now more important than the mere ability to move goods. Indeed, Britain seems to believe in free trade in goods because it believes in free trade in money. When Britain dominated world commerce, free trade meant that British conditions would apply to international commerce. Britain wrote the rules. The end of empire was followed by unsuccessful attempts to keep up the old trade linkages through the doctrines of Imperial and Commonwealth Preference.

Now, with these British rules no longer in force, Britain is once again merely an offshore part of the European continent. Its business culture occasionally pays no regard to this fact but harks back to a land of lost content when Britannia ruled the seas. Its model of capitalism is, however, still the main force driving globalisation through its impact on international financial markets.

■ A case in point: key periods in Japanese industrial history

● The Shogunate Period 1185-1867

Shoguns or military generalissimos held actual political power throughout this period. The emperors continued to rule in name only as divinely-appointed autocrats. Two family dynasties had leading shogunate positions: the Ashikagi (1338) and the Tokugawa (1603-1867).

During much of this period Japan was pre-occupied with two key threats.

Firstly, civil war involving regional warrior aristocrats (daimyos) and their retainers (samurai) each seeking to build up regional power at the expense of the centre. Secondly, the ever-present danger of colonisation as a result of the superior military technology of the Portuguese, Dutch, Americans and English and the way in which the latters' colonisation moves to date had left Japan encircled. Naturally enough, the Japanese were highly resentful of the stand on trade that foreigners (gaijin), especially the Americans, had adopted.

Conversely, Japan was a strong and self-disciplined nation. The experience of the Mongol Horde, led by Batu Khan son of Genghis, had left an abiding impression of the need for fortitude. Religious teachings divided into those which stressed militancy (Zen Buddhism) and those which advocated the doing of good works and acceptance of the settled order of things (e.g., the Jodo sect). The result was a highly-stratified feudal society with innate deference and ingrained obedience. This proved ideal raw material for the subsequent industrialisation of Japan.

● First Industrial Period 1867-1912

A group of samurai contrived the restoration of the Meiji dynasty, ending the capricious rule by shoguns in 1867. They had done this as a result of their analysis of the perilous situation in which their country was placed at the time. This did not involve any form of democracy, however, and political parties made their appearance only in 1889.

The model for industrialisation was patterned on the experiences of Germany under Chancellor Bismarck and reflected the fact that Japan could not, in the situation it found itself, achieve economic power initially through trade. Nor did it have access domestically to the wide range of raw materials it needed to build up its industry base and needed to import large volumes of commodities like iron and oil. Like Germany, therefore, Japan built up large conglomerate industrial groups (later called *Zaibatsu*), which came under heavy state supervision. It had little choice, in effect, given the relative lack of development of commerce at the time. Unlike Germany, however, the intention was that these groups would be able to rely on internal funding. Their workforces were rigidly managed and carefully protected and it is no surprise that Japanese schoolchildren even now wear some elements of Prussian design in their clothing.

The rapid technology advance that the formula permitted was the envy of some other nations. It was built on the innovation in manufacturing capability that a new entry into the market demanded; it took advantage of the skills and devotion of Japanese labour and it reflected the driving force of the Japanese government. Initially the focus was on weapons, and war took place with China in 1894-5 and with Russia in 1905. Here the Russians were soundly beaten at the battle of Tsushima. The self-protecting industrialisation of Japan continued along this track until World War II.

● **Post-war Industrialisation 1960-1983**

After its defeat in the Second World War, Japan had to rebuild. It had access to few of the resources needed by a trading/manufacturing nation to achieve this purpose but, such was its martial spirit, that it was not deterred from trying. Three things worked in its favour. Firstly, American aid was supplied to ensure that Japan would serve resolutely as the USA's first line of defence in the Pacific. Secondly, the imposition of the American decision that Japan could not make military weapons made it certain that Japan would try to seek mastery in civil products. Thirdly, the way in which the USA opened up its markets to Japanese products allowed Japan to achieve critical mass economies of scale in certain product areas.

These three macro opportunities were capitalised on by the Japanese through a corporatist approach to managing the Japanese economy and through maximised productivity. The first allowed the nation to concentrate its efforts on producing "winners" (e.g., cars, ships, consumer electronics), maintain low inflation and labour commitment and, most importantly, to protect the Japanese market-place against foreign imports and takeover threats in ways that seemed quite natural. The second, a reflection of Japanese diligence and quality-mindedness, allowed companies to invest heavily in new technology and new product development. Above all the *Keiretsu* or business alliance formula provided Japanese firms with security and the low cost of capital they needed. In terms of Japan's balance of payments in the 1980s, it was a highly successful approach. The fact that the yen appreciated in value of course made the sale of low value-added Japanese products impossible but it also helped Japan to build up its manufacturing capability in low cost regions of the world. In Britain and the USA, good assets could be acquired very cheaply with a high-value yen.

● Japanese commerce at the turn of the millennium

Japan has proved to be the economic paradox par excellence of the modern world. Following its longest-ever economic expansion in the 1980s, Japan hit the buffers when, in 1990, its stockmarket bubble burst. The Nikkei had doubled in value over the period 1985-1900 and since then has been trading at *below* its value in 1985. Despite all the fiscal and monetary policy moves that the Japanese government has made up to July 2001 – including *negative* interest rates – the economy never really moved beyond stagnation.

The primary reason for this was the level of indebtedness in the system. The expansion in the 1980s was fuelled by a massive level of interbank and bank-company lending, on the one hand, and consumer borrowing on the other. This was buttressed by the *wealth effect* derived from a rising stock market or other forms of capital appreciation. This means that, if your shares rise in value, you feel better off and you want to buy goods which show it. There is no difficulty in raising a loan for these goods as you now have the collateral to back it up, i.e., the shares whose price is rising. Should the stock market collapse, however, you are left with negative equity. And this is what happened on the grandest of scales in Japan.

The second reason has been the fact that the Japanese have tried to ignore the problem of negative equity by really pretending the economy was not in serious trouble. So far as the large corporates are concerned, this has meant large-scale bail-outs of the banking system, a heavy programme of mergers and firms' not going into receivership (which would mean long jail sentences for directors) or laying off workers in large numbers. Conversely, the low value of the yen, a result of the perceived weakness of the Japanese economy, and the buoyant USA economy has dramatically aided Japanese exports. However, the impact on smaller companies within Japan has been significant and has affected Japanese business confidence. Unemployment has grown and there is no longer the promise of life-time employment on offer to salarymen.

The system of unqualified obedience to a prestigious company, in return for job protection and status, no longer has the appeal to the young that it did to their forefathers. The degree of corporate ceremonial and ritual, too, is coming more and more under scrutiny in an increasingly materialistic Japan.

By no means is it the full-scale capitalism of the West, with its hostile take-over bids and labour shake-outs, but it is moving in this direction. And here the media, globally present, demanding instant news in their search-and-destroy missionary zeal and unremittingly mercenary, are playing a full part in achieving cultural transformation.

CHAPTER 4

An Analytical Toolkit

■ Introduction

How a national business community behaves in its distinctive commercial relationships and activities is both visible and tangible. As we have noted, many aspects of the superstructure of our business culture iceberg are plain to see. Hiring, de-selection, working conditions, pay rates, strike activity, trains running on time, money handling – all these are physical outputs from the complicated management and work systems that are governed by a nation's culture and its system of shared beliefs and values. All managers are a physical part of them, just as are all transactions. More importantly, perhaps, all business cultures are now more than ever before in the last century in a state of flux as a result of globalisation.

The bedrock of the iceberg consists of identifiable bases underlying this visible pattern of behaviours. As stated before, these are less discernible as they are sometimes amorphous and always distant from the day-to-day action. They are listed in Table 4.1 page 70.

Each of these areas brings with it a whole series of questions, the answers to which will reveal a substantial amount of managerially-useful information about a country's culture.

Our analytical toolkit will consist of issues and questions based on economics, government and economic and religious ideology.

■ Element 1: Economics

We began this book by discussing the case of the European Battlefield Taxi. Let us now pose the question of whether your foreign colleagues in the European cross-border Battlefield Taxi alliance are self-confident or ambivalent, noisy or reticent, proud or humble, active or passive, aggressive or defensive, persuadable or hard-line. Much will naturally depend on their individual personal psychologies and the profile of the company for whom they work. But it will also be heavily affected by whether their country is richer and more powerful than yours.

1	The country's physical endowments – its size, proximity to the sea, its fertility, accessibility, the nature of its borders (land or water), the balance between mountain and plain (area cultivated), rivers, ease of communication. Its people and their social, economic and demographic structures. Disparity of wealth and life chances.
2	The size, nature, productivity, growth, and growth potential of the country's economy. The nature of wealth distribution. Per capita income. The fiscal balance between direct and indirect tax.
3	The nature of the country's political system – democratic/authoritarian – and the form of, and forum for, decision-making used, i.e., market-driven v command-administrative.
4	Ideologies ranging from politico-economic (enterprise economics v communism, for example) to moral and religious.
5	The nature of the country's historic institutions (e.g., monarchy, parliament, civil service, church) and their power and authority.
6	The nature of the country's social structures. Patterns of deference, class-based behavioural ritual. Inequalities. Inter-generational social change.
7	The major influences on current behaviours arising from the country's history, particularly its experience of war, revolution, colonialism (whether as coloniser or as colony) and political mutation.

TABLE 4.1: KEY BEDROCK CULTURE BASES

Let us begin, therefore, with questions of a nation's economy. Perhaps the most pertinent issue is the relative size of the nation's output, i.e., its gross domestic product. Is the country well endowed with a superb set of natural resources and an enviable climate, geography and location? Does the ambient temperature, in particular, favour hard work? Is the country we are concerned with a G7 country, an OECD country, a World Economic Forum member or is it relatively unimportant? Is it a developed, developing or under-developed country? Has it got a well-resourced infrastructure? What is the level of growth it is currently experiencing and how far into the future can this be sustained? What is the country's track record on inflation and unemployment? What is the breakdown of consumption and investment (i.e., building roads and factories, buying machine tools etc.) and the balance between government spending and private sector spending? What are the trends in both of these?

Such an elaborate checklist is difficult to handle, unless we focus on the basic issue of whether or not the individual business person in a given nation at a given time feels wealthier and/or is getting wealthier, just feels more secure about future prospects or, in fact, is more secure. In other words, we relate the macro factors listed above to actual and potential national income per capita. This allows us to conclude whether the nation's business culture is being influenced by a mood of optimism, dynamism, pro-activity, aggressiveness – if the income per capita is rising – or the converse.

The answers to these questions will go far towards establishing the business climate that exists at that time within the national business community. A large economy, growing at a reasonable rate, for example, induces a belief in the future and a sense of commitment, dignity and pride in its citizens. It might even stimulate an inbuilt sense of power and leadership, even a certain arrogance, if the country in question happens to be the USA, Japan or Germany of today.

As part of the economic enquiry we will want to know the balance of national output among the key contributors shown in Table 4.2 page 72. We need to know the pattern of change as well as the current levels in order to ascertain the rate of business developments that is taking place. Thus we are interested in the extent to which the country under investigation produces a substantial volume of high value-added output, i.e., products with a high profit margin which are made either with high knowledge intensity (e.g., scientific invention or design flair) or high technology intensity (e.g., using high specification robots).

It may be we are interested in working with an Indian company. A study of India indicates that there will be pockets of a more advanced level of high value-added production (e.g., computer software in Bangalore, Maharashtra) but that a major portion of the country is under-developed and seeking to get by with an agricultural subsistence economy. Conversely, because the unit cost of labour is low overall and literacy among the Indian middle classes or *bourgeoisie* is very high, the business prospects for some investors in India may be particularly good. Hence, the interest of the Indian government is to attract in-bound foreign direct investment to build up the country's economic capabilities. The dominant Indian political mindset is, however, not to reward foreign investors by selling off national assets too cheaply.

Type of Industry	% Contribution to the Nation's GDP
Extractive industry	Coal, oil, gas, bauxite etc.
Farming	Grain, meat etc. Low v high technology methods.
Manufacturing	Heavy v light, OEM v assembly, low v high technology, industrial v consumer products. Export-Import Ratio.
Services	Domestic v export-oriented. Value adding (e.g., software design) v control (e.g., accountancy).
Entrepôt activities	Transport, shipping, logistics management. The country thrives because of its location at the crossroads of many international trade paths.
Rentier activities	Cross-border portfolio investment (foreign stocks, bonds) or direct foreign investment. The country gains through its overseas investments.

TABLE 4.2: POSSIBLE CONTRIBUTORS TO A NATION'S ECONOMY

Another element in the feeling of security in itself that a nation can have (or not, as the case may be) lies in an alternative, *cruder* way of figuring out the make-up of the GDP. That is to seek an answer to the qualitative questions we may pose about the quality of labour input available in the country. (See Table 4.3 page 73.) For instance, what precisely is the Brains-Brawn balance in Malaysia today? Does the country have the balance of talent it needs to meet its ambitious economic growth targets? Does the country value its brains and its brawn in equal measure?

Economic element	Contribution to the National Economy in Qualitative Terms
Brains	Scientific research resulting in commercially-attractive intellectual property which will create a long-term return. Design capabilities in scientific or aesthetic terms. The work of people who invent and design high value-added products and services.
Brawn	Superior manufacturing capability in the extractive, manufacturing or service industries and/or high productivity and/or low unit cost whichever is the more commercially viable. The work of people who make or assemble things or who provide low value-added services.

TABLE 4.3: THE BRAINS-BRAWN EQUATION

To put the argument in basic terms, Britain, as compared with Japan, the USA and Germany, significantly under-spends on long-term civil commercial research and development, except, that is, for certain industries such as pharmaceuticals and defence. This does not mean, however, that many high-grade British scientists are out of work. Not at all, since, with their relatively low rates of pay and high level of expertise, they can, all other things being equal, win research contracts placed by firms who cannot afford to do some of the volume of research needed in their own domestic markets. The ultimate patents are, of course, the property of those commissioning the research in the first place. This is one of the reasons why the USA and Japan are international leaders in this field.

Why Britain may be said to underspend in these areas is bound up with the apparent unwillingness of British investors to hazard large sums of money long-term on high-risk projects unless *super-normal profits* will result if the project succeeds. The more competitive the market for funds, the higher the rates of return have to be to guarantee availability of capital. If we then consider Britain to have, on average, a worse history of inflation control than some of its leading trade rivals, then the hurdle rate for capital investment (i.e., the return on capital employed which must be obtained) may be too high to accommodate long-term, uncertain scientific research projects. After all, it incorporates both an allowance for inflation as well as risk. The significance of this cannot be underrated as it has ramifications for the way the country's esteems and values its inventors, designers, engineers, pop stars and football players.

On such a basis, leadership in some high-cost areas of science will naturally be achieved by those competitors whose pockets are longer than Britain's or those of similar spenders. In other words, Britain's trade-off between risks and returns may differ substantially from that of some of its major competitors. The more heavily a nation's business community trades in money, foreign exchange, stocks, bonds and futures as a way of making a living, as opposed to manufacturing that is, the more likely are those involved to have a gambling orientation to their work. Britain falls into this mould, at least as far as the Square Mile is concerned. It is valuable to note that French president Chirac has described one aspect of this trading – currency speculation – as *le sida de nos économies* (the Aids disease of our economies). This comment was made by him at the G7 Halifax summit in June 1995.

The comparative shortfall in British ownership of intellectual property that had become equally obvious and unrecoverable in the 1970s inevitably provoked a crisis decision by the British government in the 1980s. It needed to sharpen up the nation's *brawn* capability. The ensuing strategy involved a powerful Thatcherite cocktail of reducing the power of the trade unions, making the British work force more flexible and ensuring that work done in Britain was cheaper than elsewhere in mainland Europe. At the same time, the government was able to capitalise on its membership of the European Union to give in-bound foreign investors in Britain powerful access to the continental market-place for the products they could assemble, if not make, in British factories. Thus, its competitive strategy has been more harnessed to brawn and location than that of some of its foreign competitors.

The ideology on which the strategy was based was a neo-liberal one which played up the importance of organised capital at the expense of organised labour and reversed the trend to socialism which had been the post-war hallmark of British politics. It is no over-statement to say that prime minister Thatcher changed the pattern of Britain's business culture.

So far, we have spoken of the business community within a particular country as if it were a monolith to be easily identified. In most countries this is not a realistic way of proceeding and there are two important qualifications to be addressed.

Firstly, in any particular country there will be those who have an interest in making money through producing products or services and those who make money simply out of owning, or making, rentier investments in, such producers. This distinction we could label the *Merchant-Maker Balance*. It is an important distinction since it deals with the extent to which some owners of capital are wedded to money-making as their supreme value whereas others treat the products and services made in their factories, and their workforces, as the most important feature. Certainly, attitudes to employees and workforces in general will be substantially shaped by this trade-off.

If you have a "merchant" orientation to business, for example, you will tend to regard a workforce as a factor of production – alongside money and machinery. You will seek to optimise cost relationships as your main priority. If need be, to increase your return on capital, you may even consider exporting work to other countries where it is cheaper. If a "maker", you will cherish your people and, especially, your scientists and engineers. Under such circumstances you may value accountants less than engineers – and pay them accordingly. Not for nothing is the title of engineer (abbreviated to *Ing* on business cards) the most honoured qualification in the Czech Republic. In the period from 1925-35 Czechoslovakia was a European leader in many areas of technology and Skoda was one of its brightest stars.

If you are, in fact, more socialistic in your views, production for itself and in your own country may rank as your supreme interest. Social solidarity and the benefit of the nation state may outweigh the personal returns you seek from your investment. Such altruism may have, as we will again see in Chapter 5, very important roots in a country's history.

A second qualification of the global expression *the national business community* relates to the type of ownership of business that exists. In what proportions are the country's major companies owned by the state, by the banks, by other national companies, by individual national shareholders, by foreign companies, by foreign shareholders? And, of course, not only how companies are owned but whether or not the owners can manage the companies in proportion to the shareholdings they have? The significance of these questions lies in the fact that (a) a company can be regarded quite differently by its various stakeholders – consumers, employees, managers and shareholders. As we shall see later in case studies, there can also be significant qualitative differences between shareholders from different countries. Some owners may hold large packets of shares but be allowed only relatively few votes at shareholders' meetings. It also lies in (b) the location of power. Many socialistically-minded countries are quite happy with international investment in their companies. But they are not at all happy with the notion that foreigners through their ownership of shares are controlling their economies. Exhibit 4.1 below shows the extent of the dilemma that China faced in 2001.

China declared in late February 2001 that it was going to relax the rules governing investment in the country's stocks and shares. Up to that time, these had been divided into two types - A and B - with local investors being only able to buy the A type. The B shares could be bought by foreigners as, although they were listed on the Shenzen and Shanghai exchanges, they were denominated in foreign currencies and did not connote managerial control over Chinese companies. They could not purchase the A type.

This has restricted their appeal to foreign companies and caused the Chinese capital market to be less liquid and smaller than was hoped. China's membership of the WTO means that China's largest companies need to be able to raise capital much more freely than before and hence need to free up the capital markets. There is even a plan to merge the stock markets to allow the free sale of stock free from political control by the Communist government.

EXHIBIT 4.1: CHANGING TIMES IN CHINA
Based on: Beijing to widen access to markets for Chinese, Craig Smith,
The International Herald Tribune, 20/2/2001

At one extreme, state ownership (as in China) could well connote a feeling that the company owned is of vital strategic importance to the economy, either because of its GDP contribution or because it employs substantial numbers of workers. Its ownership should, therefore, be protected and, if it falls on hard times, it should be heavily subsidised. At the other end of the spectrum, a foreign owner of a portfolio of shares could well be wholly value-neutral about either the interests of the country invested in and those of its workers, so long as a good return on the shares is received. The case studies of Mexico in 1994 and 2000 are a particularly good example of what happens when footloose international investment capital seeks a new home.

A key question to ask, if one of the country's major banks owns a large slice of the stock, is whether the bank sees the holding as a short-term or long-term one and whether it would be prepared to divest itself of those shares willingly. So far as Germany is concerned, so substantial were holdings in many industrial companies by leading banks, that the observer could not but form an impression of a German *bank-industry complex*. This still existed in 2001, despite the large-scale shift in the pattern of capital gains tax that the Schroeder government made in 2000, with the express intention of allowing banks to divest themselves of industry holdings. In this it may be supposed that the banks' role is to preserve the integrity and functioning of the German industrial machine, taking a return on their holding as an important but almost secondary feature of their investment.

Yet another way of examining the impact on a nation's culture that comes via the management of its economy is to examine, firstly, the nation's *Man-Machine Balance* and, secondly, its trend-line on employment. The *Man-Machine Balance* relates to the extent to which a nation produces its stock of goods and services, either through manual labour or through automation. In other words, it seeks to measure the relative extent of capital investment. Naturally, the business investor is concerned with the relative costs of these two modes of production, since he is anxious to manipulate these and the cost of capital, marketing and distribution to achieve optimum results.

The government's concern is with overall cost-competitiveness of the nation and the state of its national accounts. Perhaps the purchase of automated plant from an overseas supplier involves the exporting of capital the nation does not have and means increasing indebtedness. But the chief concern may be with the unemployment that might arise if machinery replaces labour. At all events those threatened with redundancy under such conditions may seek, all other things being equal, to accept lower wage rises than may normally be the case.

India's reputation as a safe destination for foreign investment risked a serious setback when the state government of Maharashtra demanded that the Texas-based Enron Corporation renegotiate a controversial power project at Dabhol for the second time in six years. The demand followed a stormy debate in the state assembly about the cost of the electricity produced by the facility and the prices charged by Enron. The Dabhol plant is symbolic of India's problems.

The country needs a major increase in electricity capacity today to make up for the so-called lost decade for power reforms, and multinationals like ABB, International Power and Electricite de France have been tempted. But the problem is that some states cannot pay for what they need and the multinationals have better prospects elsewhere in the world. Indeed, the cost of electricity from the plant has risen by two to three times the original estimate since the rupee has declined in value and naphtha fuel costs have spiralled.

And, on top of that, Percy Barnevik, the former head of ABB, speaking at a conference in Delhi, reckoned that India was not forcing agricultural cusomers to pay their bills and that power theft and fraudulent billing were rife. The protestors, by contrast, waved their placards outside the Dabhol plant. They read "Enron quit India"!

EXHIBIT 4.2: ECONOMICS AND CULTURE IN INDIA

Source: Indian state asks Enron to revise the power deal, John Elliott, *The International Herald Tribune*, 12/12/2000

This has the admirable effect of keeping the cost of goods sold down. Similar pressures of course apply to capital investment in new plant and machinery which might replace labour. Costs for this, too, must be kept under control. Such views would be typical of a neo-liberal government but not a socialist one. It is a vision which is wildly at variance with Exhibit 4.2 above.

A nation's range of value-added products & services which collectively adds up to its GDP

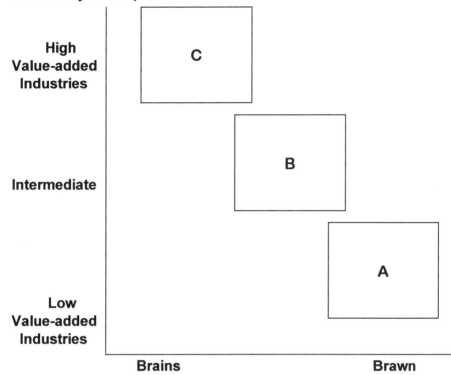

The nature of labour input in a nation's industries

Notes: A = Low value-added products (such as low-priced shoes or textiles) and services which can be produced in Europe with high labour input only if wage and non-wage costs are kept low. They can be more profitably produced in some Asia Pacific countries where unit labour costs are extremely low. Thus, if wage levels rise in Europe, jobs might migrate around the globe.

C = High value-added products and services (based on high technology or design flair) produced with low levels of high-cost labour. This is the Eldorado aimed at by leading European countries anxious to build up the value of their GDP, but involves handling rising unemployment.

Note that the commoditisation of products and services continuously downgrades the level of value-added (profit) that can be achieved just as automation reduces the volume of employment under old style technology conditions. The shift from A to C is sometimes referred to as *climbing the technology ladder*

FIGURE 4.1: VA-LIN ANALYSIS

© Terry Garrison, 2001

Note, in this connection, how some aspects of modern technology favour female, rather than male, employment. The assembly of consumer electronic products, for instance. Throughout Western Europe there is currently an unemployment crisis which is affecting young males who are unskilled and under-qualified, perhaps to a greater extent than their female counterparts. A government strategy of keeping wage rates low does have the effect of bidding higher numbers into work but may not be capable of achieving categorical success in reducing male youth unemployment because the skills of the latter are more related to heavy manual work which many modern technologies simply do not require.

So far as employment is concerned in fact, a further elaboration of our previous argument is in order. Figure 4.1 page 79 presents a situation of a qualitative trade-off between the type of labour used and the mix of products and services produced by the country making up the country's GDP. These are rated on a scale from high value-added (i.e., large profit margin) to low value-added. As the figure indicates, examples of the former could be brain scanners, jumbo jets or Versace suits (designed in Italy, made in China?). The latter might comprise low-grade footwear, plastic cups and, perhaps surprisingly, personal computers. These would now rank in this category because:

- the technology which is used to produce them has now been commoditised just as the products have been;
- there is no longer any substantial brand franchise (speciality status) in some products because of the widespread use of automation;
- the resultant general price war in the industry has driven prices down to rock bottom; and
- the products are made in the cheapest possible locations consistent with quality.

When applied to our current open world trading situation, with its lowered tariffs and free capital movement, the Value-Added – Labour Input (VA-LIN) analysis throws up the following propositions:

- that, if a government wishes its manufacturers to continue to manufacture product in quadrant A and it wants to keep unemployment down and it wants to honour its free-trade obligations <u>and</u> it is faced with low-cost competition from overseas, <u>then</u> there is no alternative but to keep the wage bill under tight control and, if possible, protect its domestic market. Britain, as we have seen, has sought to remain competitive in this sector by effectively cheapening work. Interestingly, however, it has not sought to protect its domestic market. In fact it has used openness of access as a spur to gain even more workforce competitiveness by forcing a rise in worker productivity in order to preserve jobs Furthermore, all governments after Mrs Thatcher' have omitted to pursue a policy of full employment. Marx' theory of the reserve army of the unemployed (i.e., millions of workers outside the factory gates are seeking your job) puts an interesting gloss on this approach. It should be noted that the cumulative effect of all of these factors has been to induce a mood of great uncertainty in the business community and among the nation's workforce.

- that Quadrant C is the Eldorado for all developed countries. This is the quadrant where the finest products are produced using the nation's best-qualified labour. A high profit margin allows high salaries which, in their turn, attract high quality labour in a virtual, and virtuous, upward spiral. However, it is not a quadrant to which all countries can have equal access, nor in which all countries can perform equally well. Highly-qualified labour is ultimately in short supply. Not only that, the intense pressure in this quadrant can ultimately have the effect of commoditising (or cheapening), through price competition, some of the brands that once ranked supreme. Hence, it is not necessarily a safe haven – especially when cheaper countries can also use high-grade technology at will.

- To succeed long-term here there is no alternative, in fact, to continued and high levels of investment. This may take the form of increased investment in intellectual capital, i.e., to keep up the innovative development of knowledge – or technology-intensive goods (as in Japan) or that of aspirations to marketing leadership in the industry (as in Britain) or both. Success, therefore, means continuing to move, as we say, *up-market.*

- Note, however, that some highly successful developing countries (e.g., Malaysia and Korea) are now beginning to find themselves squeezed in their Quadrant C positions. This is because their once-formidable labour cost advantage is now disappearing, in part as a function of their continuing industrialisation and economic success. This approach is particularly problematic for countries whose governments have not left the choice of which products or services the nation should produce to its businessmen but have intervened. Nations like Malaysia, Korea or Japan fall into this category. In fact, in the 1960s Japan's Ministry structure (e.g., MITI or the Ministry of International Trade and Industry), with civil service support and an over-arching strategic planning framework, laid down the range of product possibilities which Japanese industry was exhorted and encouraged to act upon. This became the archetypal *flying geese* model which other industrialising nations followed. Advanced shipbuilding, car production and personal electronics were three such areas. It was popularly called *Japan Inc.*

For many countries there is a product possibilities curve which links in quadrants A and quadrant C together. This represents a situation in which a particular country has become uncompetitive in low and medium value-added goods and services because, for instance, its costs (wage, non-wage, capital, distribution, raw materials, currency etc.) are too high. It has tried to remedy that situation by moving into higher value-added output. If the country has an adequate stock of high quality resources (especially science graduates) and a good quality product possibilities base (personal electronics, cars, specialised shipping, software, aeronautics etc.), possibly created with governmental support, then prospects may look good. It is climbing the technology ladder.

For a country which does not have a strong position in Quadrant A, a lower resource base than is needed and a government which allows strategic product possibility decisions to be wholly market-driven, economic prospects can only look good if all costs are kept under increasingly tight control.

All governments, without exception, are now faced with the need to tackle unemployment in a world where products and services are becoming increasingly commoditized and their manufacture automated. The business culture consequences of this will be immense. If the world continues to globalise its pattern of trade, and if developed nations are not legally able to protect their markets from lower cost imports, then those countries most affected have no choice but to embrace business cultures which emphasise competitiveness at ethe expense even of equity. In other words, as the Russian proverb puts it, if you live among wolves you need to learn to howl like one.

Such issues go to the heart of the mood of the nation and its business leaders. Are the latter positive and optimistic enough to invest in their own domestic market or are they taking advantage of the open trading world to export capital? Are governments defensive and trying to protect their industries against cheaper foreign imports? Are the countries' leading companies taking over their rivals or being taken over themselves? Does it matter that a country's leading companies are owned by foreign-owned companies, especially in an age of international share ownership? Such issues are of great significance for an understanding of bedrock culture.

It is important to recognise that, if a European country is becoming uncompetitive in Quadrant A, failure to take action by reducing costs or moving as quickly as possible into Quadrant B or, if possible, C will result in the lack of long-run GDP growth. To maintain or even increase social expenditures on pensions or unemployment benefit would take a larger tax slice of the low-growth GDP. This would then have an impact, in a depressing spiral fashion, by lowering growth possibilities. The consequences of such a long-term position in Europe are too serious to contemplate. Therefore, all European governments have taken steps to reform their economies.

The business culture implications of lower-than-necessary economic growth for any developed European country are substantial: it would have to begin dismantling aspects of its *Welfare State* and to change the nature of its *Social Contract* with its citizens.

■ Element 2: Government

Government and governance has to do with who rules and how. The first concerns the state where rule-systems may exist at federal, national and local levels as in Germany and the USA, but not in Britain. Government depends on either the granting of legitimate democratic authority by the citizens (democracy) to an elected authority or the usurpation of power by a person or group. So far as the latter is concerned, we distinguish between totalitarian, oligarchic and merely authoritarian regimes. The first is rule by one person or party, the second by an important clique which owes its leadership position to wealth (and sometimes military or clerical power). All three tend to claim quite ostentatiously to rule on behalf of, and in the interests of, the people.

Rule systems do, of course, exist at supra-national levels, as in the use of the European Union, the World Bank and the International Monetary Fund.

Governance has to do with the system of management of firms. It focuses on whether ultimate power and authority shall rest solely with the representatives of the owners – the board of directors – or whether other stakeholders (e.g., workforce, trade unions) should rightfully participate in decision-making in some structured way. For example, in Germany this is typically done in large companies through works councils and supervisory boards charged with ratifying decisions made by boards of directors. Note, as an aside, that the European Union's policy – the Social Charter – is to introduce works councils throughout Europe, a move strongly resisted by the British Conservative government of John Major and later welcomed by the New Labour administration of Tony Blair.

How important is government as a bedrock culture driver? It is immense. The way a nation is governed affects all the attitudes, opinions and belief systems of all its citizens because of the impact it has on their freedoms, their life chances and their prosperity. This is because politicians decide on, firstly, how to stimulate economic growth on the basis of the nation's factor endowments (its resource profile) and, secondly, having created a prosperous economy, how to divide up the national income.

How the economic cake is baked and sliced up affects all aspects of a nation's business culture.

Stimulating economic growth means making appropriate decisions on the balance between state and private ownership of the means of production, i.e., the types of firms that will be allowed to exist. Naturally, this is done in the particular time and resource-base context. In the 1960s and 1970s, for example, British governments were supportive of the notion of nationalised firms and, in many ways, comprehensive industrial state planning. The approach typically involved corporatist management of the nation's labour and financial systems on an integrated basis. Under the socialist government of Harold Wilson it even incorporated a National Plan (n.b. France still has an indicative Plan National).

By the 1980s, by contrast, the pendulum had swung wildly, under administrations led by Mrs Thatcher, to favour private enterprise as the essential route forward to create greater economic competitiveness. This amounted to a massive and speedy switch to a much more pronounced individualist culture. Each approach involved different forms of companies, different management philosophies (c.f. Harbison and Myers' model) and different government-industry relationships. Interestingly, the New Labour government in Britain, as from 1997, accented economic efficiency and competitiveness just as heavily as previous Conservative governments had done.

All governments also need to decide on the nature of competition in the country, both in principle and in terms of the legitimate sizes of firms. This may mean anti-monopolistic legislation and rules to curb the market power of large oligopolistic players. Conversely, in counties where nationalised industry has been favoured, monopolies (like France Télécom or Russia's Gazprom) have been heavily supported and come to be regarded as *national icons.*

However heavily-oriented to free enterprise the Conservative government of Great Britain was in the 1980s and 1990s, it still found that, to protect the public interest, privatisation of state utilities could not be allowed without building in an elaborate set of safeguards. The local monopolies it created in the water and electricity distribution industries and the protected duopoly status of firms sharing the electricity generation and telecommunication markets, for example, needed to be controlled in the public and, moreover, the government's political interest. The pricing of services and competition in these sectors needed to be regulated – a major paradox. To deal with this problem of regulating de-nationalised industry without appearing interventionist, the government created a set of quasi-independent regulators who did (and do) the government's work without being too closely identified with the machinery of state. It is interesting to observe that the New Labour government of Tony Blair did not reverse the previous government's stance on de-nationalisation.

France and Germany have taken different approaches over this period on the need to privatise and the manner in which privatised state companies should be managed in the public interest. Of course, the more competition-driven the county's industries are, the more likely it is that the government will be a strong adherent of capitalism, the private ownership of wealth and the means of production. And vice versa.

Political Management Systems

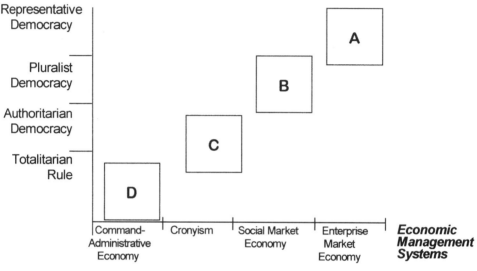

FIGURE 4.2: POLICONOMY ANALYSIS

Note:

(1)   A policonomy is a combination of a particular type of political system or polity and a particular form of economy. Countries can sometimes be located in one of the indicative A-D quadrants but are more likely to be in transition between them , following their idiosyncratic trajectories.

(2)   Examples of A are the USA and Britain. Their economies are enterprise- or market-driven to a considerable extent and they have, relatively speaking, a minimalist orientation to the welfare state. Their political approach is based on separation of powers.

(3)   Examples of B are Germany, Holland, France and Italy. Here pluralism and a social market economy are key features. They all see sectoral collaboration, i.e., government - business - labour, as important. This is referred to as a mixed economy.

(4)   Examples of C are S. Korea and Indonesia. 'Authoritarian' signifies a very heavy presidential or prime ministerial rule and 'Cronyism' means that control of industry and commerce may be excessively placed in the hands of presidential nominees, supporters, friends and family.

(5)   Examples of D are the USSR of Brezhnev and the China of Mao Tse Tung. Modern China is following a horizontal path away from D towards a market economy.

(6)   A country's position on the political management axis illustrates the extent to which it responds to citizens' demands. Its position on the economic management axis shows the level to which it is consumer-driven.   © Terry Garrison, 2001

Capitalism also lies at the heart of the question of distributing the nation's income. A strong belief in private ownership connotes *Little Government*. Why? Because capitalism is primarily concerned with the individual creation of wealth by entrepreneurs and the maintenance of private wealth by those who already have it. The socialist model of *Big Government* typically seeks, by contrast as its title suggests, to intervene through its taxation policies to change that pattern. It might curtail private ownership of production by nationalising firms or reducing private wealth or income by its taxation systems. This is done, not in the name of economic efficiency or effectiveness, but in the name of social equity. Thus, a country's business culture is necessarily powerfully shaped by the political colour of its government.

Figure 4.2 page 86 can be used to plot the policonomic position of individual countries on two scales: firstly, the extent to which they are consumer-driven and, secondly, citizen-driven. The first relates to the extent to which they espouse market or enterprise economics, i.e., have little faith in state ownership and regard consumer choice and, therefore, the market-place, as the true test of a nation's competitive capabilities. Such a laissez-faire approach involves a limited level of government intervention in industrial management and as low an accent on redistributive taxation as is feasible. In such a state, the length of your pocket would go a long way to determining your life chances.

A government which is purely citizen-driven would have such a strong belief in representative democracy that it would seek to exclude from government, again as far as feasible, any form of pressure exercised by oligarchic (i.e., powerful, but numerically small groups) organisations, be they industrial, financial, ecclesiastical or social. The people would decide, and without sectional pressure. The arguments for this rest on the

- extent to which government of any form is perceived to be in some measure an unwarrantable intrusion into citizens' private lives;
- the level to which state economic management can represent, inevitably, a more ineffective and inefficient form of resource usage than can be achieved in the private domain.

Quadrant A in Figure 4.2 page 86 illustrates a position where a government is extremely responsive to the requirements of the majority of the citizens that voted it into power. Of course, it is not feasible for a state to operate in a wholly economically and politically libertarian fashion. This is because its citizens, rich and poor, are inevitably concerned with voting for parties which represent their own interests more than those of others and the government must concern itself with conflict avoidance between these two. Hence, the political power balance in any democratic state will rest between those who uphold the existing share-out of national income and those who would change it. Democracy always equals open dissension. Political genius stops it from becoming action on the streets.

Quadrant B matches the pluralistic government system with the social market economy. Pluralistic government signifies a democratic basis, with proportional representation, rather than Britain's first-past-the-post system being the continental norm, plus an input into decision-making from other societal groups. Such groups could comprise organised labour in the form of the country's trade unions, the country's leading employers (e.g., the *Patronat* in France, the *Keidanren* in Japan), the major banks and insurers, the Church (as in Poland). The idea of this is simple: structured power-sharing and interest representation, with no national power bloc being excluded, equal more-balanced, rounded decisions which have a greater chance of being socially acceptable to the country as a whole.

It is interesting to note, by contrast, that in Britain the trade unions were, during the period from 1979 to 1997, progressively marginalised or excluded from direct intimate contact with the government. Previously they had been regarded as full partners in the management of British industry and heavily involved in advising governments. Their rise to pariah status under successive Conservative administrations was accompanied by a fall in their power as membership in them declined. It is fascinating to note, as an aside, that Britain's New Labour government has not been accommodating, either.

On the other hand, both the Conservative and New Labour governments' willingness to listen to advice from the City of London has increased markedly since 1979.

Why the British trade unions were so treated is not far to seek; in the view of these administrations they had maintained the power and cost of organised labour in Britain for too long at an economically unsustainable level. Governmental legislation in 1980, 1982 and 1984 brought them to heel. Why the voice of the City of London is now attended to more is also clear. Britain is heavily dependent in terms of international politics and its invisible trade balance on what the *Square Mile* is thinking and doing.

A *social market economy* is one where the government is pledged by its written constitution to balance its share-out of the national income among the have-nots as well as the haves. In other words, the government must take specific account of the social needs of the old, the poor, the unemployed and other disadvantaged groups in deciding on measures to create and distribute national prosperity. The more republican the government, the more likely it is to do so.

After a decade of dipping its feet in and out of the sea of capitalism, unsure of just how much Marxist-Leninist ideology it should abandon in the post-Cold war world, Vietnam has decided to plunge into the free market. It has signed a landmark trade agreement with its former enemy, the USA, to allow low-tariff exports to America and American investment in Vietnam.

The deal was signed in Ho Chi Minh city and was thought to involve a major reduction in Communist control over the economy and a shake-up of its corrupt and inefficient state enterprises.

The Vietnam government welcomed the surge in the exports of cheap clothing, shoes and toys that would take place. It would bring enormous benefits to its population of 79 million people. But The American trade union federation, the AFL-CIO, said it would fight the deal which, it said, threatened labour standards and human rights.

EXHIBIT 4.3: NECESSARY CHANGES IN VIETNAM
Source: Vietnam takes leap toward the free market, Rajiv Chandrasekaran,
The International Herald Tribune, 15-16/7/2000

The method naturally selected for creating and maintaining a social market economy is a country's fiscal policy. A country that is representative of a social market economy, like France, will use its taxation and security system to transfer wealth and income from rich to poor, whatever the complexion of government. Of course, the argument used to support this approach is that the nation's overall wealth can be increased to a greater extent if all citizens pull together in a truly collective endeavour, rather than if they each try to maximise their individual wealth. The counter argument is that such economic frictions as the need to maintain a high level welfare state simply put a brake on the country's ability to grow economically; they divert investment from production to consumption.

Quadrant C – the mixture of authoritarian government and cronyism occurs in countries which are democratic but which are led by a particularly strong leader. The tendency may exist where he or she, possibly corruptly, hands positions of power in government, industry and commerce to "cronies", i.e., friends and family.

Quadrant D represents the combination of state totalitarianism and a command administrative economy. Here, the rulers of the state decide everything – freedom/social control, guns/butter – without the need for any real form of democratic machinery. This was the USSR under president Brezhnev. Given the abject fall from great power status of the USSR in 1989, this quadrant represents for Western nations a policonomy no-go area. China is still seeking at present to combine totalitarian political rule with aspects of social market economy.

Most advanced democratic, developed nations, indeed, find themselves in Quadrants A or B. However, major differences exist between states that tend to be corporatist (B) and those that tend to be individualist (A). The former use the pluralism-social market formula as a basis and then add on to it a process for integrating the workings of industry and the economy to maximise economic benefit. In other words government, industry, organised labour and the financial authorities work together for their common benefit in pursuing the national interest. They may even use a national planning system; they may arbitrarily decide on which products and services the country should produce. Such governments are interventionist and have a tendency to be protective of their national interests and property. As we shall see later, Japan, Germany and France fit this model.

On the other hand, individualist states, such as Britain and the USA, seek a balance between capitalism and socialism (the typical corporatist creed). The balance here leans towards creating wealth, in which sphere market or enterprise economics is seen to win hands-down over corporatism. Big government, with its tendency to plan strategically for key aspects of a nation's industry, is frowned upon. The taxation system is, consequently, less re-distributive than that in socialist regimes.

It is of great importance to note again that all Western governments which have, for reasons of social justice and social solidarity, created substantial *welfare states* are now finding difficulty in funding them. Four key reasons explain the problem. Firstly, the changing pattern of demographics, with more people becoming dependent on the state. Secondly, the rise in global competition resulting from more open world trade and the growing stress of unemployment in those countries whose competitiveness is diminishing, not rising. Thirdly, the resistance of taxpayers to increasing impositions. Fourthly, the recognition by governments that high fiscal pressure on a nation's economy can have highly negative consequences. The net effect is that countries with once well-secured corporatist approaches are now finding themselves exposed to change. Deregulation, privatisation and break-up of some mutually-supportive governmental, industrial and commercial frameworks is now an everyday reality in, for instance, France, Germany, Japan and even Korea. The 1997-8 economic crash in Asia Pacific forced the last two to adopt a more liberal approach to economic management than their previous corporatism culture had ever conceived of.

In practical terms, those involved in cross-border management need to know what sort of government lies behind the partner they are dealing with. Where does the British government stand vis-à-vis the German government on direct/indirect tax, on welfare benefits, on discussions with trade unions about the economic future. These are key issues and in many ways they have created, and now, sustain, radically different business practices and, hence, cultures.

■ Element 3: Economic Ideology

The assertion underlying the use of this part of the toolkit is that ideologies shape activities and institutions, and these latter shape business cultures. This is a widely accepted notion, especially when we consider a range of economic ideologies – and particularly the contributions of laissez-faire, socialist and mercantilist thinkers.

Many of the thoughtforms which are typical of our age and which have been considered in the last section, free enterprise, market economics, shareholder value, for example, owe not a little to the theories put forward in the 18th century by Adam Smith and David Ricardo. These two are the major representatives of a school of thought whose members considered that:

- individuals were largely selfish and motivated by their own self-interest;
- the economic system of demand and supply, being profit-driven, would always function harmoniously and that, if so, government interference in the market-place was unnecessary and certain to be harmful;
- combining the division of labour (i.e., task specialisation) with adequate capital and entrepreneurial impulse would result in economic success. This, incidentally, is derogatorily referred to in France as *Fordisme;*
- the principle of division of labour could be extended to foreign trade with advantage to both partners, since each profited from the specialised expertise (and hence better prices for the output) of the partner.

Such ideas are at the heart of what has come to be known as classical economics, the basic text for which was Adam Smith's book *An Enquiry into the Nature and Causes of the Wealth of Nations*, published in 1776. It is this corpus of doctrine that is at the heart of the current policonomy management approach of the USA and Great Britain (see Quadrant A in Figure 4.2 page 86). Its tenets are so immediately appealing and correspond so closely to the Western version of economic reality that the business community and academic leaders here, such as Michael Porter (1980), typically accept it as dependable truth.

It is interesting to note that the term *laissez-faire* (let it happen), however, predates the work of Adam Smith. It was created by a group of French economists led by François Quesnay, called the Physiocrats. They rightly lay claim, particularly through Quesnay's *Tableau Economique*, published in 1758, to many of the basic ideas of classical economics. The laissez-faire element had to do with their advocacy of the need for governments "to stay out of business". The associated term *laissez passez* had to do with their advocacy of free trade: it basically means "let the goods through" without any tolls or duties being levied on them. Historically, however, the French, be it noted, have always had apparent difficulty with the notion that business issues should be left to businessmen. The British standpoint, by contrast, seems to have been (and still is) that business is far too important to be handled by politicians.

Classical economics is not the only body of theory to have held sway, however. Two other schools of thought with dissimilar views have also been highly influential. The first is Marxist, the second is mercantilist.

Several of the views of Karl Marx in his book *Das Kapital* (1867) now seem so archaic that they are hardly worth mention, never mind debate. Conversations with Russian, or even Polish managers or workers, even today rapidly reveal, however, that what we often think of as Marxist anachronisms can live on, even after democratic revolutions, admittedly in watered-down form. It is no coincidence, however, that recent elections in Poland, Hungary and the Czech republic have produced less revolutionary regimes than those voted in after 1989.

Take the concepts of *class conflict* or *surplus value*, for example. Marx's belief on the first was that capitalism was simply one stage in an evolutionary process of socio-political development and that it would collapse under the weight of its central contradiction. This was that the mass of economic power was overly-concentrated in the hands of the bourgeoisie or middle classes whilst the weight of political power was in the hands of the proletariat or working classes. They were necessarily locked in political combat as a result. The superior weight of the latter would defeat the former, he contended.

The concept of surplus value was tied up with Marx' *Labour Theory of Value*. This held that the price of a product should be made up entirely from the labour cost of the product and that, if a profit margin is then added by the capitalist, this "surplus value" has, in fact, been simply expropriated (or even stolen) from the worker. This was a concept first spelled out by the founder of modern anarchism, the French socialist Pierre Proudhon (1809-65). According to him, private property in general was nothing more than the theft of communal property. *Qu'est ce que la propriété? C'est le vol* was his classic phrase.

These two notions taken together help serve to explain why the Russian regimes under presidents Gorbachev, Yeltsin and Putin have been so slow in changing the laws governing the private ownership of land and the private employment of individuals. The law on bankruptcy has certainly taken its time. Conditions on joint ventures are also highly protective of Russian interests. The state still has a strong role as ring-master.

Socialism took stronger root in Europe than did Communism. Until, that is, the latter was imposed in Russia in 1917 and, after the Second World War, in central Europe. Indeed, it is arguable that it could only have been imposed by military force. Socialism had many forms – co-operativism (e.g., collective workshops), paternalism (e.g., housing for workers), Fabian socialism (e.g., introducing benefits to workers via the political system). In Britain, the names of Robert Owen, Seebohm Rowntree, the Webbs (Sydney and Beatrice) and Bernard Shaw are closely associated with these aspects. In continental Europe, Louis Blanc, Ferdinand Lassalle, Wilhelm Liebknecht and August Bebel were leading lights.

In all cases the Socialist wish of the time was to mitigate, if not reverse, some of the worst effects of the rampant capitalist control of European industry in the nineteenth century. The Socialist creed was adopted more readily and much faster in mainland Europe than in Britain, especially in those countries where revolutionary thinking had been, or was, in the air. Its focus was on a rejection of the *economic Darwinism* that many saw as inherent in the nature of capitalism. For most socialists in West Europe the central thrust was the role to be played by the state in managing social provision rather than in creating any form of social market economy.

In Germany Bismarck effectively hi-jacked Socialist ideas on worker insurance (e.g., the Reich Liability Law of 1871) to build up Germany's industrial base and secure a dependable labour force for its future empire. The creation of trusts, Konzerne, and Konglomerate – giant, almost wholly-integrated industrial enterprises like I.G. Farben or Krupp – was one eventual result. These firms typically managed massive workforces with a mixture of high-grade paternalism and iron-handed control, both of which were backed up by state insurance schemes. Note, in passing, how the pre-war Japanese *zaibatsu* (large all-purpose conglomerates) were the mirror image of such German companies in intention, size and scope. This should not surprise as the Japanese model of industrialisation from 1870 onwards, government-industry collaboration, bank-industry co-ownership, absolutist workforce control, was heavily patterned on the

German approach. Indeed, today's *triple-B* culture formula in Germany – Bund, Bank & Beamte – owes its existence to it. The Bund is the trade association to which your business must belong: the Hausbank is the bank on which your business relies; the Beamte is the stable employment model of the civil servant which serves as the German employment paradigm.

Socialism, throughout Europe, meant a balance between the interests of capital and the interests of the working class which was to be maintained by the government. At times, the balance was heavily weighted in favour of the working classes or *proletariat* as Marx called them. Pensions and accident insurance legislation, universal education, state health services, statutory protection for organised labour in the form of trade union legislation – these were gains achieved by them at diverse times from 1870 onwards, especially as a result of the experience of war. The experience of the 1920s and 1930s taught Europe the particular need to secure as high a measure as possible of full employment. Again, this was a major step forward for the working classes.

A by-product of this was a phenomenon many would certainly now find remarkable: the tolerance of cartels. In the Europe of this period market-sharing deals, especially in heavy industry, were considered quite normal and politically and economically acceptable. If there were not a well-structured approach in existence, excessive competition would result (it was thought) in international, beggar-my-neighbour pricing strategies. These, it was felt, would ultimately be in no-one's interests as they could lead to a re-run of previous and highly costly European wars.

In fact, anti-trust, pro-consumer thinking (c.f. American laws such as the Sherman Antitrust Act of 1890, the Clayton Act of 1914 and the Robinson-Patman Act of 1936) prevailed much earlier and much more extensively in the USA than in Europe. In a divided European continent the interests of the workers (jobs and pay) and government (full employment) ranked before the interests of the shareholders (dividends) and consumers (value for money) in not a few countries. The more such countries in the 1930s were intent on preparing for war, the more pronounced this phenomenon became.

Cartel-type thinking is still not absent from the European mainland as recent European Court cases in the steel and cement industries testify. Indeed, it is only in recent times in Russia that gigantic conglomerates (like Zil or Kamaz) with their bloated workforces, their cartel mentality, their market-place domination and state-backed financing have come to be questioned by the Russian government on the efficiency and effectiveness of their economic contribution. (Ekonomika 1989)

The *Mercantilist* approach to economics was also orientated to the role of the state. This was a set of doctrines dating from the 17th century and embraced widely by the French and English governments of the time. They aimed at raising the prosperity and power of the state by:

- building up the nation's reserves by exporting more than was imported;
- exploiting colonies exclusively for the benefit of the mother country via a trade monopoly; and
- achieving economic self sufficiency (*autarchy*) by building up an empire which would supply the necessary raw materials.

The chief proponent was Thomas Mun whose magnum opus, *England's Treasure by Foreign Trade*, appeared in 1664.

Germany applied Mercantilist doctrines in the 17th century, when the approach was known as *cameralism*. They received a major boost in the 19th century under the inspiration of the economist Friedrich List whose chief work, *The National System of Political Economy* appeared in 1840. Whereas Adam Smith had taken the individual to be the central economic player, List gave that role to the state. The purpose of increased economic activity at the time was to create a unified or "normal" nation, a vital goal in view of the fact that Germany since 1618 had never been united. For this a conception of the state as an industrial giant with a complex economy – an *Industriestaat* – was vital. And that meant collaboration among the business, commercial and agricultural sectors. The state's leadership in this co-operation, together with protection of the country's industries until they could be strong enough to compete, was mandatory. As we shall see later, Bismarck accepted both of these ideas, in order to create the basis for Germany's industrialisation, and the imperial leadership role that went with them. His actions in helping to create the Deutsche and Dresdner banks in the early 1870s, and give them the mission of aiding the country's industrialisation, was also rooted in them.

It was quite natural for these banks, therefore, to own major equity stakes in the country's major firms.

Elementary mercantilist thinking, in the form of advancing the state's interest before that of the individual business investor, is still present in the approaches of certain continental European countries. France's individualistic attitude to its own military defence, for example.

■ Element 4: Religion

At first sight it might seem strange to deal with religion side by side with economic doctrine. One religion, Protestantism, has, however, given its name to a business phenomenon so profound that the linkage seems quite reasonable. The phenomenon in question is *The Protestant Ethic*.

The phrase is used by Max Weber in his monumental book, *The Protestant Ethic and the Spirit of Capitalism.* (Weber 1930) It covers the elegant notion that, as from the start of the sixteenth century in Western Europe:

- those disaffected with the hierarchy and prescriptions of the Catholic faith were ready and anxious to think and act differently about worship and morality;

- this new thinking impacted on traditional capitalism, which began to develop a new spirit effectively allowing the (previously unthinkable) disassociation of wealth creation and religious belief;

- the spirit was to be found in its heaviest concentration in Northern Europe, and not in Southern Europe, and allowed materialism and hedonism into money-making as never before. It gave an enormous fillip to the economies of those nations that had embraced Protestantism and retarded the development of those which did not.

Hierarchy is ingrained

The leader unilaterally supports, consults, decides, disposes especially if he is a Tai-Pan (business tycoon) and clan chief like Hong Kong's Li Ka-Shing, Chen Yu-Tung or Lee Shau-Kee. Often the rule is absolute, frequently patriarchal (as in Korea and Bangladesh) and sometimes charismatic. In India, for instance, a leader is seen to be gifted with "mana" or superior spiritual insights and benevolence, both of which quite naturally command respect. The problem of nepotism or cronyism is widespread in Asia and particularly marked in Indonesia where excessive dependence on leadership (i.e. lack of self-starting entrepreneurship) is called "surat keputusan".

Groupism is universal

Each member of the organisation functions as part of a social machine, treating all other members with the respect and deference which is their natural due (c.f. Thai "kreing chai") Group solidarity is widespread in Indonesia ("gotong ryong") and in Japan where individualism and independence are seen as selfish and immature organisational phenomena. In the Philippines "pakikisama" or "getting along well together" is regarded by many as a more important indicator of organisational health than efficiency or effectiveness.

It is the groupism of some Asian business societies that makes it impossible for the Western business person to penetrate through to the ultimate decision-making structures. In China, for example, it is widely thought that without "guangxi" or "the right connections" satisfactory deal-making is impossible. Naturally, in some countries the word "connections" has significance beyond simple inter-personal relations of the social sort.

Religion is a meaningful guide to action

All Asian religions (e.g. Buddhism, Hinduism, Confucianism, Taoism, Shinto and Islam) pay much attention to two specific societal factors. Firstly, the common good as opposed to individual benefit. Through your life, and not just through ancestor worship, you pay a debt of gratitude to (as, for example, in China and Japan) your forebears. You also treat those whom you regard as members of your fellowship with respect and dignity. They are the targets of your strong sense of duty. You quite naturally also accept the natural pecking order that exists within your social context. Note, however, that this may connote a degree of antagonism to those who are not seen as part of the in-group whether it be nation, caste, sect or business organisation.

As an example of this it is possible to cite the traditional Hindu law of Mitakshara which has quasi-religious force. This law underpins the working of what is known as the Hindu Undivided Family (or HUF) according to which all family members of the extended family have a duty to keep the family together in terms of food, residence and worship for as long as is feasible. According to this particular law, a family living together (i.e., parents, sons and daughters, sons- and daughters-in-law and their children etc.) cannot separate legally whilst it contains a potential mother. As will be easily understood, the possibility of creating exceptionally strong family firms is continually increased as a result of this enforced social bonding.

The second focus is on the extent to which society is a divinely-ordered cosmology in which you live out the fate that has been laid down for you (c.f. the Hindu concept of karma) rather than one in which you create your own exclusive and particular destiny. In such a scenario the importance of the individual human life in societal terms is low. Such fatalism obviously underpins acceptance of high power distance structures and social solidarity.

EXHIBIT 4.4: THREE BUSINESS CULTURE TENDENCIES IN ASIA

At this point we need to take stock of the personal contribution that King Henry VIII of England (1491-1547) made to this process of replacement of Catholicism in England with what later (and speedily) became the Anglican Protestant faith. The refusal of Pope Clement VII to annul Henry's first marriage to Catherine of Aragon (in order to allow him to marry Anne Boleyn) provoked a truly cataclysmic chain of circumstances. These involved:

- a decision by the king to break with the church of Rome and establish a new, but still Catholic, religious order which would grant him the required divorce;
- a nationalisation of religion in England which gravely weakened the central authority of the Pope (e.g., in respect of rules on money lending); and
- major socio-political and economic consequences, such as the furtherance of democratic and liberal economic thought and the increasing strengthening of the bourgeois class;
- sequestration of church property.

It is hardly likely that Henry VIII in his haste to acquire a new wife could have foreseen the ultimate impact of the move: he it was who poured oil on the bonfire that could be said to symbolise the growing business culture differences between England's approach and that of continental Europe (except for the Netherlands). Henceforth, Britain's co-ordinated strategy of shipbuilding, trade finance and exploration-colonisation would become possible as a legacy of his rule.

In other words, the Protestant reformation may be asserted to be the very heart of the superior economic development in later times of the Netherlands and Great Britain as against Spain and France, in particular.

How could this be? In three distinct ways. Firstly, the Catholic church's organisation structure was nothing if not rigidly hierarchical (high power distance in Hofstede's terminology), with pope-cardinal-bishop-priest linked together in a linear fashion within the doctrine of *papal infallibility*. In this, it had, incidentally, an absolute parallel with the structure of most European medieval states where the top-down power linkage was king-baron-landowner-serf. The obedience required in the latter was, if anything, just as great as in the former. Land was exchanged for military service according to strict rules, the serfs were slaves (Latin servus = slave) and the over-arching doctrine was the *divine right of kings*. Clearly, the maintenance of social order was maximised if the temporal or state powers (the *sword*) and the spiritual or religious powers (the *robe*) worked in tandem to manage government and economy.

The conclusion of this is that acceptance of Catholic dogma was likely to remain universally high in Catholic Europe, i.e., France and Spain, particularly. And in fact did. Furthermore, it underlined the acceptance of these countries of the doctrine of papal infallibility. Where the authority of the Catholic church was rejected, new forms of religious thinking were introduced. These involved strong elements of democratic thinking on free will and a rejection of absolutist, top-down hierarchical structures.

Secondly, some of the key statements of Catholic dogma in the medieval period militated against the creation of any widespread money-focused business ethic. For example, the Catholic church's negative attitude to usury or lending money at high rates of interest (viz. Gratian's Decretum of 1149), its anxiety about the appropriateness of high merchant profits, and its insistence on the need for price control of everyday commodities, including money, i.e., through the *pretium justum* or morally right price. (Swain 1958) It is noteworthy that interest payment on debt was illegal in France before the French Revolution.

It was the fact of the sinfulness of lending money that allowed the Jews a privileged (but exposed) position in early medieval times as often quasi-monopoly money-changers, money-lenders and pawnbrokers. They were not Christians and, therefore, not subject to Catholic rules. Their only competition in medieval Catholic Europe came (as we have seen) from the Lombards, a generic name for clans of Italian money-changers and bankers. Their prominence rose as the power of church doctrine over matters of usury declined and as the papacy became more malleable. So also did the financial power of the Knights Templar, who became, somewhat paradoxically, bankers to several European kings. This was, in part, due to the geographical spread of the order and the role they played in the Crusades.

Even so, the Lombards were at this time, like the Jews and later the Templars, at the mercy of their political overlords. Italian bankers took elaborate note of the fate of their Jewish competitors as, for example, in

13th century England, when the Jews were first expropriated, then expelled from the country, and then charged to come back in. They were also mindful of the fact that in Spain in 1492, as we have seen, the Spanish Inquisition managed to get all Spanish and Portuguese Jews (the Sephardim) expelled from the peninsula. It requires little imagination to grasp that this did little for the development of Spanish banking and undeniably damaged the subsequent development of Spain's colonisation of the New World. Especially as the Jews were welcomed with open arms by other more commercially-minded countries like, as we have noted, England and the Netherlands.

Thirdly, the extent to which social advancement in pre-Reformation Catholic Europe was strictly controlled by the church and state is also of great importance. It was, in fact, so constrained that inheritance and the possession of land were the only keys to social status. Jews were, for this reason, not allowed to own land and the bourgeois class – whose merchant skills were often disparaged rather than praised – was not regarded as having aristocrat potential.

By absolute contrast, from the time of the Protestant queen Elizabeth I onwards, the key to ennoblement in the English, and then British, system has been, to one extent or another, wealth. She herself had no compunction about making aristocrats of people who had *stolen* money from England's Spanish enemy. The merchants of the city of London gained immeasurably in economic and political status as a result of this. Undeniably, through this formula of allowing wealth creation in whatever form to be entwined with aritocratisation, Queen Elizabeth I established the mercenary pattern of British business culture that has endured to this day.

The banking and insurance systems that came into existence in the late 17th century in Britain dovetailed exactly with the country's rising shipbuilding capability and its colonising thrust. The machinery of trade and industry was operated by a new, rich and powerful bourgeois class, which had no parallel in continental Europe, except for the Netherlands.

It is noteworthy that Protestantism blossomed on soil that had already many traces of democracy. It could also be said to contribute to democracy itself as it is a permissive and entrepreneurial faith. By contrast, Catholicism was, and is, an authoritarian faith with spiritual leadership vested in the Pope.

(1)	The extent to which a believer in this religion is free to pursue his own destiny and create his/her own heaven by living a good life on earth or whether that individual's duty is simply to live out a life that has already been pre-programmed by fate with grace, dignity and strict moral compliance.
(2)	The extent to which the religion has formal ritual and mandatory beliefs or whether the doctrine is less dogmatic.
(3)	The extent to which any rule system is administered by a spiritual hierarchy which demands obedience or whether the religion's structure is more egalitarian.
(4)	The extent to which the religion's teachings on morality seem to fly in the face of economic realities.
(5)	The extent to which the religion places a high value on the life of the individual person.

**TABLE 4.4: KEY CULTURAL QUESTIONS FOR
PARTICULAR RELIGIONS**

We should not, however, lose sight of the fact that *all* religions, because they require obedience to a code of ethics, create stylised patterns of behaviour, rigid organisational structures and self-contained cultures. The Amish in America are a good example of this. Where a religion demands conformity with the existing social order, it typically buttresses the government's rule. In 19th century Germany, for instance, the rigid social structure was much supported by the Triple K culture. This applied only to women and stated that their place in society depended on Kinder (having children), Kirche (attending church) and Kuche (cooking). How times have changed!

Confucianism provides a contrary picture in those Asian countries where Western Europe long had colonial interests and investment. Like Protestantism and Catholicism, it is deeply ingrained in the culture of nations. In this case, however, its centre is the Asia Pacific region where it shares place with often-similar religions – Buddhism, Taoism and Shinto.

This religion differs from Western religions and Islam in having less concern with inherited teachings and wisdom about God and more to do with the development of divine insights through meditation and self-purification. On the other hand, Confucianism is very much taken up – as is Catholicism –

with maintaining social order. Here, however, the approach is for the individual to accept the rules and regulations governing life from within, rather than to have them imposed from outside by others.

The rules in question are concerned with role management and go a long way to explaining aspects of Asian business culture. Each man has five basic relationships (WU LU) to manage. They are ruler-subject, father-son, older brother-younger brother, husband-wife and senior friend-junior friend. Each connotes mutual obligations, respect and a sense of duty and corresponding commitments. The more structured, balanced and measured these relationships, the more likely will social harmony result (i.e., high uncertainty avoidance to use Hofstede's term). Social disharmony is to be avoided at all costs. Note that Confucianism accepts and endorses social stratification (power distance) but tries to reduce any frictions arising through this by playing up the individual's sense of moral duty.

Another key aspect of this is the notion of shame. In a high context culture (such as that of Japan) people develop an inbuilt sense of proprieties: the subtle nuances of socially-correct communication and action. Failure to behave with due propriety in a given context will create a sense of shame and embarrassment. Breaches of the code lead, thus, to *loss of face*, i.e., to a loss of personal dignity. By losing face, you lose the respect of others. This is something highly undesirable, since your key purpose in life is to merit the regard of others.

To do this you typically conform to precepts such as those of Confucius and you dutifully fulfil your commitments to others. You will not for example, thrust yourself forward; you will willingly work in teams; you will accept the duties given to you without question; you will serve with dignity and obedience; you will enjoy life within a collectivist culture. You will willingly be a *salaryman* working excessively long hours for your Japanese employer.

An intriguing gloss on the issue of Asian religions is the extent to which they achieve obedience and commitment from believers without having the formality of doctrine and hierarchy that exists in some other religions. Certainly, the standard of belief is no less high. They place consistent emphasis on the nature of man's duty, as opposed to his personal wishes and inclinations. It is this feature that gives Asia Pacific workforces in countries like Japan their devotion. It is also an element which encourages a sense of family membership in each manager – as in the typical Korean chaebol (large conglomerates like LG or Samsung) – and sometimes a disdain for the foreigner (viz. the Japanese view of the *gaijin*). At the very least, it is possible to distinguish in cultural terms between those who belong to an *exclusive* culture (i.e., includes no foreigners) and those who do not. Thus, it is not over-exaggerating to suggest that the role of Confucianism, quite apart from its religious aspects, is to act as a sort of social machinery, regulating civilised life in Pacific Asia for its believers.

Another form of social machinery that had immense significance for Japan was *Bushido* – the ethical code of the samurai or military caste. This warrior's code, now considerably played down, long supported the feudal absolutism of the shogunate rule which lasted from 1192 to 1867. It demanded total obedience to one's superior, acceptance of one's personal destiny and a willingness to accept self-immolation. It seems apparent that the experience of shogunate rule has left its mark on the Japanese in terms of their willingness to accept discipline, either from within or without, and in terms of their obeisance rituals. When Japan industrialised from 1870 onwards, it was able to capitalise fully on such internalised self-discipline.

Islam has shaped, and is still shaping, business cultures also. The economic growth of Malaysia, for instance, owes much to the racial tolerance preached by this religion and the spirit of co-operation among its diverse population – indigenous Malays or *Bumiputra*, Muslim, Chinese and Indian. It is a simple religion with a strict moral code and a deep sense of purpose which has also served the country well in steering forward its massive programme of economic development.

Conversely, the detail of the visions of the Prophet Muhammad and his teaching about divine will, which are recorded in the Koran, are currently creating substantial disharmony within the Islamic faith between the fundamentalists and those who are somewhat less rigid in their observance. Given that the Arabic word Islam means "surrender" or "submission" and that its imperatives include pilgrimage (to, for example, Mecca) and worship, clothing and punishment rituals, such a split is highly problematic.

In certain countries, like Iran and Libya, increasing religious fundamentalism has led to political revolution and a wholesale re-casting of economic structures and commercial life. In turn, because of the strategic situation of both these oil-rich countries, such changes came to be regarded by the USA, the leading world military power, as highly significant and hugely negative. Their net result has been the virtual political ostracising of these two countries.

Economic thinking in Islam does not particularly concern itself with those causal relations which neo-classical economics treats as objective and scientific laws and tendencies. It is essentially prescriptive... Economic hypotheses have to be based on assumptions derived from the Shari'a (Islamic law). Economic objectives such as optimisation, maximisation.... cannot constitute desirable criteria of assessment... They can only become useful if they contribute to the attainment of Islamic objectives...

Since the objectives of the Islamic system... are incompatible with those of economic man, the practical success of Islamic economic theories hinges on the... universalisation of the Islamic man's outlook and... the prevalence of an Islamic individual and social psychology... This in turn is dependent upon a conducive social environment, the creation of which necessitates an Islamic state capable of promoting and upholding the Islamic value system.

EXHIBIT 4.5: THE BASIS OF THE ISLAMIC ECONOMIC SYSTEM

Source: *Islamic Economic Systems*, Farhad Nomani and Ali Rahnema, Business Information Press, Kuala Lumpur, 1995

The enmity thus created has established these countries as leaders of the fundamentalist camp. But this has not meant that all Islamic nations support their vision of doctrinal purity. Indeed, there is, and has been for many centuries, a major political split in the Islamic nations between the Shi'ites and the Sunnis, the former being the more fundamentalist and the more orthodox. As Exhibit 4.5 above indicates, the importance of orthodoxy to adherents of Islam cannot be overstated.

There are two areas in which religious over-riders on economic decisions are especially important in the Islamic faith. These are pay and lending.

So far as the first is concerned, the chief principle is not worker productivity but the Islamic social consciousness of the employer. He will apply to decisions on pay the three standards of:

- what is just, i.e., morally right;
- inflicting no injury on other human beings;
- giving priority to social benefit over private benefit.

In fact, an Islamic producer might come to regard existing market wages as unfair and adjust pay upwards to what he sees as right. The second feature also represents a major difficulty as the most orthodox form of Sharia law prohibits usury. As Nomani and Rahnema point out, *a radical Islamic interpretation of social justice... takes a hard line against the capitalist system and the market allocation of resources. The market system is condemned, since it gives free reign to exploitation (via excessive interest payments) and increases injustices by rewarding those who already possess more than their share.* (Nomani & Rahnema 1995)

The divergences from straightforward western business approaches that are indicated by these aspects of Islamic and Confucian thinking are of considerable significance. They point to a world in which practices and behaviours will be quite alien. And so, in fact, they are.

■ Conclusion

The elements in our tool-kit are extremely diverse yet valuable pointers to what to look for in our examination of how other countries go about their business affairs. It may sound absurd that an engineer – such as a member of the Battlefield Taxi group – should concern himself or herself with the impact of history or economic theory or even religion. Yet is it beyond dispute that to understand modern Germany we need to know how it was industrialised and how it has been affected by war; without an understanding of feudalism, Catholic doctrine and Revolution much of the French approach cannot be fully appreciated. So far as Britain is concerned, it is the rise of Protestantism, democracy and the country's merchant ethos that need to be investigated. Certainly, the thrust towards economic development that has motivated Malaysia cannot be fully appreciated unless the analysis covers Islamic thinking.

CHAPTER 5

Work Systems and Behaviours:
A Culture Perspective

■ Introduction

We are now in a position to turn our attention to the super-structural features of the business culture iceberg, the theoretical model introduced in Chapter 2. Whilst the bedrock elements we have just explored can be seen to have a major influencing role on national culture, we are still faced with the task of isolating and exploring the key features of the *visible* elements of culture. These are, as will be recalled, the behaviours of people:

- as individuals, dealing with their own countrymen and with foreigners;
- as employees, operating within an organisation and subject to standardised work systems.

The first deals with such things as the manner in which people communicate with others, their gestures and mannerisms, their style of dressing and eating and the nature of their etiquette. It also with the nature of the *organisational glue* that gives the necessary bonding to groups within a nation, much of which has its origins in the religion(s) practised within the country.

In the *organisational glue-pot* we find such coherence-raising methods as

- language – Does the group speak a separate language which gives it a separate identity (like the Basque nation) or use particular words and phrases which mark out group members as special?

- dress – Do group members have a form of dress or clothing that shows they belong (like the cardinals of the Roman Catholic church who received the insignia of their office in March 2001 from the Pope)?

- food – Do group members eat certain foods and avoid others (like Muslims and Jews)?

- ceremonies – Does the group in question maintain a variety of traditions, rites and rituals (like the ceremonial parades in honour of Independence Day in the USA or the Chinese New Year)?

- beliefs – Is it axiomatic that, in order to show they belong to a group, members have to demonstrate their understanding and acceptance of certain beliefs (the Koran, the Bible or Marxism-Leninism, for example), even if, in some ways, the (perhaps uninformed) outsider may criticise the code of belief as *mumbo-jumbo*?

- personal habits – Do members have to follow certain behavioural rules (like the Sikhs, covering their hair, or the criminal Yakuza in Japan who cut off the tip of their little finger to show belongingness to the fraternity) or have particular gestures (salutes, greetings) that indicate group membership?

Such features are all of a highly personal nature and can differ markedly from one nation to another.

The second covers the way in which organisational work is done in a particular country. The focus here is on how organisations in particular countries typically recruit, train, reward and de-select employees within a specific system of corporate governance.

■ Values

All the personal elements of the cultural glue-pot depend on the values that people hold. People can hold certain values – concepts or things they esteem and which serve (to use an Edgar Schein metaphor) as anchors for their behaviours:

- as the result of conscious and intelligent choice made independently about what is important, spiritually and emotionally, or

- as the result of the need that individuals have to belong to a group or groups because they are unable to tolerate ostracism or alienation.

In our analytical framework, values translate themselves into behaviours. The word *visible* is of significance here, because all of these business culture features are tangible, observable and capable of being monitored and dissected. This fact makes it possible for us to compare and contrast the way in which people in different countries, and more especially typical companies in them, go about their business activities. As Exhibit 5:1 below shows, knowledge of how this happens is of great importance.

The USA economy is slowing but Mexican retailers are on the march above the border. The reason: immigrant incomes are rising in the USA and a local beachhead provides a hedge against a weakening peso and cooling consumer demand in Mexico. The home appliance vendor Famsa is one such. It opened its first USA store in San Fernando, a Latino suburb of Los Angeles, in 2001.

Trying to make himself heard against the noise of a mariachi band during the store opening, Famsa president Humberto Garza Valdez said the company wasn't trying to "take on the Americans" so much as to focus on "the Hispanic market". In California there are over two million households with at least one Mexican-born member.

In fact, even though it's in the USA, Ignacio Toussaint, CEO of Grupo Gigante, another incomer, considers Los Angeles itself to be "truly a Mexican city". Its attractions were the density of the population and the buying power of what is still an immigrant community. Famsa operates a "Mexico showroom" where its customer can feel at home when they buy.

EXHIBIT 5.1: THE MEXICAN WAY IN THE USA
Based on: Mexican retailers enter USA to capture Latino dollars, Joel Millman, *The Wall St Journal, Europe*, 9-10/2/2001

The Iceberg Model is, in fact, one of several that can be used to encapsulate the notion of the value pressures which interact to shape and mediate a nation's culture. Lessem and Neubauer (1994) use a tree image to link together the way in which the earth (institutions, policy, religion), the tree trunk (frameworks, ideas and images) and the branches (attitudes and behaviours) each interact with the others to shape a management culture.

A particular orientation in their model is towards the way philosophy can pervade national culture. The four most salient European philsophies they select on the basis of that continent's history are:

- **pragmatism** and **wholism**. Taken together these would amount to a highly factual, unemotional and empirical way of managing harmonious parts-whole relationships. In more basic terms, people are more down to earth in how things are done. They believe, for instance, that "there is no such thing as a free meal".

- **rationalism** and **humanism**. Rationalism deals essentially with abstract eternal principles whilst the humanist is concerned with perfecting the state of mankind. Espousers of such creeds believe, as did Dr Pangloss in Voltaire's Candide, that either "all is for the best in this best of all possible worlds" or we can set ourselves on the way to such a nirvana.

Ranking of value in terms of perceived importance	Japanese Self-image	American Self-image	French Self-image	Arab Self-image	Malaysian Self-image
1	Relationship	Equality	Self-reliance	Family security	Family security
2	Group harmony	Freedom	Freedom	Family harmony	Group harmony
3	Family security	Openness	Openness	Parental guidance	Corporation
4	Freedom	Self-reliance	Relationship	Age	Relationship
5	Co-operation	Co-operation	Time	Authority	Spirituality
6	Group harmony	Family security	Spirituality	Compromise	Freedom

TABLE 5.1: SELF-IMAGE – AN ADAPTATION OF THE ELASHMAWI AND HARRIS VALUES STUDY

Their arguments are not dissimilar from those expressed in Chapter 3 and relate to the extent to which, even today, certain European countries manifest cultural traits rooted in their particular philosophical histories.

More specifically, Christopher Leeds (1994) associates pragmatism with Britain. Here, he finds the inhabitants are heavily concerned with fact and reality and are restive with big designs and grand theoretical concepts. They are empiricists: they make things work by infinitely adjusting them in the light of experience. Their behaviours reflect this practical way of managing challenges.

Millions of Japanese graduates hunting for jobs this month have been told that if they want to get ahead they should keep their hair black.

As the recruitment season gets under way, corporate personnel managers are advising young men and women that following the fashion for chapatsu, or brown hair, may seriously hurt their chances of employment.

"Anyone with dyed hair, male or female, is not suitable for our company," a spokesman for Ito-Yokado, a big supermarket chain, said. He was echoing the horror being felt throughout corporate Japan at the youthful trend for bleached and coloured hair.

The trend, blamed on American styles, is abhorred by company managers since it implies a casual approach to life. Their objection, in a country where "the nail that sticks out gets hammered down", is that employees with dyed hair will stand out from their colleagues. This is seen as detracting from corporate discipline and efficiency. Ito-Yokado, like most big firms, offers lifetime employment, but does not tolerate dyed hair, earrings on either sex, or beards.

EXHIBIT 5.2: GET YOURSELF A JOB

Source: Bottle Brunettes banished to Japan's corporate fringe,
Robert Whymant, *The Times,* 11/7/96

The thinking expressed in these philosophical categories underlines yet again the extent to which physical behaviours are expressions of people's values. But the results of an empirical study of comparative value systems, based on respondents' self-images, carried out by Elashmawi, Harris and Majeed are more relevant. (1994) These are shown in Table 5.1 page 112.

Wa Kon Yoh Sai	The post-war combination of Japanese spirit & western technology that many Japanese thought unbeatable.
Keiretsu	Literally, business alliances. These are massive industrial groups which are the linear descendants of the old pre-war conglomerates, or Zaibatsu which the Americans sought to break up. There are six leading Keiretsu, all distinguished by the intensity of the internal relationships between their subsidiaries & divisions - Mitsui, Mitsubishi, Sumitomo, Fuji, Sanwa & Dai-Ichi Kangyo. Each subsidiary of a Keiretsu maintains especially tight relationships with that Keiretsu's banking subsidiary (its housebank), which, with the exception of Mitsui, is numbered among the world's top 20 banks. There is evidence to suppose that this "housebank" model was taken from German practice in the late 19th and early 20th century, following its sponsorship by Chancellor Bismarck & the creation of the Deutsche & Dresdner Banks.
Zaikai	According to Prakash Sethi, Zaikai is the Japanese establishment i.e., "a politico-economic group of wealthy financial leaders who can exert tremendous influence on government & politics". The group includes the Keidanren, the Federation of Economic Organisations, the Japanese civil service, key ministries like Finance, MITI (Ministry of International Trade & Industry) & JETRO (part of MITI) are also held to have decisive power.
Kuromaku	Sometimes lower-level, & possibly covert, organisation leaders in politics & business who are known to call the tune in policy matters. They typically are power brokers who "fix things" behind the scenes & before the event so that those who attend meetings follow an action scenario that has already been scripted for them. They are "the power behind the throne".
Yakuza	The immensely important Japanese mafia whose criminality lies at the heart of recent scandals such as the Recruit, Nomura and Kuibin Sagawa episodes. They are noted for their ruthlessness, organisational cohesion – Miata clan members all have highly distinctive body tattoos, for example – and penetration of all reaches of government &business. The Sokaiya is a subset of the Mafia. According to Kevin Rafferty, "these are people who demand money from companies in return for guaranteeing a peaceful annual shareholders' meeting".
Ringi	The process of organisational consultation between superiors & subordinates on important decision issues is an old practice in Japan. It dates back to feudal times when its blame-spreading effect could allow some senior leaders to avoid censure and blame for some of the mistakes to which they might have been party & for which suicide by disembowelment (Hara-kiri) might have been the punishment. Now it symbolises the groupist nature of Japanese industrial & commercial society. Nemewashi ("binding up the roots") is the poetic name given to the wide-ranging consultation among such operational luminaries as a Bucho (department head) & a Kacho (section head). Individual agreement with the overall plan is signified through one's personal seal (Hanko). Typical issues that are subject to Ringi debate are Kaizen (continuous quality improvement) & Kanban ("just-in-time" management).

Oyabun-Kobun	This is the idealised father (Oya)-child (Ko) relationship that optimally exists at all levels in any Japanese corporate hierarchy between superior and subordinate. The former is expected to look after the interests of the latter in exchange for obedience & due deference. Social deviance is not well-regarded & the phenomenon of the subservient &, to us in the West, docile Japanese "salaryman" may arise. This is the derogatory term given to lower-level managers in Japanese business who naturally put the demands of their job – including its inevitable socialisation aspects – before their home life. It is a matter of record that organisational automata like these may (& have been known to) die through overwork (Karoshi).
Amae (depend-ence) and Ie (family)	Every Japanese is bound by a deep sense of duty (On) and obligation (Giri) to his/her family. The company is just such a family and it is vital to preserve harmony (Wa) with all its members. Part of the manner in which this is done is for outward appearances to be kept up at all times (Tatemae) and for ultimate truths which might damage relationships (Honne) to be kept firmly under wraps. It is noteworthy that respect for individuals (Nenko) can depend on their age and length of service. It is not a function of youth, exuberance or contrived organisational visibility.
Menmoku O Ushinau	This means "loss of face". It is what happens to a person when the awful truth is revealed. The individual thus compromised feels a deep sense of shame at the total loss of self-dignity. The outward show ("face") has been ripped away and there is no longer any defence. The individual and societal compulsion to avoid such a disgrace is clearly massive. It may account in part for another Japanese practice which is widespread, that of constantly apologising. The Japanese, says Professor Richard Bowring of Cambridge University, say sorry (Sumimasen) "about fifty times a minute. It's their way of oiling society". Naturally, an enormous range of expressions of sorrow exist and these are tailored to the situation and to the age and rank of the person being apologised to as necessary.

EXHIBIT 5.3: A GLOSSARY OF SELECTED JAPANESE BUSINESS CULTURE TERMS

References: *Japanese Business - Social Conflict*, Prakash Sethi, Ballinger, Cambridge Mass, 1975. 'Japanese extortion gangsters turn to murder', Kevin Rafferty, *The Guardian*, 19/10/94. 'A language riddled with etiquette and nuance', Edward Pilkington, *The Guardian*, 15/8/95

It is noteworthy that their research indicates the extent to which national values can change over time. For example, a set of younger Japanese respondents indicated that their top value was, in fact, freedom. Perhaps this is not surprising if we consider the situation described in Exhibit 5.2 page 113.

Of course, what we are predominantly interested in is not so much our self-image as how other nations perceive us. Compare, in this regard, the rankings given in Table 5.1 page 112 with those in Table 5.2 below, again findings from another Elashmawi and Harris study (1994). Note the Japanese view of the Number 1 Chinese value.

Exhibit 5.3 pages 114-15 sets out some of the most potent attitudes underlying Japanese behaviour.

The issue of globalisation is again germane to our discussion at this point. To what extent are individual national values, affecting work systems and behaviours, being modified by countries' exposure to trading in the global village? Once a multinational firm moves from a one-centre, hierarchical structure with an explicit chain of command to being a global company with a many-centre, organic structure the value systems of all its employees are affected because their work systems alter. The more technology intensity grows, the more global integration will occur, and with it a certain level of value shift. Pressure of this nature leads such firms from what Bartlett and Ghoshal (1995) call a *global* to a *transnational* strategic mentality. By this they mean that central management is not just co-ordinating standardised global operations from the centre but following strategies which are locally responsive as well as being globally integrative. For such firms an understanding of cultures is paramount.

Value Ranking	What Malaysians say other cultures value		What Japanese say other cultures value	
	American	Arabs	Chinese	Arabs
1	Success	Family	Bicycles	Religion
2	Power	Community	History	Allah
3	Relationship	Creation	Health	Koran
4	Material possessions	Brotherhood	Obedience	Status
5	Openness	Respect	Family	History
6	Profit	Power	Money	Family

TABLE 5.2: OTHERS' VALUES – AN ADAPTATION OF THE ELASHMAWI AND HARRIS VALUES STUDY

As we have already seen, this need is most strongly felt in cases of global alliances, generally, and joint ventures, specifically. Another theoretical framework is of value in this context. Wendy Hall's Compass Model (1995) of cultural styles draws attention to two sets of behavioural characteristics, manifested alike by individuals and by their employers, which can be grouped, according to her model, under the two value-orientation headings of *assertiveness* and *responsiveness*. The diverse characteristics themselves are listed in Table 5.3 below.

Her theory indicates that the researcher can isolate particular styles of corporate (as well as national) culture according to the extent to which various levels of assertive and responsive behaviours are typically used in the business context. Depending on the patterns of ratings for the characteristics that make up each behaviour type, firms can be classified as having a culture style which is:

North:	low assertive, low responsive	=	**"analytical"**
South:	high assertive, high responsive	=	**"expressive"**
East:	low assertive, high responsive	=	**"amiable"**
West:	high assertive, low responsive	=	**"driver"**

As will be seen later, this model has affinities with those of other scholars like Handy and Goffee and Jones.

Assertiveness	**Responsiveness**
(Can be evaluated on a range from high to low depending on demonstrated behaviours of the following types)	(Can be evaluated on a range from high to low depending on demonstrated behaviours of the following types)
☐ individualistic ☐ pushy ☐ demanding ☐ taking control ☐ challenging ☐ hardworking ☐ quick-moving ☐ decisive	☐ sensitive ☐ loyal ☐ compromising ☐ trusting ☐ team player ☐ unpredictable ☐ qualitatively-oriented ☐ emotional rather than factual ☐ people-oriented rather than task oriented
A company is rated on each dimension. If it has a tendency to be very demanding, it would score highly on this dimension of assertiveness. A highly assertive company would have a high average score over the complete range of dimensions.	A company is rated on each dimension. If it has a tendency to be very trusting, it would score highly on this dimension of responsiveness. A highly responsive company would have a high average score over the complete range of dimensions.

TABLE 5.3: KEY BEHAVIOURAL CHARACTERISTICS IN WENDY HALL'S COMPASS MODEL

Reference to Table 5.3 page 117 indicates the sort of behaviours that a "driver" company would reveal in its cross-cultural dealings. Its senior management would be decisive and demanding, hard working and fast on their feet. They would concern themselves with facts rather than emotions and certainly lack a people-orientation. Nor would they, unlike the South type of company, make particularly good team players. Naturally enough, such culture style analysis indicates that twinning together East and West in a joint venture will lead to culture clashes that will need to be managed very carefully indeed.

■ Work Systems

The work systems in which a nation's culture approach is most clearly revealed are those of hiring and firing (or, less ethnocentrically, deselection), training and rewarding employees within a particular framework of corporate governance. Of course, some companies have cultures which are quite distinct, perhaps on the grounds of the technology they use, from those of the nations in which they are based. Here, for sake of simplicity, we are discussing the average firm which does reflect national culture in its work practices.

■ Hiring and Firing

One problem we immediately have in any cross-cultural debate is with the word *firing*. It has Anglo-Saxon connotations of treating the *workforce* (not the employees) as if it were a mere factor of production to be dispensed with when business conditions indicated it was no longer needed and to be employed or re-employed to suit the demands of the firm. Indeed, one politically-incorrect American version of this is to look upon those to be de-selected as *extra*, that is, no longer needed.

Countries do differ markedly in their approaches to the technicalities of selection and de-selection, to use the more value-neutral terms. Their stance does indeed depend basically on the extent to which the worker is regarded as an economic or social resource and treated in an objective, unemotional manner or as an important player in a socio-economic team. So far as recruitment is concerned, issues arise as to the importance of hiring recruits from the families of employees, or other tightly knit (e.g., ethnic or religious) groups. In India, especially, it is the practice of employees to push forward other family members to their employers as potential hirees, just as it is the practice of firms to seek to create a family of its employees.

For the past 36 years Mano has been a bonded worker, in southern Pakistan. His job has been to work day and night tending the cotton and sugar cane crops of his landlord – a member of the hated zamindar class. Although bonded labour was made illegal in this country in 1973, an estimated 2m haris (poorly-educated, poverty-stricken dirt farmers) are still forced to work in the farms of Sind and the Punjab to pay off their debts to the owners of the farms from whom they borrow money. They are victims of the feudalism that still fuels the wealth of Pakistan's élite, as, once they accept a loan, they find that they can never pay it back.

The bonded labour system is part of the centuries-old way of life known as rawaj or the tide of the river. Mano himself is a low-caste Hindu, an untouchable, from the Thar desert near the Indian borders and is 65-years old. He escaped from his landlord last month and now lives in Kotri camp, one of four refuges set up by Pakistan's independent Human Rights Commission.

EXHIBIT 5.4: HOW THE OTHER HALF LIVES
Based on: Bonded workers bid for freedom, Rory McCarthy,
The Guardian, 17/7/2000

Then there is the question of the extent to which the employer can legally discriminate against unwanted job applicants on the grounds of, say gender or age or sexual orientation, as well as the fraught question of how pay is determined. Some countries allow pay to be set by the market-place for work, a fact which can favour the employer. Others try to insist that employers have obligations to pay minimum wages on the grounds of political concern with the workers' livelihoods. See Exhibit 5.4 above for an instance of the exact opposite of this situation.

Such countries as these may also be heavily pre-occupied with the difficulty of unemployment. Considerations of the political and economic impact of worklessness can lead governments to consider employers not as maximisers of profit (as would be the case in laissez faire economies) but as providers of work and up-holders of the nation's social fabric.

Even in countries where there is no religious impulsion in this direction, socialistic forces can be very powerful not just in government but also among trade unions and even employers. The end result is the concept of a *job-for-life* or lifetime employment, once commonplace in Japan and South Korea among employees of those nations' big conglomerates, the *keiretsu* and the *chaebols*. See Exhibit 5.5 below.

It was clearly a major headache for the Korean government. The founder of the bankrupt Daewoo Motor Co., the country's third largest carmaker, Kim Woo Choong, was on the run. He was charged with embezzling 20 trillion won, destruction of family lives, threats against the survival of employees and paralysing the national economy. Ford and Fiat, having looked at the possibility of stepping in as saviours, had both walked away. Perhaps not surprisingly, as the company's debt was now known to be a multiple of the original $10 billion unmanageable debt that had caused the collapse in 1999.

From the trade union viewpoint, however, the worst thing was that the company's car factory at Puyong had actually been forced to stop working – they had been making just for inventory up to this point. Redundancy notices had already been issued to 1750 workers, the plan being to eventually slash the entire workforce by one third. The result was uproar with employees furiously blockading the plant and smashing the factory gates.

In fact, four thousand riot police had to be used to deal with the problem. The employees resistance to layoffs was said to be extreme and based on the fact that they couldn't understand how it was possible to lose their jobs. Whilst loudspeakers played union songs, Kim Il Sop, company union president pulled no punches "We will keep on striking" he declared "until the government abolishes the layoff plan". His red headband spoke volumes: it read "Fight to the Finish". The government's hope now was that General Motors would step in and save the company.

EXHIBIT 5.5: THE FATE OF DAEWOO
Based on: Don Kirk, *The International Herald Tribune*, Police roust workers
from Daewoo plant, 20/1/2001 and Seoul steps up effort to court GM
as Daewoo rescuer, 21/2/2001

Countries which have a socialistic attitude to work management are placed today in a considerable quandary over the question of strike action by workers. Given the principle that strike action is a legitimate expression of trade unionists' basic rights, what should the state do (if anything) if the action threatens the country's economic performance, especially, if the strike is called over pay and conditions of work This was a question confronting France in 2000 as Exhibit 5.6 below reveals.

The three-month-long programme of strike activity that the technicians of the Paris National Opera (Palais Garnier & the Bastille Opera) began in November 2000 was very impressive They certainly meant business as their previous disruption of performances of Prokofiev's War and Peace had shown. They started off the programme by refusing to change the sets on Mozart's Magic Flute and Donizetti's Lucia di Lammermoor which both went ahead in concert version. What was wrong?

At the heart of the dispute with management was the 1998 Loi Aubry that reduced the French working week from 39 hours to 35, with no loss of pay. The Paris Opera is finding it extremely difficult to negotiate the implementation of this law, given the fact that it employs a permanent orchestra, a chorus, a ballet corps and an army of technicians. Here, four of the six different technicians' unions were demanding a 32-hour week spread over four days, accompanied by a ten percent wage increase over three years. Management said that this demand would hit quality and reduce the number of scheduled performances appreciably. Hugues Gall, the director of the Paris Opera, declared that, in this situation, "it is up to the government to assume responsibility for what happens".

EXHIBIT 5.6: LABOUR AND ART
Based on: Strikes over 35-hour week hit Paris Opera, Alan Riding,
The International Herald Tribune, 28/11/2000

Wherever countries are pre-occupied with job protection over a long period of time, whether for political, socio-economic or even religious reasons, there is a tendency for powerful political forces to interact to create a bedrock institutional framework to handle it. Socialistic systems persist over time and become ingrained in popular attitudes to work and productivity at work and can be very difficult to dismantle. In the worst cases, and Russia in recent times was one, work and pay become dis-associated in the popular mind in such a way that pay is received for attendance at work, rather than for working. In such a context, the political and social consequences of individual job loss can outweigh the economic results and people are given jobs (and kept in jobs) for socio-political reasons. Almost certainly, state ownership of industry, or the state's protection of it, is present in such cases.

As Exhibit 5.7 below shows only too well, the policonomic transition from a Socialist economy to a market economy can be fraught with difficulty. The managers who ran the system in totalitarian times garnered a harvest of systems knowledge and capital which became invaluable when the change occurred. The old leaders in many cases became the new leaders and tended to rule both arbitrarily and despotically, if not criminally.

Slovakia is a small and impoverished country that split off from the Czech Republic in 1993. From small beginnings, the government has tried to push through crucial economic restructuring, deregulating old monopolies and privatising state assets. This improved the country's credit rating and revived exports but it also tempted those with criminal intentions. Some senior managers in the newly-privatised embarked on a process called *tunnelling*. By creating a maze of affiliated companies around the mother company that few can understand or check on, you are able to syphon off assets for nefarious purposes. The mother company collapses.

US Steel was warmly welcomed when it took over the bankrupt VSZ mill in 1999. It had more than 120 affiliates and, under the leadership of Alexandr Rezes, a close associate of Slovakia's first prime minister, had lost millions in dubious investments. For US Steel the new acquisition was a major move. It accounted for one quarter of the company's entire production capacity and employed 17,000 workers, twice as many as the company employed at its biggest American sites. So, in a country where unemployment averaged 20 percent, it was a major employer. The benefits for US Steel? Apart from access to the European market place, the wage costs were highly favourable also – $2 per hour in VSZ as opposed to $35-42 in their USA mills.

EXHIBIT 5.7: A CALCULATED BET ABOUT GLOBALISATION
Based on: US Steel saves a mill in Slovakia, Edmund Andrews,
The International Herald Tribune, 1/12/2000

The converse situation is one where industry hires the best people for the job on the basis of competition (among employees to obtain work) and a realistic perception of marginal economic productivity. That they are de-selected when no longer of economic value, testifies to the relatively distant role of government in supervising the working of the economy. It smacks of private industry and shareholder value.

■ Training and Rewarding

Whose responsibility is it to educate and train the workforce? In some developing countries, like India, there is an inescapable obligation for this role to be filled by the firm. Even private sector firms like Tata or Godrej have this duty. Inescapably, because of the numbers of people they employ and the economic power they have, such firms are paternalistic and have to remain so. Education, and housing too, may have to be provided for a workforce that has no possibility of recourse to the sort of elaborate social security mechanisms that workers in many advanced and rich countries enjoy. In such countries, firms have a social as well as an economic balance sheet to worry about. Here, education and, to a lesser extent, training are public goods, widely available to all needing it and either free (i.e., paid for by public taxation) or realistically priced. Either way, employees are already educated when hired by companies and the firm itself decides, on the basis of economic value, what, if any, extra training is needed.

Pay is another issue where different countries have different perceptions and systems. Do you, in fact, pay people strictly in accordance with the value of their output, specifically rating performance and tying reward to it? Or, is the system more oriented to seniority in terms of length of service or towards non-pay rewards? To discover the attitudes underlying these approaches, we need to investigate what a nation does in terms of short-term contract working, part-time employment and so on.

Theoretically, laissez-faire economists are prone to link the average pay levels of countries that are exposed to the rigours of free and open international trade to employment opportunities. The lower the first, the higher the second. The experience of the UK and the USA in the 1990s is used as an indicator of this truth. Certainly, it must now be the case that their competitiveness is increased as pay restraint is practised. But are pay increases in the USA and the UK being held back by some form of government intervention, and not just the demand-supply pressures of the market-place? One form of this might be a reluctance to believe in full employment as a socio-political good on the grounds that, if it is known that a government seeks minimum unemployment, trade unions and wage seekers will drive up wages accordingly. Marx referred to this, as we have noted, as the *reserve army of the unemployed* phenomenon. This army, which could be drawn upon at any time by employers, kept the wages of those in work down.

Of course, it would perhaps be dangerous for any government to proclaim that it was no longer interested in reducing unemployment. From a political standpoint, governments which seek fair wages for employees to safeguard employment systems, so that arbitrary sackings cannot take place, and which maintain elaborate social security systems for unfortunates would certainly be better regarded.

The business cultures of nations in the developed world whose governments espouse this last line of thinking is, however, under threat. One reason is the extent to which high levels of social security are tolerable in a climate in which taxpayers and companies are simply loth to pay extra taxes for unproductive purposes and where governments increasingly are being driven to good housekeeping solutions to economic management. By this, we mean reduction in public expenditures, maintenance of the value of the nation's currency and so on.

■ Governance

The issue of governance in business culture terms has to do principally with the extent to which the workforce is represented in the decision-making process. The Anglo-Saxon model places responsibility for managing firms that are owned by shareholders firmly in the hands of directors appointed by the shareholders, and no-one else. A system of this form is no more nor less than a reflection of pure capitalism, according to which ownership of the resource connotes total command over its use. The UK use of the Japanese practice of *ringi,* in-depth consultation on business issues with the workforce, and its focus on *empowerment* do not detract from the degree of shareholder control of the firm. The first has to do with achieving technical improvement; the second with improved organisational productivity.

So entrenched in the UK is this *capitalism-in-control* thinking, for example, that recent debate on governance has been taken up with reforms in the duties and role of boards of directors, rather than their extended membership. In continental Europe the situation is different: in France and Germany strategic decisions affecting the future of the workforce in large-scale companies and made by the companies' directors are reviewed formally by bodies made up of shareholders and elected employees, as well as by works councils (Betriebsrat, Conseil de l'entreprise). For these countries it was unthinkable that workforce interests would not be protected in this way in a new Single European Market. Hence the reason for the inclusion of the Social Chapter in the Maastricht Treaty. France and Germany, in particular, simply do not accept the unequivocal dominance of capitalism as a defining ethos for industrial and commercial management.

■ Conclusions

If you enter a joint venture with a foreign partner, it is vital to do so in a spirit of optimism and with your eyes wide-open. As Wendy Hall's compass model indicates, different companies, taking their cues from national cultures, may have different approaches to many aspects of the HR management system. Some, indeed, may not even use the term *human resources management* to describe the field. There will be those companies who are *drivers*, perhaps short-term profit maximisers, who see the workforce as simply an expendable resource. Their focus could well be one where trade unions are unwelcome, pay is performance-based and redundancy is a management decision. Perhaps the government supports this neo-liberal orientation, seeing in it the right way to raise national competitiveness. But, there will also be those firms whose systems are more worker-friendly. For them, amicable union-management relations are of critical importance, jobs are protected wherever possible and the human resource is well-rewarded. As an instance of the challenge, just look at the characteristics included in East and West in the Hall model and then imagine the sort of diametrically-opposed systems that could be entailed in companies, say, in Britain and Malaysia. Note also the extent to which the Indian Management approach as described by

Putti (Figure 5.1 below) reveals features of both.

It is useful to employ a more simplistic model of the work systems we have covered to place countries' approaches on a range from *materialistic* to *communitarian*. The first group would see work predominantly as a matter of pay and profits in a laissez-faire market-driven context. Productivity thinking would dominate all aspects of work systems and job protection would be a lesser consideration.

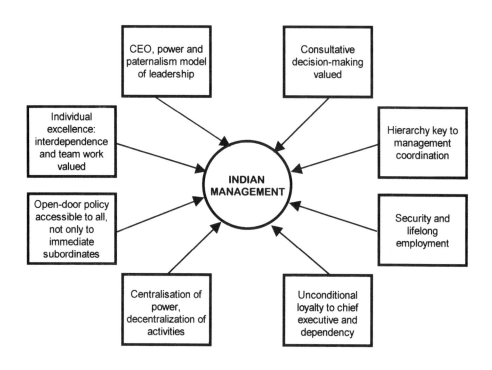

FIGURE 5.1: CHARACTERISTICS OF INDIAN MANAGEMENT

Based on: Joseph Putti, *Management Asian Context*, McGraw Hill, 1991

The word communitarian implies, by contrast, that work is a matter of social as well as economic importance and how people are employed must not be left to the laws of supply and demand.

In the next chapter we shall present a series of questions which allows us to gauge the orientations of nations and companies in this area.

■ Personal Behaviours

The term *personal behaviours* in the cross-cultural business context relates to a variety of situations ranging from first-time business introductions to the management of subordinates in a country by a non-domestic manager. They cover all forms of communication, verbal and non-verbal, gestures and actions, spatial orientations, etiquette and form. There is no other business arena where divergences from what every single nation regards as the natural way to do things are so obvious, and yet so often ignored. At home in our own cultures, each of us greets, eats, talks, smiles, laughs, looks and gestures in ways that are immediately recognised as standardised approaches and are responded to in kind. Depending on the nature of our cultures, we benchmark people by such individualistic features as full eye contact, friendliness, openness, directness, action gestures, formality in greeting, modesty and avoidance of giving offence. Even the extent to which we keep a spatial distance between ourselves and other people comes into the equation.

So excitingly diverse are the different types of anthropological and sociological behaviours exhibited by mankind that it is impossible to expect adequate real cross-cultural harmony between business representatives of different nations to follow instantaneously after a business deal. Nor is there any rule book which prescribes accurately how an American businessperson (say) should deal behaviourally with a Korean businessman (say) for optimum success, or vice versa, before, during and after the deal.

What we, therefore concern ourselves with is not the specifics of a nation's approach but

- broad categories of generalised behaviours;
- key differences among the broad categories.

Both of these are highly are instructive in that they alert the business traveller, negotiator or manager to some of the cultural differences which may manifest themselves and which need to be managed.

Let us, therefore, range over some of the differences in behaviours between nations that need to be anticipated by using the framework presented in Table 5.4 page 129. Note that we shall be dealing with only behavioural tendencies. Note also that we are assuming that business-folk within enterprises do conform to national *mores*. We shall deal with behaviours by using two models which we will label *open* and *closed*.

■ Open Model

Verbal communication takes place in face-to-face conversations, presentations, negotiations, telephone calls, letters. and so on. Logically, one's style clearly should be always tailored to the event, the nature of those taking part and elementary standards of diplomacy and politeness. Most business people also are sensible enough to tailor the approach to the purpose to be achieved, recognising that there are situations where a strong style may avail more than a deferential manner, or diplomacy win out against forcefulness. Given this, however, there can be substantial *culture-bound* differences between our two models which are hard, if not impossible, to overcome.

For example, some people are unconsciously direct in content and manner. They do not *beat about the bush* and *they tell it as it is*. They use active, rather than passive, tenses of verbs and colourful imagery. They may also tend to speak relatively loudly and to emphasise their key points by raising and lowering the voice for dramatic effect. They want to impress you with their forthrightness and action-orientation. They also want results from their exchanges with you and they want them quickly. Such people may be less concerned with building a long-term relationship with you than in achieving beneficial short-term pay-offs, whatever these may be. Stereotypically, Americans seem to possess such traits. So do some Europeans. Such people may be lacking in an elementary sensitivity in relations with foreigners or may make a show of their rude simplicity.

There may be a tendency for the body language gestures of those conforming to this culture style to be in line with such a forthright communicational manner. If so, the finger may be pointed, the arms folded, the stance more erect, the hands employed dramatically to strengthen the effect of the words. Even the manner of walking can be used in this way, to give the impression of urgency. So also moving one's chair or changing one's posture can assist with the effect sought.

Open cultures favour firm handshakes and looking into people's eyes. Dismissive gestures, like rolling one's eyes, are to be avoided, as is excessive touching or getting too close.

Typical Feature	Americans	Arabs	Asia-Pacific	Europeans
Communication: Language approach	Direct, informal, friendly, talkative, even brash	Indirect, formal, flattery, talkative	Indirect, formal, little talking, indeed occasional silences	Direct, informal, talkative
Communication: Non-verbal approach	Firm handshake, direct eye contact, active gestures. Can seem aggressive and sometimes confrontational	Direct eye contact, expressive body language. Tone of voice important.	Bowing, formal gestures, self-control. Minimum of facial expressions. Non-confrontational	Direct eye contact, expressive body language, facial expressions
Spatial orientation	Maintain distance. Each person keeps personal space intact	Much greater intimacy. Informality. Warmth vital. Manages to maintain inner distance	Groups maintain a structured distance. Low levels of intimacy. Ever self-effacing	Maintain distance. Each person keeps personal space intact
Focus on	The individual, job and company	The company, the job and individual	The company the job and the individual	The company, the individual and the job
Information exchange	Speedy and open. Step-wise data sharing	Lengthy process of data sharing. Can't be rushed	Data seeking. Little data given	Step-wise data sharing
Closing action	Commitment-seeking. Action-oriented. Specific	Gradual build-up to agreement. Can't be rushed	Non-specific response. No commitment given. No semblance of urgency	Less urgent than American approach but in line
Involvement in discussion	Informal. Everyone joins in. Cross-table discussion preferred	Seniority of great importance	Strictly organised on basis of seniority. Formal. Preference for circle. Stage managed	Formal and informal. Task-oriented
Self-image of participants	Equal, competitive, independent, "a winner"	Harmonious, patient, consensus-oriented	Modest, group oriented, respectful, dignified	Independent, competitive but a team player
General cultural values	Action-orientation, openness, informality, directness, clarity	Hospitality, formality (ritual), keeping status, harmony, indirectness	Objectivity, respect, listening, harmony, passivity, indirectness, opaqueness	Action-orientation, openness, formality, directness

TABLE 5.4: STEREO-TYPICAL CULTURAL BEHAVIOURS IN CROSS-CULTURAL EXCHANGE SITUATIONS

Such a cultural style is basic to those who regard themselves as independent-minded and who are restive with protocol and hierarchy. They typically do not like excess formality since it can smack of pomp and artificiality. They make a virtue out of their openness and expect others to measure up to their approach.

Hence, they may not favour formal clothing or forms of greeting, beyond, that is, the firm handshake. Naturalness is their watchword.

Note, however, that all this does not mean friendliness or even intimacy. Those with a cultural style of this nature are typically more concerned with the economics of the relationships they are creating and not with the social webs the relationships might ultimately entail. It may even be the case that the openness is, in fact, artificial in that it hides the secret intent of the cunning negotiator.

Whatever else, those who act in this way tend to see their approach as the most natural, spontaneous and correct in the world and, when confronted with foreigners who follow an entirely different behavioural paradigm, they can suffer from a sense of disbelief that other people can act the way they do. Culture shock is what we call it.

■ Closed Model

The history of the USA is one of open spaces, ever-expanding state frontiers, non-stop immigration, civil war and masterful political and economic growth. The country has developed to become the dominant world power, exercising global sway in economic, technological, military and cultural domains. These features all imply for its citizens a pride in national achievement and a self-image of the utmost rectitude. *The American way is the right way.* An open model of cultural behaviour most reflects this standpoint.

What of a closed model? Other parts of the world do not share the heritage of the USA. Some countries are hemmed in geographically, economically and politically to the extent that their inhabitants are natural followers rather than leaders. They can be prisoners of, or escapees from, their historical past and suspicious of all foreigners. Their social structures may have produced, and do sustain, hierarchies and patterns of total obedience rather than equality and total lack of deference on grounds of birth. Religion may have played, and still play, a substantial role in determining societal linkages and bonding behaviours. Wherever also countries were faced with the prospect of war, civil or foreign, the nation may have evolved approaches to task management of a communitarian form which have endured over time.

If a nation has undergone such experiences, as Japan has done, then its cultural behaviours will be strongly marked by them. Stereotypically, Japanese businessmen manifest in their individual behaviours in cross-cultural contexts a pattern wholly distinct from that of the Open Model. They do not parade their individuality or the forcefulness of their personalities; they do not seek to impress and win instant success. Their communicational style is quiet, self-effacing and diplomatic, seeking clarification and more and more information. Their gestures are humble and stylised to an exceptional degree, for example, in the habit of bowing. Whatever else, it is vital for each member of an organisation to keep harmony (*wa*) with other members. You need to keep reality (*honne*), in terms of feelings etc., hidden behind a mask of outward appearance (*tatemae*). Japanese are, in fact, deferential in all matters connected with hierarchy, such as eye contact (looking downwards) and sitting down (when a superior allows it). The impression formed is one of a mixture of studied politeness and heavy inscrutability. In Japan in particular, and in Asia Pacific in general, being a subordinate is a position of honour; being a superior is a position of trust. A flavour of this comes through in Table 5.5 below.

Qualities of Managers	Most Important Quality (%)
Ability to guide and advise	15
Ability to inspire and set example	17
Understanding and sensitivity	25
Ability to persuade and motivate	25
Firmness and decisiveness	16
Ability to look ahead into the future	10
Ability to withstand considerable pressure	3
Most competent person	9

**TABLE 5.5: QUALITIES EXPECTED OF MANAGERS IN A
MULTICULTURAL SOCIETY – SINGAPORE**
Source: Joseph Putti, *Management Asian Context,* McGraw Hill 1991

Inscrutability is, of course, the precise intention behind this cultural style, whether concious or subconcious. Directness and openness were not winning cultural strategies within Japanese society during most of that country's samurai-dominated history. The period of Shogunate rule was itself so harsh as to force social inferiors into patterns of total obedience and secrecy in order to avoid dire punishment. It can even be conjectured that *loss of face* has much to do with the loss of one's ability to keep oneself out of the public gaze, a difficult thing to do in some of the most heavily-populated parts of Asia Pacific. Certainly, silence became a virtue and risk-taking a danger for ordinary citizens quite early in the Japanese nation's history.

Other countries who are fearful of losing out in negotiations with trade partners deemed cleverer or more powerful may adopt a cultural style of such a nature. It cloaks their intentions by making them impenetrable; it slows down the danger of losing out by dragging out the discussions. More positively, of course, it allows the Closed Model partner to try to establish a more meaningful basis to the trade relationship. Trust is the key ingredient here, and a Confucian version of trust at that.

Five orthodox Jewish students, due to begin their undergraduate degrees at Yale University next week, are demanding an exemption from the rule that obliges all freshmen to live on campus, likening the dormitories to "Sodom and Gomorrah".

The students, told by the university's authorities that they had a choice between staying on campus or taking their degrees elsewhere, have threatened to sue Yale if their demand is not met.

The university, however, is adamant that it will not bend its residential rules, regarded as an essential part of a freshman's "character-forming package", as well as contributing to Yale's esprit de corps. Richard Brodhead, the dean said: "If you allow all groups based on affiliation or conviction to separate themselves from the whole university community, you open the door to all kinds of self-segregation that this place has worked very hard against."

EXHIBIT 5.8: CULTURE SHOCK
Source: Jewish students take Yale to task over domitory rule,
Tanku Varadarajan, *The Times*, 11/9/87

The danger is that, whilst each partner is seeking a positive relationship outcome, their behavioural styles are so divergent that truce (a temporary agreement to get on together) replaces trust (an agreement to work together permanently in harmony). Note the difficulties that Yale University has recently had with orthodox Jewish students as illustrated in Exhibit 5.8 page 132.

By taking Japan and the USA as examples of extreme behavioural stereotypes, we can be accused of over-simplification. It is not the case that all members of the two nations' business communities behave like this and the categorisation is self-evidently lacking in precision. On the other hand, these extremes lay down useful markers by which we can evaluate in broad terms the behaviours of other countries. For instance, where do Germany, Russia, Brazil and Korea stand with regard to the behavioural characteristics we have addressed? What do companies from these countries need to know about the behaviours of potential partners before signing joint venture deals? This information can only come from a comparison of data obtained from them directly. That is the subject of Chapter 8.

CHAPTER 6

A Focus on Company Culture

■ Introduction

Companies, like nations, have cultures. They operate at a given time as economically-driven, cohesive groups on the basis of shared value systems and collectively-accepted interpretations of organisational matters. Or, so theory would suggest. In fact, nations have sub-cultures of (say) the young or the old, the rich and the poor, the South and the North. Each may differ from a national norm, to a lesser or greater extent. And so, too, do companies.

A commercial organisation will have an over-arching culture profile, but this may then be occasionally or even continually influenced by types of sub-cultural identity, based, for instance, on functional activity or level of decentralisation or its type of technology (manual or automated). The resultant corporate culture will, at all events, be the outcome of a synthesis of all these subcultures and will be as static or dynamic as they are. If the multinational company is made up of warring tribes, each worshipping a different god, its culture will reflect this throughout the world and operate all its functional activities, its factories and its financing in exactly the same manner.

Culture is, after all, a pattern of thinking and behaving which is common to a group of people. To greater or lesser degrees, members all tend to share the same thought-forms and see the world in the same way and to share identical ways of dealing with issues in their working systems. Culture is not just about *groupthink* and *groupways,* however. It is about behaviours such as gestures and verbal and non-verbal communications, ceremonies, rites and rituals which, by making the group cohesive and separate from other groups, give it identity. It is therefore, as we have noted, about o*rganisational glue.*

A group's culture can be rich or poor, strong or weak, dynamic or static. It is _rich_ if there is an abundance of *groupthink, groupways and organisational glue* that marks it out from other groups and gives great depth and complexity to life within the organisation. The more intricate the rituals, the more demanding the belief patterns which members accept, the more extensive the particular ways of in-group communication, the more the group member can become immersed. If all members are wholly committed, the culture is _strong_. This culture feature tends to become more salient if entry to the group is voluntary, if there is a detailed entry requirement (perhaps a rite of passage of some description) and if banishment from the group is seen by members as a matter of great significance. The rewards for group membership, beyond that of the sheer psychology of belonging, may, in fact, be outranked by the pain of not-belonging. The culture is _static_ if it resists change. This can occur if members are so committed to their existing culture that they refuse to alter it; they are virtually prisoners of the past. The age profile of members and their ability to assimilate new ideas and emotionalism obviously plays a role here.

A culture is distinguished not only by the existence of the group of people who share it, willingly or unwillingly. It is made separate by the extent of the *behavioural orthodoxy* required. There are right ways for group members to act and wrong; things they must do and should not; things that are obligatory and things to be avoided. The rule book may be unwritten but the behaviour codes will still exist. It could be that some members do not actually know that they are living within a particular culture framework and, therefore, accept that their culture is either *real life* or *the proper way to live,* or *both.*

The degree to which orthodoxy is stressed is counter-balanced by the extent to which some members will rebel against dogma and form sub-groups with sub-cultures. Schisms of this sort can occur in strong and rich cultures, as power-play is a key human behaviour pattern which affects all groups. The more the culture of the group is perceived to be managed by an in-group or clique for its own ends, the more likely are such schisms.

We can therefore polarise cultures qualitatively and in general terms as rich/poor, strong/weak and static/dynamic.

Hence, for example, a major multinational could have a strong business culture because it uses the same technology throughout the world and operates all its functional activities, its factories and its financing in exactly the same manner. The technology it uses obliges compliance with the main features of its operating systems, such as time to market and tight financial objectives. Even country culture features which normally are quite pronounced can cease to be significant. In the case of the car industry, it does not matter whether we are talking Ford or General Motors, Peugeot or Renault, each needs to have internationally consistent ways of operating since, with globalisation, a car is a car, a car factory is a car factory and car financing is car financing the world over. Indeed, in some industries, the fact of rising globalisation can simply iron out faster any country-based culture differentials that do exist. Indeed, many such companies are obliged to accept what we could call a *Model-T* culture: a corporate culture that is predominantly technology-driven. The use of automation, information technology and logistics management is so standardised that its culture tends to be homogeneous (see Table 6.1 page 138).

Conversely, the multinational may be

- active in many different markets and product lines;
- have major operational differences between how it carries out its key functions of manufacture, marketing, R&D, human resources management and finance;
- have substantial differences in its resourcing activities and in the strategic management of its divisions;
- have a high degree of centralisation in some divisions, but quite the reverse in others, possibly using wide-ranging, differing technologies.

Hence, such an organisation will possibly find itself operating globally with a range of different ways of thinking and acting, which are difficult to accommodate within one single business culture. Worse, the sub-cultures may all be jockeying for position, each claiming supremacy, locally if not internationally, and they may be evolving at different speeds

In such companies there is always an issue of power politics, as to whose values will prevail in a given context or as to how to achieve a modus vivendi between *culture competitors,* which will allow the firm to move forward constructively as an entity. This can occur when a cosmopolitan leader (see Table 6.3 page 141) takes over from a local leader and the workforce are upset by the notion of ill-considered changes that will upset their cosy lives.

Culture Model	Key Features
Technology-driven or *Model-T Culture*	The company's culture is primarily driven by its work technology. This is the combination of production automation, information processing systems and logistics management. All branches of the company use exactly the same approach. Culture standardisation results.
Money-driven or *Model-M Culture*	This is a form of culture where all that matters is money. A typical modern example would be a professional football club in Europe where everyone – managers and players alike – is for sale. The social life of the club's shareholders is characterised by the intensity of the pursuit of instant success and people are saleable assets. Another is the world of pop music. Both the football and pop worlds have strong and rich cultures – uniforms, songs, rituals abound. They are heavy in emotion.
Virtual Business-driven or *Model-V Culture*	Organisations which have outsourced much of their peripheral activities and downsized many of their core functions to the point of becoming a shell organisation that orchestrates a network of actors who do the work of production, marketing etc. Such shell companies attempt to search for a cultural soul to embed in the enterprise but find it difficult. The company simply has no social substance outside its choreographing of work to be done by teams of outsiders. The matter of interpersonal chemistry is unimportant compared with that of network optimisation. The culture is poor and weak.
Knowledge-driven or *Model-K Culture*	There is a recognition that the knowledge that a company has – whether hard (its accumulated wealth of patents) or soft (its workforce's know-what and know-how) – is of greater importance than its physical assets (buildings, machinery etc). Hence, the cerebral skill and creativity of innovators is valued, often at the expense of organisational discipline. An e-commerce start-up would have a typical Model–K culture…strong and rich.

TABLE 6.1: CULTURE FORMS IN TODAY'S WORLD
© Terry Garrison 2001

Individual Excellence	Each partner is strong in their own right and makes a positive contribution to the alliance.
Importance	The linkage is important to both. Each wants to make it work. Do not be greedy.
Interdependence	The partners need each other. Do not be the first to play games.
Investment	The partners are making an investment, physical or symbolic, in each other.
Information	Partnership must mean open communication especially on critical data and any trouble spots. Don't try to outsmart your partner by being clever.
Integration	The points of organisational inter-connection between the two organisations need to be carefully managed.
Institutionalisation	Roles, responsibilities, authority and accountability need to be clearly spelled out.
Integrity	The partners need to trust each other and behave honourably.

TABLE 6.2: THE EIGHT "I"s YOU NEED FOR SUCCESS IN OPERATING A BUSINESS ALLIANCE

Source: Rosabeth Kanter, *Harvard Business Review*, July-August 1994 and Johnson R. And Lawrence P, Beyond Vertical Intregration – the Rise of Value-adding Partnerships, *Harvard Business Review* July-August 1988

Even in such technology-stereotype companies as Ford or Renault, there are bound to be value conflicts at board level as to where investments should be made for best long-term results and as to the level of risk that can reasonably be tolerated in novel contexts, like outsourcing, opening up new markets or diversification. Given the stereotypical profile of *Marketing Man* (focussed on sales targets) and

Bean Counter (focussed on accounting controls), inter-divisional discord may be endemic.

And yet, it is incumbent on the directors of the enterprise – multinational or local, small or large – to inculcate in employees a standardised and consistent culture, if they can and if it will lead to better performance. As Edgar Schein (1997) indicates, if the workforce does not conform to, and assimilate, the dominant corporate culture and sign up for the *psychological contract it involves*, they may be unable to act as a successful team or even achieve the necessary systems co-ordination to allow proper work-place co-operation. This means not just sharing a time-based hierarchy of value priorities. It also means having a common view of how, for instance, to solve problems or manage resources, as well as an organisational language that all understand. With these come, we hope, a sense of belonging, a sense of identification, a sense of pride and a sense of self-fulfilment *within* the firm.

Our focus in this chapter is to explore a variety of concepts and techniques which are used academically and in the consultancy world to explore the company culture phenomenon and to examine ways of appraising it.

■ Corporate Culture Manifestations

In order to systematise the thinking and behaviours of people in an organisation, their leaders will have recourse to a variety of age-old cultural manifestations, common to all extensive socially-structured human groups. They may seek deliberately to introduce new pride symbols (logos, company flags, brand names, office decor and furniture, company uniforms, ties) and forms of ceremonial behaviour (involving rites and rituals like parties at Xmas or when someone leaves, the singing of the company song before the start of the day's work or parades). At all events, they will be faced with the existence of the *grapevine*, the system which all organisations have for the dissemination of unofficial information, and the manner in which managers and employees use it, carefully or carelessly, to spread tales about people or activities.

Form of leadership in the organisation	Culture Consequences
Hedgehog	The organisation is led by people who have a mastery of situational detail. They know the company and its industry because of their long experience in both. They occupy their positions because of the organisation's need for stability. The problem is their inability to accept change, a problem exacerbated by organisational introversion. The impact on culture is to create a feeling of separateness about the firm, *we are special*, and to make the firm's external relationships difficult. The more cohesive and powerful the feeling of difference from the rest, the greater will be the cultural reinforcement of the differences – to the point of pathology. Here we find *rich* and *strong* company cultures. The Russian novelist Tolstoy called those who know only one thing, but in great depth, ***hedgehogs.***
Fox	The firm's management has been around. They have travelled widely and worked in different jobs in different industries. Their frame of reference is wide and they seen many things. They are in post because of their sensitivity to change and their ability to create innovation. The culture within firms led in this way tends to be thin as social relationships tend to mutate quickly and the firm has no solid core of long-term employees. Company loyalty is worth less than marketable skills. Here we find poor and weak cultures. To Tolstoy, those who know many things, but only superficially, are *foxes*.

TABLE 6.3: THE CULTURES OF THE HEDGEHOG & THE FOX - THE INFLUENCE ON CULTURE OF LOCAL & COSPMOPOLITAN LEADERSHIP

Based on: Cosmopolitans & Locals: Towards an Analysis of Latent Social Roles, Alvin Gouldner, *Administrative Science Quarterly,* Dec 1957 & March 1958. Note also: *The Hedgehog & the Fox,* Isiah Berlin, Mentor, New York, 1965

Embroidered and exaggerated as they are by the human beings spreading them, these stories can take the form, over time, of myths and legends, sagas and folk tales about corporate heroes and villains. We need also to take into consideration Schein's view (1997) that people within organisations draw cultural lessons from the way see decisions being taken above and around them and focus particularly on the criteria which they see guiding these decisions. Fairness in rewarding people and allocating resources within the firm is one such prominent criterion.

Taken together, these culture manifestations amount to the sort of *organisational glue* that cements a company together, or not as the case may be.

Types of culture manifestation	Features of manifestation
Ceremonial	Various forms of ceremonial exist. A rite is a single, official celebratory event that occurs at intervals e.g., "The Salesman of the Year" award. It could take the form of (say) a rite of passage welcoming a new recruit, or conflict reduction, CEO addressing the Works Council. Rituals, such as board meetings, dressing-down on Fridays, singing the company song or holding leaving parties – are repetitive "positive behaviour" re-enforcement opportunities.
Pride symbols	Behaviour triggers which foster the corporate image and group identity. Personal artefacts such as clothing, logos, expensive company cars etc. Corporate assets like buildings, facades, furniture, décor and brand names.
Tales	Stories about important company happenings and people. Instances of corporate courage, suffering, challenges overcome or corporate taboos (things you must not speak of or do) etc. They can even become *legends* about inspirational leaders, like Sir Richard Branson, or, if over-embellished, myths. Used in the military to raise *esprit de corps*.

TABLE 6.4: CULTURAL MANIFESTATIONS

As with pride symbols and ceremonials, the tales can embed themselves so deeply within the organisation's psyche that they become synonymous with the company. They are, in short, what it stands for. Like those about the legendary Jack Welch and GEC. The more famous the company's heroes, the more famous its commercial exploits, the greater its suffering to achieve success, the more likely is it that the company's value system will be integrated around them. All three will be used to cement behaviours within the company and as part of the image the company projects to outsiders. They are used as examples of exemplary behaviour – to be emulated – or worse-case scenarios, to avoid. They are, thus, deliberate *reifications* (ways of making things real to people who have difficulty dealing with abstractions) of desirable models of how to think, talk and act.

The danger, of course, is that the ethos of the firm can be fixed in time by the prior accumulation of its pride symbols, ceremonials and tales. Such an array of cultural practices can be a blessing for all those firms, which continue to enjoy business success through technological innovation and value creation for customers and shareholders alike. But, they can be an enormous burden for a company whose products have become dated or whose technology is anachronistic. In such a case, employees will then be faced with operating, for instance, with out-of-date systems, and forced to honour a logo which the market disdains and heroes who are no longer recognised. A company's culture is subject, therefore, to life cycle pressures.

Of great importance is observation that an excess of cultural baggage in a company that is set in its ways can lead to what can be called *strategic myopia* – an inability to think about changes in strategy to deal with the challenges of the future.

The culture of the firm must, as a consequence, be consistently up-dated if it is to be meaningful as workforce integrator, motivator and quality-monitor. This means renewal of behavioural norms hitherto based on shared beliefs and experiences.

This is easier said than done, of course, on two grounds.

- Firstly, because of the need to have a cultural ambience in the organisation which is *natural* and not dictated, or seen to be dictated, by management. In fact, if company management is perceived to be explicitly manipulating the culture – using pride symbols, ceremonial and tales etc. – for organisational purposes, the result will almost certainly be counter-productive.

• Secondly, because once a corporate culture becomes enshrined and dominant within a company, it has its supporters who have gained much from adherence to the norms used (e.g., their power positions) and much to lose if the company starts to worship new gods. Dyer suggests (1986) that a culture crisis within a firm is likely to be more more immediate and impactful if it arises from an external trigger (e.g., a dramatic loss in the firm's market position) than an internal trigger (e.g., a change in internal management). Certainly, achieving a shift in corporate culture is likely to be a struggle because it involves new values, new ways of thinking and a possible new power structure. This is the realm of the organisational Machiavelli.

There are two additional issues to be considered: the newcomer and Edgar Schein's concept of the life cycle of corporate culture. (1997) In joining a particular company, the individual begins by willingly subscribing to its cultural ethos and conforming to its mores and customs, he or she is accultured. As the job develops, for as long as there is no conflict between his/her personal value system and that of the firm, the culture will serve as a behavioural reinforcer. If, however, there should be value conflict (job dissatisfaction; pay perceived to be inequitable; personality differences etc.), then cultural alienation may commence. Clearly, it will occur more speedily in those who have seen more of the outside world and have worked for a short time with the firm, than it will for long-serving employees. The alienation may take the form of a willing suspension of disbelief – as when he/she starts to question all cultural practices and *see through them* as artificial – or a flat rejection of all the company stands for.

So far as the life cycle of corporate culture is concerned, we have the problem of those with long-service within the company to consider. They grew up with the corporate culture *as it has been* and possibly profited from the status that it conferred on them. Maybe they are responsible for some of the rites and the rituals; possibly they were there when the myths and legends were hatched. A changing world, new bosses unfamiliar with the old corporate ethos, changes in the technology position (e.g., IT) – all these mean discomfort and discomfort can turn itself quite rapidly into cultural alienation. The Old Guard may be a liability in such circumstances, as, whatever else, the world moves on. And, as in any marriage, old and young partners might find living together something of a strain.

It follows that not only must the managers of the organisation seek to maintain the modernity of the corporate culture, but ensure as far as possible a fit between the culture and the reward and work systems that underpin it. This applies not only to existing employees, but also to the newly-hired who will undeniably be bringing with them the cultural baggage from their previous employment and occupation.

Such new employees need to be *accultured* as quickly and painlessly into their new firm as possible, if culture shock is to be either minimised or avoided. It goes without saying that the danger of shock is significantly increased if the individuals' former employer had a less explicit and weaker culture than the new. The image of Walmart's German employees singing the company song before starting their daily work springs to mind.

The Cameron and Quinn Competing Values Framework theory (1999) throws this issue into sharp relief. In their model, the term *clan* is given to a culture where (a) the firm is focussed internally and (b) there is a mixture of organisational flexibility and integration. Thus, a newcomer would be accultured into a family-style ambiance and would, hopefully, begin to show the characteristics of a devoted clan member. By contrast, a corporate context in which there is a mixture of an internalised focus and a stability and control management thrust is described as a *hierarchy* culture. The danger for Walmart is that their German staff will think they are being accultured into a hierarchy and not a clan.

■ Typologies of Corporate Culture

There are many types of analysis which can be used to assess, gauge and possibly calibrate a company's culture – some commercial and used in consultancy, some used, on the basis of relevant questionnaires, in social science research. Five of the most prominent formulae have been selected here as indicative of the range.

❏ **Charles Handy's Organisational Culture Typology**

Feature		Depends on
Central source of power Tough & Abrasive Selection of 'right thinkers' Few rules & procedures Decisions by influence Results matter High turnover of "losers"	Power	Trust and Empathy People think the same way Speedy decisions – right or wrong Quality of individuals Risk taking Faith in individual Manageable size
Procedures & Rules Co-ordination at top Position not personal power Slow to perceive need for change Relatively inflexible Bureaucratic	Role	Stable environment Control or monopoly Predictability of staff performance Team players, not individuals, matter Confidence in the future Obedience
Matrix structures Getting the job done matters most Task-focused Experts main roles Team culture Project thinking important	Task	Flexibility and entrepreneurship Quality staff Co-operation in allocation of resources Individual responsibility Adaptability
Cluster of individuals Creativity Few controls and rules Shared responsibility Personal Chemistry matters	Person	Individual experts Common Interest Little structure No controlling managers Charismatic individuals

**FIGURE 6.1: THE HANDY TYPOLOGY OF
ORGANISATIONAL STRUCTURES** (1991)

Charles Handy emphasises four particular varieties of organisational culture, each specifically related to the nature of work being done and the size of the organisation. These are listed in Figure 6.1 page 146. Two of the cultures – *power* and *person* – are to be found in relatively small organisations, whilst the *role* and *task* cultures are typical of the larger organisations. Of course, it is quite possible that a unit of a company, i.e., a section or a division, might have a culture appropriate to its small size, whereas the rest of the firm conforms to the large size model.

If we were to examine companies typical of the New Economy, characterised by their being high tech, fast to market, entrepreneurial and *employment minimalist,* we should find that many employ a person culture. What matters to the company are the people they have and their creativity. This is expressed not only in their work, done in a context of few rules and a free-form structure, but in the personal chemistry that binds the team together to seek a common and exciting purpose.

We should also find somewhere that a power culture rules. This is typically a firm where you have a formidable leader (maybe the owner or the head of the family owning the firm), who may well have founded it; a range of senior and middle managers who conform to the obedience pattern expected by their CEO; a workforce that share the thrills and spills of driving forward quickly, willy-nilly along the business success trackway decided by the CEO. People who do not *fit in*, leave or are de-selected quickly.

A role culture is typical of large organisations whose operating environment is stable or slow moving. Public sector or civil service structures with long-established work patterns and large trade union memberships produce predictable results. They have to, since they are bound by law to operate in such a manner. They have little need of charismatic or forceful leaders, as compared with their requirement for inflexible bureaucracy and rules governing most action contingencies, and managers derive their authority from the role they have, more even than the job they do. It is an inflexible, ponderous organisation with no sharing of knowledge except at the very top. It works well in changeless times.

Many large firms, faced with a dynamic market place and the need to keep abreast/ahead in technology development, cannot afford a role culture. They must have adaptability and entrepreneurship in order to innovate. Teamwork is mandatory, but in a way that is highly responsive. For Handy, a task culture exemplifies this requirement, with experts (leading project teams) co-existing in a matrix structure with line management.

It goes almost without saying that any attempt through M&A or joint venture or business alliance to amalgamate diverse organisational cultures or, even worse, to force one organisational culture on another is fraught with danger. If cross-border, the situation may quickly become irredeemable. This is not because the people in the companies who are trying to co-operate lack goodwill or even skill, but because the basis of each organisational culture is so different, as Table 6.3 page 141 suggests, that they cannot be combined.

❑ **The Blake & Mouton Managerial Grid Typology**

The managerial grid was the creation of Robert Blake and Jane Mouton (1990) and is a numerical approach to capturing the management orientation of a company, rather than its cultures. However, it can be used to good effect in this area as it provides quite a comprehensive formulation of leadership styles in small units of a large organisation. In its most modern format (see Figure 6.2 page 149) we are dealing with the two standard dimensions of people – and task – orientation but in a clear and exciting model. Thus, the 1.1 'do nothing manager' does precisely what his title suggests, producing a culture of inactivity and lack of concern motivation. The social tone of the organisation is not so much alienation as indifference. The antithesis of such a culture is that generated by 9.9 the 'team builder'. The culture he/she creates is one where people are successfully integrated into the organisation unit and commitment to organisational goals and morale are high.

The culture of **a country club manager** is represented by the score of 1.9. Here the manager is concerned only with the needs of people and has no interest in getting the job done. The more output is difficult to uncover or the more the firm is insulated from market place pressures, the more lively is such a pre-occupation with the internal dimensions of the company's life.

The 9.1 **production pusher**, by contrast has little concern with the human team he manages. Efficiency and task achievement are what count.

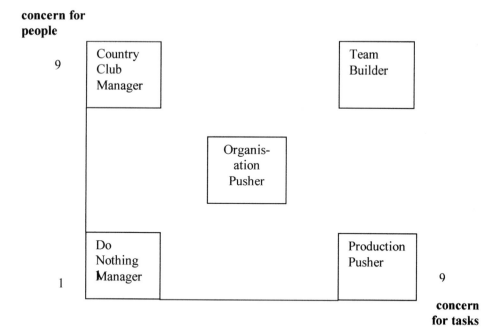

concern for
people

9   Country
     Club
     Manager

                              Team
                              Builder

                    Organis-
                    ation
                    Pusher

     Do
     Nothing
     Manager

                              Production
                              Pusher

1   9

                              concern
                              for tasks

FIGURE 6.2: THE BLAKE & MOUTON MANAGERIAL GRID
Source: Robert Blake, Jane Mouton and Anne McCanse,
Change by Design, Addison Wesley, 1990

❑ The Goffee & Jones "Double S" Cube

The organisational culture theory advanced by Rob Goffee and Gareth Jones (1998) in their powerful book *The Character of a Corporation* is based on the trade-off within an organisation of the levels of *sociability* and *solidarity* that exist, whether by management design or by the accretion of organisational history. Sociability relates to the ease with which people build and maintain positive intra-organisational relationships, whether of an inter-personal, inter-sectional or inter-divisional nature. By a positive relationship the authors mean a situation of caring and sharing, without undue regard to personal gain. A sociable firm has no zero-sum players.

Solidarity, state Goffee and Jones, is " based not so much in the heart as in the mind... with one of the hallmarks of high solidarity being a certain getting-the-job-done ruthlessness". They see solidaristic relationships as being based on "common tasks, mutual interests and clearly understood shared goals that benefit all the involved parties, *whether they personally like each other or not*". Hence, win-lose thinking is germane to all solidaristic relationships within the organisation and X support Y's moves only insofar as they allow X to win. If they do, X and Y will work together "like a well-oiled machine", emphasising achievement. High solidarity cultures do not allow the deviant or defective individual to get in the way of task fulfilment. By definition almost, the company makes a common front in the face of external forces that can affect its destiny – competitors, customers and suppliers.

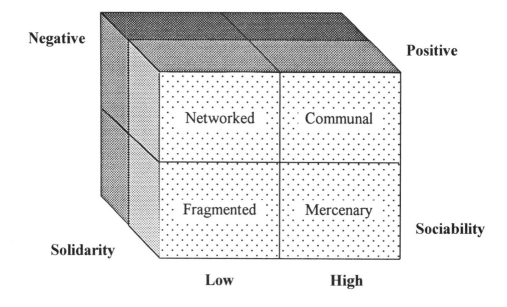

FIGURE 6.3: GOFFEE & JONES TYPOLOGY

The Character of a Corporation, Rob Goffee, Gareth Jones, Harper-Collins, 1998.

The Cube notion covers the permutations that can exist in an organisation where, firstly, you have varying combinations of high and low sociability and solidarity and, secondly, where the combinations are functional or dysfunctional. Functional in this context means helping to achieve a positive, successful organisational outcome. Naturally enough, the main focus of the message is on this.

As Figure 6.3 page 150 suggests, there are four combinations of high and low sociability and solidarity that can exist as culture forms:

- A *networked* culture is high on sociability and low on solidarity. People get on well together and make a point of doing so, on the job and off the job, e.g., in sports clubs. There is a relative absence of rigid formality, but not correctness, with regard to hierarchy, inter-personal relationships and communication. There is "a lot of talk", "office doors are open" and "excessive displays of personal difference are resisted". Obviously, there is a danger here of dysfunctional employee goal-displacement. The company is such a happy place that enjoyment rather than profitability becomes the primary focus.

- A *communal* culture is high on both dimensions. Here, one lives to work and the company is the ultimate reality. Loyalty is fierce and there is large-scale bonding. "Logos, symbols and war cries abound" and you even wear clothes with the company's logo on them. Work-time ceases to be counted and communication literally flows. Few work-space barriers exist. Thus, the individual identifies, for better or worse, with the company.

- A *mercenary* culture is characterised by the individual urge to win. It is, as can be expected, a combination of high solidarity and low sociability. Personal relationships, communication patterns, resources are seen as exploitable for individual or departmental gain rather than for company benefit. "Ultimately, attachments are instrumental" and time is both money and power so it is not wasted on building victories for the undeserving. Note that is not necessarily a negative culture insofar as intra-firm rivalries can make the whole organisation more aggressive and sharper. However, there can be a persistent tendency to dysfunctional and unedifying inter-departmental squabbling.

- A low sociability, low solidarity combination is termed *fragmented.* It is a problematic corporate culture because it inhibits organisational relationships. People tend to do their own thing, accenting their personal freedom and individuality and finding rules and regulations decidedly irksome. Employees mix poorly at work, staying in small cliques, and do not mix outside at all. You talk only to those who are "worth talking to". One's main focus is clients and professional peers *outside* the firm.

It is important to bear in mind two further observations that Goffee and Jones make about the Double S Cube. The first is minor, namely that there is no one culture that is necessarily good or bad: they are only so to the extent that they fit in with the company's competitive environment. The second is that there appears to be a life cycle to the four cultures. Profit-driven companies, they say, often start out as a communal culture, with a high-energy, clear-vision founder seeking deep commitment from *his people.* Work does not stop at the close of business; the pace is frenetic, the involvement intense. It is a case of the Gazelle start-up company in high-tech Silicon Valley and the 80-hour week.

A growth in company size and technological maturation bring a tendency for the culture to become networked, difficult in that many of the members of the original workforce will want to socialise in the old ways. But, merely employing large numbers of differently-skilled people means change. The danger of a networked culture is, of course, that it is difficult to manage a matrix, multi-dimensional firm with the right mixture of motivation and control to improve performance consistently. Should the organisation sprawl, complacency and/or disunity may set in (an organisation at war with itself) and a fragmented culture will result.

Those reviewing the possibility of cross-border link-ups will, therefore, need to be alert not only to the stage that a partner has reached in the postulated culture *life cycle* of the firm, but also to the extent of any transition that may be currently taking place or in prospect.

❑ The Deal and Kennedy Typology

It is noteworthy that the typologies of Handy, Blake & Mouton, and Goffee and Jones all deal with the organisational trade-offs arising from employing a "run a happy ship" and "get the job done" orientation.

The Deal and Kennedy approach (1982, 2000) is based, conversely, on the world outside the company. It relates to the *degree of risk* associated with the company's key strategies (and all associated activities) and the speed at which companies find out how well or badly the strategies are working – *the pace of feedback* from the market-place. Their typology, unlike those of Handy and Goffee & Jones, is related to the interface between the company and its business environment and not to the social architecture of the firm.

They distinguish among the four types of culture outlined in Figure 6.4 page 154. The first is the **Tough Guy** culture in which we find a combination of high risk and fast feedback. The world of such a macho approach is typically unforgiving – the entertainment industry is a case in point – insofar as the risks are high and the recognition of how well you are doing is rapid if not instantaneous. Companies which need a "quick hit" or, more properly, instant success need such a culture. At the other end of the spectrum we find the **Process** culture. Here the risks of failure are relatively low and there is little or no feedback of the instantaneous variety. A public utility shielded from the market-place or a large traditional bank would fit the bill. Of course, with the rise in consumerism and the massive deregulatory moves that have been taking place in the industrial market-place, the analogy is weaker than it used to be. However, firms with such a low risk-low feedback profile tend to concentrate on optimising internal processes rather than finding new and attractive things to do *outside* the firm.

The **Bet-Your-Company** culture is typical of the high technology world of the pharmaceutical industry where a company can find itself taking a multi-million dollar research decision today in the anticipation and hope of multi-billion dollars sales after a period of several years. But without certainty, as the R&D effort may not succeed. The bigger the R&D gamble in any capital goods industry, the more the directors may be said to be "betting their company". Not only that, they are consistently gambling with high stakes.

Finally, we have the **Work Hard-Play Hard** culture used by all orgnisations that focus on activity, productivity and efficiency. The firm runs relatively low risks – its product is known and respected and its market is stable – and feedback on success or failure is speedy and routinised. So, the gross uncertainty and big gamble features of the Bet-Your-Company culture are absent. Here the company seeks the same success every single day.

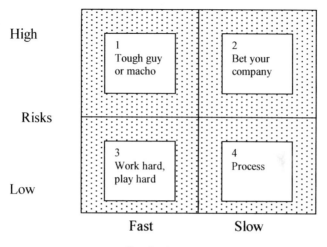

Feedback about company decisions

FIGURE 6.4: DEAL & KENNEDY TYPOLOGY

Terrence Deal and Allan Kennedy, *Corporate Culture, The Rites and Rituals of*
Corporate Life, Addison Wesley 1982 and
The New Corporate Culture, Texere, 2000

In their book *The New Corporate Cultures,* Deal and Kennedy are at
pains to point out that

- economic and technological change is fast changing the corporate
  landscape and eroding traditional cultural patterns such as those
  described;
- it is extremely difficult for organisation leaders to let go of the
  strong culture that helped make the company great, just as it is for
  employees who yearn for the good old days to change their ways;
- it is vital to try to rebuild "cohesive cultures" in companies whose
  global world, due to M&A, joint ventures and business alliances,
  resembles a virtual *Tower of Babel.*

In particular they stress the need for companies to create and maintain
what they call robust company cultures, reflecting in this the early 1990s
research of Harvard academics John Kotter and James Hesketh. (1992)
This found a strong correlation between culture strength and economic
performance. What is meant, therefore, by "robust"? A definably-

different, people-rich organisational *glue*, which creates inspiration, cohesion and commitment and which is almost tangible. This is likely to contain a wealth of ceremonial rites and rituals, a treasury of tales of corporate derring-do and leadership. These are people who sing company songs and wear company T-shirts.

❏   The Trompenaars and Hampden-Turner Typology

Egalitarian

Fulfillment-oriented culture INCUBATOR	Project-oriented culture GUIDED MISSILE
FAMILY Person-oriented culture	EIFFEL TOWER Role-oriented culture

Person ─────────── ┼ ─────────── Task

Hierarchical

FIGURE 6.5: TROMPENAARS & HAMPDEN-TURNER TYPOLOGY

Riding the Waves of Culture, Fons Trompenaars and
Charles Hampden-Turner, Nicholas Brealey, 2nd ed. 1997

In addition to isolating the cultural scales that characterise national cultures (for instance, universalism v particularism, achievement v ascription), Charles Hampden-Turner and Fons Trompenaars have also advanced a schema of four types of corporate culture. (1993) They concede that their typology is ideal and may possibly caricature, rather than accurately describe, but find it useful. As Figure 6.5 above shows, their focus is on the balance between hierarchy and equality, on the one hand, and between the company's orientation to the person and the task on the other. Each of the four types is a metaphor illustrating the way in which in different organisations "employees learn, change, resolve conflicts, are rewarded and motivated". It is a richer corporate culture model than the first three we have investigated.

In the *Family* culture we find a mixture of hierarchy and person-orientation. The leader is possibly equivalent to a caring father (or mother) in situations where the authority system is implicit and obeyed by everyone, as in Indian or Japanese companies. Indeed, the social fabric of such organisations is based around relationships, which carry natural and inescapable obligations, both vertical and horizontal. You are pleased to obey because it is your duty and, even where the leader is more authoritarian, obedience is still the watchword. The pressure for conformity with what the leader requires is immense and bonding is obligatory. The boss-subordinate relationship might reach beyond the confines of the workplace and economic values into private life.

The *Eiffel Tower* is what it suggests: a highly bureaucratic, rigid and formal work environment. You obey not because of a sense of social framework but because *rules are rules.* They are perceived to be truly necessary because the organisation with this culture faces the same tasks every single day and needs an optimal way of coping with them. The "best" means rules governing what is done, when, where and how; it means prescriptions on efficiency and effectiveness.

Relationships are, thus, specific (not diffuse as in the *Family* culture), status is ascribed and job titles matter. "Conflicts in this culture are seen as irrational – pathologies of orderly procedure and offences against efficiency". Time management does not necessarily mean "faster"; it means "orderly". The oil which runs the organisation is not the inspiration of a charismatic leader nor even a sense of familial respect. It is regulations and systems. If you want to effect change, you need to alter the rule book.

Whereas the *Eiffel Tower* metaphor signifies a static culture focussed on hierarchy and task, a *Guided Missile* culture operates in a different world. First, it is task-orientated but focussed, not on the means of getting the job done, but on the ends. Second, it is non-hierarchical, insofar as the people involved see themselves as equals and naturally take their reference point to be the professional standing or role importance of others rather than their organisational position.

> The *Eiffel Tower* operators have an algorithmic culture; they have found the best model and they work with it. Perhaps they even have a philosophical backing for what they do and how they do it.
>
> The *Guided Missile* crew, by contrast, have a heuristic culture. They persistently experiment and do not believe in an optimum scientific result. They do not even like big ideas if they don't fit in with real life.

EXHIBIT 6.1: ALGORITHMIC AND HEURISTIC CULTURES

This culture fits organisations that do many different things on the basis of teamwork and project management. Innovatory thinking, based on distilling the wisdom of past experience, is vital, as is the ability to alter organisational form to suit the job in hand.

The fourth culture form is the ***Incubator***. Here, the employee is free to express himself or herself with the minimum of constraints. What matters is team contribution and self-fulfilment in a positive, possibly super-charged atmosphere. The culture is typical of small Silicon Valley teams or clusters of scientists on Route 128 in Boston. The individual enjoys coming to work because social dynamics and the strong possibility of personal gain in the future – maybe through an Initial Public Offering of Stock (IPO) in three years time when the invention being worked on becomes a break- through.

■ Conclusions

As Table 6.5 page 158 suggests, the culture focus of the five typologies we have investigated varies considerably. Three are a function of the internal operations of the company, whilst the Deal and Kennedy model draws its logic from the results of what the company does.

In reviewing these approaches, we need to bear in mind, of course, the extent to which, in cross-border relationships, individual partners can achieve an acceptable culture balance to facilitate their co-working. (See Table 6.2 page 139.) Hence, we need to consider the extent to which, as a generality, company cultures are becoming more similar. The evidence suggests very strongly indeed that such a process is happening, and fast. We need to list merely the pressures arising from:

Researchers	Basic Culture Focus	Corporate Culture Types
Charles Handy	Structural	Power, Role, Task & Person
Robert Blake and Jane Mouton	Leadership Type	Do nothing, country club, production pusher, team builder
Rob Goffee & Gareth Jones	Sociability & Solidarity	Networked, Communal, Fragmented & Mercenary
Terrence Deal & Allan Kennedy	Risk & Feedback	Tough guy, all or nothing, work hard/play hard, bet your company
Fons Trompenaars & Charles Hampden-Turner	Equality/hierarchy & Task/person	Family, Eiffel Tower, Incubator, Guided Missile

TABLE 6.5: FIVE POPULAR CORPORATE CULTURE TYPOLOGIES

➤ globalisation: As individual country markets are opened up to trade, a function of international trade agreements and consumer demand, companies are much less able to protect themselves from competitive pressures than ever before. There is nowhere to hide from best-practice world-class business systems which emphasise productivity and efficiency;

➤ global technology transfer: It is now possible to move technology round the world in a search for new, more profitable production locations much more easily than in the past. Countries which vie for urgently-needed inbound foreign direct investment are prepared to adjust work practices to suit the new investors;

➤ global technology standardisation: There is only one correct way to make cars today; to use the most advanced automated equipment and schedule all work around the demands of the dominant multinational producers. The same is true of all technology-driven industries – telecommunications and pharmaceuticals being good examples. Should you deviate from the world-standard approach, you will be ostracised by consumers and shunned by potential partners;

> ➤ the international financial markets: The easy transfer of capital world-wide obliges all companies to *compete* for capital, whether debt or shareholders' funds, and, to do so, use the commercial logic of the world's most profitable companies. A future poor ROCE performance, as in a "profits warning" is instantly punished by a falling share price. Ergo, no company can afford to be commercially out of line. No wonder that, for some companies in the developing world, globalisation really does mean Americanisation.

This means that we need again to factor in the extent to which the culture of the company we are investigating is *technology-driven*. Is it the case, because of the type of firm and what it does, that managers have very little choice over the firm's aims and objectives, work systems, planning and the tempo of work and use of automation? Indeed, has the firm become a player in a value chain system for an entire industry – using an integrated software system to link it to "suppliers" and "customers" and, possibly, to "co-optitioners" – and has ceased to be an independent company? If the answers to these two questions are "yes", then we must draw the inference that the company's business culture must have strong similarities with that of other companies doing the same work in the same industry.

As a consequence, we need in our research into particular firms to examine the culture linkages between the extent to which their corporate culture is technology-driven and the extent to which it is:

- robust (to use Deal and Kennedy's term) or strong and rich in its social chemistry yet subject to the ageing process;
- commercial, i.e., driven by profitability and mercenary thinking and possibly, therefore, tending to de-accent matters of the firm's social capital;
- world-standard. If so, the company could be said to have a mature, cosmopolitan, "best-in-class" approach to management and not to suffer from any defects caused by unawareness or parochialism of whatever form. In other words, having a highly standardised culture.

The danger is, that with the onward rush of technological change generally, and the New Economy in particular, that a homogenous company culture becomes a thing of the past. Deal and Kennedy write of their recipe to put "fragmented cultures" back together. They call it "rebuilding the social context of work". (2000)   It consists of getting right all the factors that make people want to work and building a continuous learning environment for them. Easier said than done in our mercenary age. Perhaps the real answer is Cameron and Quinn's *adhocracy* culture. (1999) This allows the individual a maximum of organisational flexibility and discretion, within a framework of a heavy corporate focus on the external world and a desire for the greatest possibility independence in it.

CHAPTER 7

Examples of Intercultural Research

■ Introduction

The fact that cross-cultural research is technically problematic does not inhibit the thousands of investigators working at business schools and universities around the globe on this fascinating topic. Their output, in books and learned journals, is considerable. Sadly, however, and all too frequently, a bridge between their work as theory creators and validators and that of practitioners managing cross-cultural teams cannot be constructed. This is because their focus on *constructs* (concepts and conceptual frameworks) and on *social science research methodologies* can make their work appear abstruse to the layman.

This chapter seeks to redress this situation by covering five important and representative examples of research studies, each of which illustrate the usefulness of intercultural research, and concluding with an overview section. We shall throughout be focussing on the aim and nature of the studies cited rather than on the methodology. However, given the importance of producing valid data on which the practitioner can rely, we shall also cover, in a rudimentary manner, issues of how the research was carried out.

It should be noted that the cases chosen are used only for indicative purposes and many other examples can be found in (for example) *The Journal of International Business Studies*, *The Academy of Management Journal* and *The International Journal of Commerce and Management.*

■ Culture Research Case No. 1: entrepreneurship and culture

(A case for comparative entrepreneurship: assessing the relevance of culture, *Journal of International Business Studies,* London, Second Quarter, 2000)

This study, by Anisya Thomas and Stephen Mueller, was undertaken to meet two interlocking requirements:

- the demonstrable need for comparative studies into the conditions that encourage entrepreneurial activity around the world, as this is a primary way of stimulating economic growth
- the equally important need to remedy what they see as a shortfall in integrative "typologies and paradigms" (classification schemes and explanatory models) to ensure more coherent research activities in this area.

Irrespective of the needs, the task is a challenging one because, firstly, most of the research that has been done on entrepreneurship has been done in the USA and Western Europe and its transferability to contexts where "the task and psychic environments" may be vastly different remains in question. Secondly, it is difficult to undertake, since it is often difficult to gain access to entrepreneurs in other countries, it is costly and there is often a lack of reliable published data. Thirdly, much of what we associate with the concept of entrepreneurship carries assumptions about capitalism and the Protestant work ethic, harking back to Max Weber and the influence of the Calvinist ethic on "the entrepreneurial spirit", which may simply not be applicable in other countries. (Jaeger, 1990)

The core question driving this piece of research was, therefore, "Are entrepreneurial attributes universal or do they vary systematically across cultures?" The authors find persuasive arguments in the literature for supporting both propositions. Some attributes seem to be constant or universal in the countries researched, whilst the presence of others is contingent on the particular situation in the country in question. For instance, all entrepreneurs require "foresight and energy, passion and perseverance, initiative and drive". However, whilst the US entrepreneur can be stereotypically characterised by "rugged individualism", his counterpart in south-east Asia is more likely to rely on familial ties, (Redding, 1993) as evidenced by the *bamboo network* of overseas Chinese and Indian families.

The research methodology consisted of a comparative empirical investigation based on:

- a review of the literature to identify the key traits or attributes of entrepreneurship which made up the profile under investigation. These were specified in the study – on the basis of the relative degree of their coverage in the literature – to be the four traits of *innovativeness, risk-propensity, energy level* and *internal locus of control (the entrepreneur taking charge of his own destiny);*

- a comparable sample of international business and economics students in nine countries. The *dataset* contained 1800 responses to the questionnaire. It is noteworthy that the sample did not consist of actual entrepreneurs;
- a recognition that the study did not purport to be a comprehensive investigation.

The research instrument (the questionnaire) covered respondents' biographical data, their attitudes and perceptions (on free markets, competition and contribution of entrepreneurs) and a reflection on their personal values. There were 64 items (questions) in the instrument of which 34 were used to construct four scales to measure the four traits referred to above. Items and scales for innovativeness, risk-propensity and energy were adapted from the Jackson Personality Inventory, (1994) whilst those for the locus of control were adapted from Rotter's I-E scale. (1966) Cultural measures were derived from Hofstede's work. (1980) The study thus involved computing the cultural distance (deviation) of each country from the USA for each trait (profile characteristic) using multivariate logistic regression analysis.

The results indicated that :

- *innovativeness* is a universal trait in all cultures, i.e., this attribute of entrepreneurship did not vary systematically with cultural distance from the USA;
- the *internal locus of control* and *risk-taking propensity* traits, by contrast, did vary – and in an interesting manner. The greater the cultural distance between the country in question and the USA, the lower the degree to which the entrepreneur feels himself to be in charge of his destiny and is modest in risk-taking;
- the investigation of *energy* as a trait yielded results which were not conclusive.

Despite such valuable results, the researchers are still left with three central questions. The first relates to the extent to which any research in this area is bound to be ethnocentric, given that the very conception we have of entrepreneurship is defined predominantly by the USA model.

The second concerns the validity of the assertion that "entrepreneurship is the domain of achieving societies that adhere to the Protestant ethic". (McClelland, 1961) The third covers the thorny issue of motivational differences across cultures – especially between "live to work" and "work to live" cultures. (McGrath *et al.*, 1992)

■ Culture Research Case No. 2: marketing and culture

(Marketer acculturation: the changer and the changed, *Journal of Marketing;* New York; July 1999; Lisa Penaloza and Mary Gilly)

One of the key challenges to the international marketer of products and services is how to sell to customers whose culture is different, culture being defined here as "the shared meanings, practices and symbols that constitute the human world". Lisa Penaloza and Mary Gill's research study focuses on this issue by

- dealing with a small, real and closely-circumscribed example of the challenge;
- using, as the example, an ethnic market place in the US. The research site was, in fact, a major urban shopping street in the city of San Pueblo in southern California. Here there is a mixture of retailers from different cultures (Latinos, Asians and Middle Easterners) and different occupational backgrounds and a range of customers (predominantly working-class Mexicans and occasional Anglos as either individuals or festivity-oriented groups);
- carrying out a *longitudinal study* of marketing relationships between the retailers and their customers, i.e., a study over a long period of time and allowing for before-and-after data comparisons. This involved closed-ended questionnaires and open-ended interviews;
- using supplementary *ethnographic methods*. These comprised participant observation, depth interviews and photography as data collection techniques. So far as data for interpretative analysis were concerned, the researchers employed a mixture of field notes, diary entries and artifacts (business flyers, cards and local newspaper cuttings). These methods provided a descriptive overview of the *fieldsite* and participants' attitudes and practices;
- developing an empirical model describing how marketers in this

shopping street adapted their approaches to fit the clientele by, for example, using the correct language and appropriate cultural customs;

- ending up with a dataset of transcribed interviews, photographs, field notes (343 hours of fieldwork) and a 507-page journal;
- contributing to marketing theory and practice by "furthering substantive understandings of intercultural market dynamics".

The starting point for the research was an in-depth review of the literature on the topic. This threw up a variety of important conceptual issues. For example, there is the paradox of a global business environment, which we can all recognise as increasingly multicultural and, yet, in which "discrete sub-national ethnic, religious and racial parts are far more in evidence". There is also the question of the degree to which marketers, selling to customers of different cultures, and consumers buying from them can and do *acculturate* each other or assimilate the other's culture, i.e., adopt the other's frame of reference on business issues and adapt their behaviour patterns accordingly. There is evidence that whist the latter have been noted to acculturate, the former have not. Hence, this research project which found that marketers did effectively seek to *enculture* themselves into their consumers' culture. Finally, in this case, there are issues of the extent to which ethnic and cultural differences between marketer and consumers were not conducive to business success or community development, especially where there were culture-based patterns of economic discrimination or segregation.

How did the enculturation process manifest itself in down-town San Pueblo? Given the Mexican clientele, the signs outside the stores – Venta! Credito Facil! No Enganche! (Sale! Easy Credit! No Down Payment!) – and the language spoken by owners/managers and/or hired staff had to be Spanish, whatever their backgrounds. The degree of cultural rapport with customers had, also, to be deep and, hence, marketer acculturation meant intensive listening to, observing and interacting with clients. The product lines sold in the shops had to be appealing and suitable in all senses to the target market. Overall, "merchants' cultural heuristics (everyday guidelines for appropriate behaviours) involved critically important and pervasive skills, yet so subtle were these to the merchants themselves that they appeared inconsequential".

Among the particular skills of merchants were *code switching* between USA and Mexican market customs (choosing one's behavioural approach to suit the individual client), awareness of gender roles (in the Mexican culture, the woman decides and the man negotiates and pays) and empathy with consumers' economic and socio-cultural circumstances.

Such skills are just as germane to the multinational marketing managers as they are to the retailers in San Pueblo.

■ Culture Research Case No. 3: management concepts and culture

(Can American management concepts work in Russia? A cross-cultural comparative study, *California Management Review,* Berkeley, Summer 1998, Detelin Elenkov)

Detelin Elenkov's study shows just how difficult it can be to apply management concepts, created and widely disseminated in one country, to another. In this particular instance, certain concepts and management approaches were found to be portable between the USA and Russia but, such were the differences in managerial values between the two countries, they were still difficult to apply.

It is received wisdom that foreigners find the Russian business climate and Russian business people difficult to deal with. If we add cultural difference, says Elenkov, we have a most challenging mixture to cope with.

The aims of the study were, therefore

- to check on the extent to which managerial values were similar or different in Russia and America, to calibrate the extent of the difference (if any); and

- to draw inferences from any such variation on the relative viability in Russia of American management and organisation concepts.

The theory behind the study was, of course, that the bigger the value differences, the greater the likelihood of Russian difficulty in accepting USA management approaches. (Terpstra & David, 1985)

Six measures were identified for use in this project to compare the USA and Russian situations. The first four were drawn from the work of Hofstede (1980) and were

- the power distance scale;
- the individualism/collectivism scale;
- the uncertainty avoidance scale;
- the competitive orientation or the masculinity/femininity scale.

The second set of two measures were derived from the work of Bollinger (1994) and Berliner (1988) and were the degree of

- political influence orientation; and
- dogmatism.

Hofstede's measures are classical and well known. His power distance measures the degree to which power is distributed unequally within a society; the individualism/collectivism scale is concerned with the extent to which society welcomes individuality or regards individualistic traits as "socially undesirable and destructive of group harmony"; the uncertainty avoidance scale deals with a society's tolerance for uncertainty and ambiguity. Roughly speaking, the typical Hofstede values for Russia for these three measures are high to relatively high and for America low to moderate. Use of the Hofstede construct of masculinity/femininity as a proxy for competitive orientation proved more difficult.

The traditional importance of political influence in Russia is well-attested. The Shaw, Fisher and Randolph study (1991) indicated that nepotism was rife, performance and rewards were not inter-dependent and you needed to be loyal and "right-thinking" if you wanted promotion. This last depended, in the former Soviet Union, on a whole host of specifically political factors, like party membership, protection, connections and *blat* (personal influence). (Madonna *et al.*, 1989 and Zook, 1985) The USA is patently far removed from this situation.

Machievellianism (M for short) is one of the most widely used methods for handling the political influence phenomenon. It seeks to calibrate the extent to which managers and/or companies base their strategies on their contacts (whom you know) or their activities (what you do); on deviousness or straight talking; on using informal channels or the more formal authority structure. A company can thus be said to have a high M culture (it tends to try to *fix things* in advance so as to win) or a low M culture (it is a *plain dealer*). (Berliner, 1988)

Dogmatism, thus, refers to the extent to which people are prepared to accept new ideas.

The survey method was used for this study. Participants were selected from two discrete manager populations in Russia (St Petersburg area) and the USA (Northeastern region) on the basis of a multistage sampling plan. Complete surveys were returned by 178 Russian managers and 147 USA managers. A sequence of statistical tests was used to examine the 47 cross- national differences. The main findings were that:

- American managers are more individualistic than Russian;

- USA management culture scores lower than Russian on power distance, uncertainty avoidance and political influence orientation;

- Russian managers are significantly less dogmatic than their US counterparts;

- There was no significant difference in competitive orientation between the two cultures.

Using these results, Elenkov then proceeds to investigate the transferability of concepts such as leadership styles, motivation, performance appraisal systems etc. The approach is to base the analysis on the particular combination of the six values that he regards as conducive to a certain concept's relevance and attractiveness. For instance, an amalgam of the high power distance and low individualism scores would be an indicator of the likely appeal of authoritarianism as a type of leadership style). To the discussion, he adds in other theoretical dimensions, such as French and Raven's social power framework (1960), as required.

This framework is an interesting one. According to Elenkov, it allows us to develop a deeper understanding of effective leadership in the context of Russian culture as it comprises two power categories (legitimate power and referent power) which are the most effective sources of influence for Russian managers. The first relates to the role holder's power in the organisation as a function of his/her formal position and authority, whilst the second refers to the power enjoyed by a leader who is liked/admired by his subordinates.

The two other forms of power in the Raven and French typology are reward power and expert power. These are comparatively less accented in Russia compared with the USA. Here the power of a leader to bestow tangible or psychological recognition on his followers and power exercised through specialised skills and knowledge are paramount.

On the basis of the accumulated evidence, the main conclusion of the study is that any *universalist assumption* about the easy transfer of USA management techniques is bound to be erroneous.

■ Culture Research Case No. 4: cross-border team-working and culture

(Long-term cooperation prospects in international joint ventures: perspectives of Chinese firms, *Journal of Applied Management Studies,* June 1998, Abingdon, Roger Chen and David Boggs)

Current developments in world trade demand more and more collaboration among joint venture partners. Co-operation among partner firms within one nation can be difficult; even more so if it is cross-border where, it is asserted, the determinants of long-term co-operation remain inadequately understood. This is a research study about Sino-foreign collaboration as seen through the eyes of a sample of Chinese managers of joint ventures in the Liao Ning province of China. Not only is it intended as a positive contribution to the literature in its own right, it is a powerful counterbalance to other studies which have treated the subject from a Western management perspective. This is so, even if studies like those of Eiteman (1990), have thrown a powerful light on the topic.

The study probes, therefore, how various factors (*the independent variables*) influence the prospects for successful co-operation between partners in a joint cross-border venture (*the dependent variable*), as seen through the eyes of one particular partner.

Various hypotheses emerge from the literature which relate to the dynamics of the relationship between the co-operative partners. There are issues to be considered, for instance, of the nature of any "informal psychological contract and sense making" between the partners, expectation for long-term co-operation, degree of cultural similarity and environmental characteristics. Additionally, elements from transaction costs theory and social exchange theory (Gomes-Casserres, 1990) can be used to good advantage within an international management context, drawing as they do on core concepts such as trust, reciprocity, opportunism and forbearance. In this regard, it is interesting to note that the Osland and Cavusgill study (1996) indicated that there is even a lack of knowledge in the West on the "criteria Chinese managers use to evaluate joint venture success".

Because the existing literature is not clear on the components of success in long-term co-operation, Chen and Boggs employed an aggregate concept for discussing prospects which has already been widely used in the study of joint ventures. (Gomes-Casserres, 1990) The theory they employed is called Environmental Uncertainty Transactions Costs Theory (EUTCT) and it argues in circular fashion that:

- firms will be committed to co-operation so long as it reduces their transaction costs;
- firms may have to pay extra for assets which are specific to the joint venture or for organisational procedures to monitor the working of the joint venture (and particularly any opportunistic behaviours on the part of partners) on top of the costs of making formal collaboration contracts. Such costs are referred to as uncertainty costs and are part of the overall transaction costs;
- Reducing uncertainty costs is, therefore, vital to improving the prospects for long term co-operation.

The empirical tests that were carried out to assess the validity of the hypotheses advanced were based on a survey of Chinese joint venture managers taken during 1996. In order to control for geographical differences – China having major differentials in regional economic performance – the researchers picked one of China's top ten foreign investment hotspots. 40 joint ventures were investigated randomly and controlled for the Chinese ownership stake.. Since the detailed components of the prospect for long tern co-operation are not perfectly clear (due to inadequate study in the literature), Chen and Boggs *operationalised* it as respondents' prediction of the probability of the joint venture co-operation would continue for the next ten years. This was the dependent variable and a high value indicated JV success and satisfaction.

Multiple regression analysis supported three of the five hypotheses advanced, with two of the four control variables registering as significant. The main findings were that:

- Environmental uncertainty (measured by difficulty of predicting market change) *does not* necessarily damage the prospect of JV co-operation;
- Culture differences, and in particular the absence of trust, *do*. Western reliance on contracts in a China characterised by weak property rights laws, powerful informal relationships and a dynamic environment may not be enough for trust building;
- Certainly, the appointment of an expatriate general manager to run the joint venture may be indicated to ensure better resource provision and access to the western partner.

The researchers were clearly disappointed with the findings and treated their study as an exploratory one, stating that its generalisability remained in question.

■ Culture Research Case study No. 5: hybrid teams and culture

(Creating hybrid team cultures: an empirical test of transnational team functioning. Christopher Earley & Elaine Mosakowski, *Academy of Management Journal*, Mississippi State, Feb. 2000).

Earley and Mosakowski's focus was on team membership and the impact of different sorts of teams on group working. More specifically, it was on the extent to which a hybrid team culture was a facilitator or inhibitor of group interaction. The review of literature on team heterogeneity suggested a variety of perspectives on the issue

- Team similarity is positively associated with team effectiveness and interpersonal attraction; (Tsui, Egan & O'Reilly, 1992)
- Homogeneous team members generally report stronger affinity for

their team than heterogeneous; (Ibarra, 1992))

- Heterogeneous teams have a variety of perspectives, values and skills that contribute the benefits of diversity to their team working. Indeed, a small amount of heterogeneity (one dissenting opinion) can enhance the team's functioning, depending on the task. (Nemeth, 1986)

Considerations of this nature led the researchers to hypothesise that that there is a curvilinear relationship between team heterogeneity (THET), team homogeneity (THOM) and effective team performance. Team culture in this context is defined as "an emergent and simplified set of rules, norms, expectations and roles that team members share and *enact*", providing for "a group-specific sense of identity" which forms the basis for team-member self-evaluation. Thus, THET would constitute, in effect, a *hybrid* team culture which might, because of the fact of differences among members, deviate from this model.

However, instead of hypothesising an inverted U-shaped relationship (with a moderate level of heterogeneity being optimal), Earley and Mosakowski postulated an upright U relationship, asserting that high and moderate THOM and high THET would result in better team working than moderate THET.

Crucial to the research was the isolation of those key factors, which cause teams to work well or badly.

Following Turner, (1985) the researchers here reckon that nationality has a meta-effect on individuals' traits hierarchies, i.e., it shapes one's value system, and is a "superordinate determinant of a person's self-identity". This accords with the view of Hughes (1971) that nationality is the primary status-determining trait as it controls communication patterns.

Tajfel's Social Identity theory (1982) indicates that you join clubs with people like yourself and, in so doing, create in-group sentiments which are important for team cohesion. Once perceived, "these similarities are over time contrasted with members of the *IN-GROUP* with the perceived dissimilarities of outsiders, members of the *OUTSIDER-GROUP*, to enhance self-construals... and to strengthen group *entativity* (degree of group bonding) and shared worldviews".

Lau and Murnighan (1998) suggest that demographic faultlines, arising from team members' personal and societal backgrounds, can underlie the positive appearance of team diversity and affect their functioning adversely. In THET teams you are always going to get "multiple subcultures" asserts Hambrick *et al.* (1998) So, in a moderate THET, reckons the Hambrick research team, the danger from external challenges (difficult tasks that the team cannot cope with, for example) is one of "retreat towards pre-existing subgroups for ego protection". They also consider other traits such as race, gender, religion and profession as secondary determinants of teamwork performance.

The literature seems to suggest that if you want good teamwork, you pick THOM or High THET teams.

The methodology for the research was extensive and involved two studies, the second being a check on the first. Here, we are concerned only with the field observations and survey work (open-ended and structured interviews) carried out with members of five transnational teams in a large clothing manufacturer which operated in the US, Europe and Asia Pacific. The study was a longitudinal one and focussed on the views of sales and marketing teams meeting in Bangkok as the central location.

The primary salient distinction in the make-up of teams was nationality and most team members had comparable functional, work and educational backgrounds. Four teams were high THET and one was low THET. The research test was to rate team effectiveness rating as a function (f) of mediating variables such as

- group members' normal interaction patterns, based on formal and informal group norms governing the styles of interaction (pattern of communication, procedures for meetings – seating, discussion, agenda handling etc.;
- group members' conflict handling approaches e.g., suspension of politeness, terseness in speech, shifting position in chairs and other negative body language, lack of eye contact, rolling eyes, personal confrontation etc.

The researchers found that the issues involved were more complex than originally thought. In sum, however, there were indications that the initial stage showed that high THET had a detrimental impact on team functioning during the start-up phase of team formation and initial work. But, over time, the high THET teams' capability and cohesion became more positive as they *forged common identities*. The low THET group revealed throughout many communication problems, relational conflict and low levels of team identity.

So, the hypothesis that there may be a curvilinear relationship between team heterogeneity – a hybrid team culture – and effective team performance was sustained, even if the results were not regarded as generalisable.

■ Overview

These five cases do scant justice, it must be said, to a powerful and growing body of literature and so does the form of *reductionism* that has been used here to summarise the important features of elaborate research. Any realistic overview dealing with the relevance of theoretical studies to the needs of the practising international manager should also consider the wide range of topics studied by a long line of prominent researchers such as Philippe Lasserre, Ket de Vries and Sheila Puffer. We have clearly omitted much important work.

Additionally, however, among the more exciting and noteworthy recent contributions we can note:

- Lipeng Deng's study (1997) of the intercultural aspects of Japanese foreign direct investment in China, which was based on aggregate data, literature frameworks and two field trips;
- A fascinating piece of research entitled "the Seven faces of Singaporeans" by Jung Kwon, Jochen Wirtz, Soo Jiuan Tan and Ah Keng Kau. (1999) This produced a seven-cluster typology of Singapore consumers – Traditional Family Oriented, New Age Family Oriented, Entrepreneurs, Aspirers, Materialists, Pragmatists and Independents. A discriminant analysis showed that the typology was patterned by value-based demographic variables such as family values, entrepreneurial spirit and status;
- The Osland, Bird, Delano and Jacob study entitled "Beyond Cultural Stereotyping" (2000) which deals with cultural myopia and, more particularly, paradoxes. These are phenomena which come as surprises to external *observers* who are accustomed to thinking that situational *actors* will always behave in a culturally-prescribed, true-

to-form manner, e.g., materialistic, individualistic, self-reliant, America being the world's biggest charity donor. Their research found that the construct of *value trumping* gave a good explanation. This occurs when there is an implicit value conflict (individual v group, for instance) in a given context and where one value unexpectedly (for the observer, that is) takes precedence over others. In other words, when one value trumps – outweighs in importance – another. We can only make sense of culture, therefore, if we disregard some of the simplicity of "Western either-or dualism" and start to generate theories of culture with room for "holistic maps", say the researchers.

Notwithstanding these contributions, however, the field is still under-ploughed and much work remains to be done. Writing of the challenges ahead, Philippe Hermel (1999) questioned the extent to which any firm's traditional management methods can serve it well in a dynamic global environment with its ever-increasing number of changes, interaction of business variables and uncertainty, each demanding greater cross-cultural understanding. "The vastness of the field of analysis" is manifest, he said. And so it is.

CHAPTER 8

A Country Culture Audit Using the Triangle Test

■ Introduction

The treatment of cross-cultural analysis in this book has ranged widely over matters practical, theoretical and historical in an attempt to create a basis for investigation of business cultures in business alliance situations. In this chapter, we now turn our attention to a simple and practical method of auditing cross-cultural differences: the *Triangle Test*. It is so named because it consists of three sectors requiring investigation: **bedrock, work systems and behaviours.** It is simple and practical because the questions asked go right to the heart of those differences in the culture of nations which cross-border management teams need to know about at the very start of their collaboration. In addition, the statements can be applied to many of the case studies in this book to good effect.

The fact that we are assuming that differences between national business cultures do exist should not blind us to the fact that international business culture is undeniably tending to become more and more homogeneous on a global scale. The pressures to improve competitiveness are now common to all trading nations. The negative economics of continuing to finance entrenched high-cost welfare mean that all developed countries thus affected need to economise. Unstoppable technological developments bring in their train standardised work solutions that do not allow for substantial cultural differences. **In other words, the entire world is under the threat of being gradually shoe-horned into a mass-market, world-standard business culture**. Mass materialism, market fundamentalism and shareholder value are, in particular, on the march. But we are not yet, however, at the point where in-depth analysis of a team-partner's attitudes and opinions is not to be recommended.

■ The Triangle Test

As Figure 8.1 page 179 indicates, the Triangle Test can be used in a variety of situations, for example:

- where a management problem/project/task needs to be dealt with by a team, whose members are from different nationalities and whose collaboration is vital to the success of the mission;

- where a take-over bid or merger/alliance/joint venture plan is being considered or appraised;

- where a strategic move into a new market is being evaluated.

It is a questionnaire which needs to be completed by those involved in the process, the assumptions being that they will be truthful in their responses and that their responses will be at least sound indications of the culture of their country. We would aim to have responses from all the different nations who might be involved in the cross-border move, whatever it is. Naturally, these assumptions may not be fulfilled, but we have to be optimistic.

By scoring the degree of respondent agreement to sets of questions, the analyst can easily find out whether national attitudinal differences exist and, if so, whether they are significant in any cultural area which is of critical importance. Of course, for the sake of social science purity, we should need a statistically-valid approach if we were to make any claims about accuracy. The nature of the task we have set ourselves and the simple survey procedure preclude this. Our approach is to collect *indicative* data and build up a representative picture.

Thus, from this perspective, the linking of the scores on Figure 8.1 page 179 allows a culture triangle shape to be constructed for each of the countries involved and the size differences between, say, the triangles to be appraised. It can be a matter of great interest for engineers, particularly, to note the extraordinary extent to which many apparently value-free, technical discussions are subject to cultural over-riders and constraints.

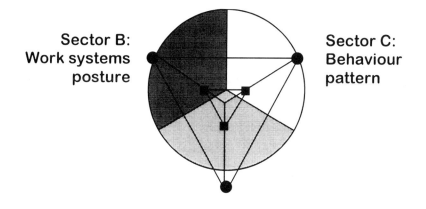

Sector B:
Work systems
posture

Sector C:
Behaviour
pattern

Sector A: Bedrock

FIGURE 8.1: THE TRIANGLE TEST INSTRUMENT
© Terry Garrison 1996

Note: the Triangle □ — □ — □ shows the average scores of one partner in a fictional joint venture. Its partners' scores are represented by the triangle O — O —O.

Auditing Procedure

The procedure for applying the Triangle Test is for a sample of executives in each of the partner companies to complete a questionnaire covering their own behaviour, the nature of their work systems and features of the way in which their nation operates in terms of politics, economics and religion. A sample size of 20 is usually found adequate for our indicative purposes. The assumption is that the responses of the executives in the firm give a reasonably correct picture of their nation's culture.

Of course, the identical audit approach could be applied to one single company or organisation to test out its cultural orientation.

Each statement in the Triangle Test is prefaced by the question **"Do you agree that, in your country ..."**, which each respondent must answer on a scale from 1 ("I disagree entirely with this proposition or statement") to 5 ("I agree totally with this proposition or statement").

The statements in each part of the Triangle Test have been carefully designed to be as neutral in social science terms as possible but, given the conversational format that has been chosen for them, there is always some possible bias.

Indeed, in some nations, merely asking a cultural question may be enough to elicit an overtly emotional response, since the act of questioning may be seen per se as value-laden. The reason for this is easily understood: culture is more about personal values and feelings than personality and both sides in a relationship need to know the key areas in which the deepest held values exist. Questions or statements deemed to be provocative are problematic. Again we need to be optimistic.

Hence, chosen executives from each company respond to the ten questions posed in each of the three sectors of the questionnaire – **bedrock, work systems, behaviours**. The scoring method is very simple. You simply take the average of the scores out of 50 for each section of the tests. For example, if the total number of points for the bedrock section is 36, then the score is 36/10 = 3.6 and so on.

This enables the three scores to be plotted on the Triangle Test diagram where the centre of the Triangle = a score of 1 and the apex of the Triangle = a score of 5. The intention, as we have seen, is to obtain a triangle shape for each country investigated and compare the shapes of the countries as we require, noting the differences that exist.

Figure 8.1 page 179 indicates that one partner's team (□) has scored "very low" for each of the three sectors whilst the other (O) has recorded scores which are "extreme". The culture map that results shows how wide apart they are and how difficult partnership would be.

■ **Bedrock**

In this section of the Triangle Test we are seeking to establish the extent to which the national culture (as represented by the company) is **individualistic** or **corporatist.**

Question 1 in the first sector of the Triangle Test refers to the extent to which capitalism is the dominant economic philosophy in the country. Each team of respondents is invited to agree/ disagree on the scale of 1-5 with the following statement *"shareholders are, by far, the most important stakeholders in the business"*

Question 2 refers to the perception that exist within the business community about the relative importance of company directors and workers. Again the format is "Do you agree that, in your country..." and the response scale is from 1 (I don't agree at all") to 5 (" I am in total agreement"). The statement is *"differences in the pay of employees and directors are fully justified by their relative economic contributions to the business".*

Question 3 is intended to gauge the relative contribution of the state to providing welfare benefits – and hence its demands for high social security contributions from employees and businesses. The statement is that *"the charges for tax and social security seem to be comparatively low, when compared with countries which are known to be relatively high-cost, like Germany and Sweden".*

Question 4 examines the impact on working practices that arises from religion. The statement is that *"religion has very little influence on how things are done in business".*

Question 5 focuses on the financial aid companies may receive from either the government or friendly banks. The statement is *"as a rule, companies which are in financial trouble neither expect nor get much help from either the government or banks with whom they have commercial relationships".*

Question 6 deals with the relationship between government and industry. The statement reads *"government does not try to manage business by such mechanisms as a National Plan or government-industry pacts to create jobs".*

How decisions are made in business is the focus for Question 7. The statement reads *"most business leaders think that the best way to run the company is **not** to allow the workforce to participate in the strategic decision-making process (through works councils, for example)".*

Question 8 addresses the issue of the basis on which pay is negotiated: *"wage and salary levels rates in industry sectors like engineering or retail are usually based on the individual company's ability to pay and do not depend on industry-wide pay deals between federations of trade unions and employers".*

The extent of the role of the civil service is sought in Question 9: *"the civil service, with its traditional bureaucratic systems, has a relatively small role to play in regulating the way business is done, e.g., on licensing business start-ups".*

Finally, Question 10 in the bedrock section takes up the question of strike action and other forms of industrial disputes. The statement says: *"industrial disputes, such as strikes and other forms of mass action by workers, are relatively rare and ineffective".*

A total score of 50 (i.e., an average of 5) would indicate that the country under examination is wholly **individualistic** in its bedrock culture, whereas a score of 10 (i.e., an average of 1) would reveal a nation that was **corporatist.**

■ **Work Systems**

The work system questions are designed to elicit whether the country we are examining has a **materialistic** or a **communitarian** culture. The first signifies that most business issues revolve around questions of money: the second signifies that firms seek to run their affairs on an inclusive, family-type basis where finance can be secondary to, say, job satisfaction or continued employment.

Question 1 is concerned with the degree to which the country tries to stop foreigners from buying its large companies, i.e., the extent to which the country is capitalistically-orientated: it reads: Do you agree that, so far as your country is concerned *"there are very few barriers to foreigners' buying into companies here, apart from regulations on the need to maintain competition".*

In Question 2 we refer again to the issue of who owns companies. It reads: *"Large-scale private control of the means of creating wealth (i.e., shareholder ownership of companies) is seen by most people as perfectly acceptable and natural".*

Work systems involving the management of people cover the next three questions:

3: *"Typically, a person's salary and his/her promotion chances are strictly related to on-the-job performance".*

4: *"Business leaders look upon the labour market as precisely that – a market".*

5: *"Technology progress and acceptance of change often seem to matter more than people's happiness at work".*

Question 6 focuses on the acceptance of trade union membership within companies. It reads: *"most employees, even in big firms in the private sector, simply are not interested in belonging to trade unions".*

The comparative size of the nation's social security safety net is addressed in Question 7. It reads: *"the government, in contrast with some other high-tax, high-spend countries (like France, for example), does not pay out what might be called large social security benefits to people who are ill unemployed or retired".*

Question 8 reads: *"firms simply do not believe in maintaining uneconomic jobs on grounds of supposed loyalty to their workforce and will readily move factories to cheaper locations".* It measures how committed employers are to employment, as opposed to profitability.

Question 9 is about who wields influence in business circles in the country: it reads *"it's not whom you know that matters, but what you know".*

The last Question, number 10 in this section, deals with the extent to which entrepreneurship is the key driver for business. It asks for a view on the proposition that: *"business leaders are typically driven by the need to achieve results which meet the short-term demands of their shareholders".*

■ Behaviours

Our section of questions on behaviours is aimed at classifying the culture of the country we are researching as **open** or **closed.** An open culture is one that is comparatively easy for any foreign business-person to enter and to feel relatively at home. Notice that we are not using absolutes to define our terms. "Closed", by the same token, means a culture which is comparatively stylised, rich in rites and rituals and very hard for foreigners to immerse themselves in to the point of total acceptance by the local business community.

Of course, an American might find the Japanese or Saudi business culture *closed* in our terminology, and perhaps a Chinese or an Indian might find the western cultures relatively *open.* We are, however, in the Triangle Test, not focusing on foreigners' views of a country's culture but whether the countryman/woman rates his own culture as *open* or c*losed.*

Question 1 in this section asks about how different nations communicate. It reads: *"business people are usually very straightforward and direct in how they communicate verbally, both with each other and foreigners".*

Question 2 follows this line in addressing the issue of emotion in business: *"most company executives do not suffer social disgrace, shame or loss of face if things go wrong in their business affairs".*

The next two Questions are designed to test the extent to which teamwork is seen as all-important:
3: *"people do not habitually meet with colleagues outside work simply to improve work relationships, as Japanese salary-men are said to do when they go out drinking with the boss every evening after work"* .
4: *"firms are strongly in favour of individual effort and entrepreneurship, especially when it involves dynamic young managers who want to get on".*

The nature of management is the focus of the next two questions. Question 5 reads: *""the manager" is typically "in charge" but there is no sense of a leadership cult where the "boss" is naturally seen as all-knowing and all-powerful".*

6: *"there is an absence of a macho culture (where jobs are typically divided up in gender lines and top jobs are almost exclusively filled by men) but we are not yet egalitarian in our approach to employing women".*

Questions 7 and 8 deal with the issue of social glue:
7: *"companies typically have such things as flags, badges and company ties but these are more for building up the company's image than for getting people to bond together socially in work teams"* and
8: *"companies, as a rule, do not oblige people to wear a company uniform (or even a dark suit) or sing a company song or anthem or even do early morning callisthenics".*

Questions 9 & 10 address the often-fraught question of the social obligations that can exist in business in some countries. Question 9 states: *"people like foreigners, especially those who invest heavily in the country".*

The final Question, 10, asks whether you agree with the assertion that *"people don't seem to have the same sense of social obligations to each other (like having to find a job for an employee's cousin) as they seem to do in some other countries, like India for example".*

■ Conclusion

The Triangle Test is laid out in full on pages 187-189 and scored on Figure 8.2 page 190. Completing it offers a concrete way of synthesising many of the wide-ranging discussions we have had on the subject of the business culture of different nations. Our description of a country that achieves an overall low score in the Test would be that it had a tendency to **Triple C culture.** It would be Corporatist, Communitarian and Closed. A country that scored highly would tend to have an **IMO culture** (or more popularly an I'm Ok culture!). This would be a blend of Individualism, Materialism and Openness.

Although the Triangle Test does suffer from being *reductionist*, it is nevertheless a powerful consultancy tool that can be employed to good effect in a variety of diagnostic circumstances. It provides a workable picture of the key dimensions of a country's culture and indicates the relative divergences between cultures that can occur. The statistics gathered so far from tests indicate that there are manifest differences between the bedrock and work systems cultures of the Anglo-Saxon countries and the continental Europeans but little divergence on behaviours. On the other hand, the differences between East and West on all Triangle Test dimensions are large.

We now add to this concrete framework for studying country culture a range of case studies illustrating these and other dimensions in a practical fashion.

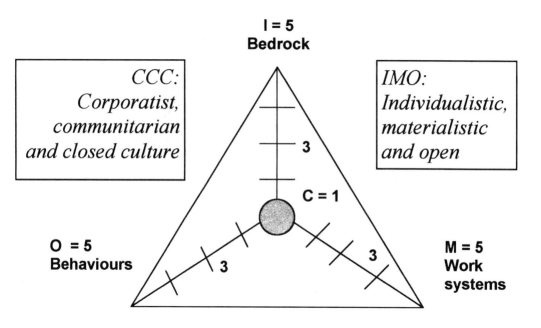

Figure 8.2: THE TRIANGLE TEST INSTRUMENT SCORING

© Terry Garrison 1996

Table 8.1: TRIANGLE TEST QUESTIONS

Question number	Bedrock – do you agree that in your country…	Respondent	
		Score out of 5	Average score
1	shareholders are, by far, the most important stakeholders in the business?		
2	differences in the pay of employees and directors are fully justified by their relative economic contributions to the business?		
3	the charges for tax & social security seem to be comparatively low, when compared with countries which are known to be relatively high cost, like Germany & Sweden?		
4	religion has very little influence on how things are done in business?		
5	companies which are in financial trouble neither expect nor get much help from either the government or banks with whom they have commercial relationships?		
6	government does not try to manage business by such mechanisms as a National Plan or government-industry pacts to create jobs?		
7	most business leaders think that the best way to run the company is *not* to allow the workforce to participate in the strategic decision-making process, through works councils, for example?		
8	wage and salary levels rates in industry sectors like engineering or retail are usually based on the individual company's ability to pay and do not depend on industry-wide pay deals between federations of trade unions and employers?		
9	the civil service, with its traditional bureaucratic systems has a relatively small role to play in regulating the way business is done, e.g., on licensing business start-ups?		
10	industrial disputes, such as strikes and other forms of mass action by workers, are relatively rare and ineffective?		
	Average score for Bedrock		

Table 8.1continued

Question number	Work Systems – do you agree that in your country…	Respondent	
		Score out of 5	Average score
1	there are very few barriers to foreigners' buying into companies, apart from regulations on the need to maintain competition?		
2	large-scale private control of the means of creating wealth (i.e. shareholder ownership of companies) is seen as perfectly acceptable and natural?		
3	typically, a person's salary and his/her promotion chances are strictly related to on-the-job performance?		
4	business leaders look upon the labour market as precisely that – a market?		
5	technology progress and acceptance of change often seem to matter more than people's happiness at work?		
6	most employees, even in big firms in the private sector, simply are not interested in belonging to trade unions?		
7	the government, in contrast with some other high-tax, high-spend countries (like France, for example), does not pay out what might be called *large* social security benefits to people who are ill unemployed or retired?		
8	firms simply do not believe in maintaining uneconomic jobs on grounds of supposed loyalty to their workforce and will readily move factories to cheaper locations?		
9	it's not whom you know that matters, but what you know?		
10	business leaders are typically driven by the need to achieve results which meet the short-term demands of their shareholders?		
	Average score for Work Systems		

Table 8.1 continued

Question number	Behaviour – do you agree that, in your country…	Respondent	
		Score out of 5	Average score
1	business people are usually very straightforward and direct in how they communicate verbally, both with each other and foreigners?		
2	most company executives do not suffer social disgrace, shame or loss of face if things go wrong in their business affairs?		
3	people do not habitually meet with colleagues outside work simply to improve work relationships, as Japanese salary-men are said to do when they go out drinking with the boss every evening after work?		
4	firms are strongly in favour of individual effort & entrepreneurship especially when it involves dynamic young managers who want to "*get on*"?		
5	"the manager" is typically "in charge" but there is no sense of a leadership cult where the boss is naturally seen as all-knowing and all-powerful?		
6	there is an absence of a macho culture (where jobs are divided up in gender lines and top jobs are almost exclusively filled by men), but we are not yet egalitarian in our approach to employing women?		
7	companies typically have such things as flags, badges and company ties, but these are more for building up the company's image than for getting people to bond together socially in work teams?		
8	companies, as a rule, do not oblige people to wear a company uniform (or even a dark suit) or sing a company song or anthem or even do early-morning callisthenics?		
9	people like foreigners, especially those who invest heavily in the country?		
10	people don't seem to have the same sense of social obligations to each other (like having to find a job for an employee's cousin) as they seem to do in other countries, like India for example?		
	Average score for Behaviour		

Now transfer all three average scores to the Triangle Test instrument and plot the shape of the triangle.

REFERENCES
Chapters 1-8
alphabetical by author's last name, then date (earliest first)

Bartlett, C. and Ghoshal, Sumantra (1995)
Transnational Management, New York, USA: Irwin

Berliner, J. (1988)
Soviet Industry from Stalin to Gorbachev, Ithaca, USA: Cornell University Press

Berry, J.W. (1983)
Acculturation: a comparative analysis of alternative forms IN Samuda, R.J. &
Woods, S.L. (eds) *Perspectives in Immigrant and Minority Education,* Lanham,
MD, USA: University Press of America

Berry, J.W. (1984)
Cultural relations in plural societies IN Miller, N. & Brewer, N.J. (eds) *Groups in
Contact,* Orlando, FA, USA: Academic Press

Blake, Robert, Mouton, Jane and Adams McCanse, Anne (1991)
Leadership Dilemmas - Grid Solutions, Houston, TA, USA: Gulf Publishing

Bollinger, D. (1994)
The four cornerstones and the three pillars IN *The House of Russia Management
System, Journal of Management
Development,* 13/2

Cameron, K. and Quinn, R. (1999)
Diagnosing and Changing Organisational Culture, Reading, MA, USA: Addison
Wesley

Chandler, Alfred (1990)
Scale and Scope, Boston, USA: Harvard University Press

Chen, Roger and Boggs, David (1998)
Long-term cooperation prospects in international joint ventures: perspectives of
Chinese firms, *Journal of Applied Management Studies,* June 1998, Abingdon

Deal, Terrence and Kennedy, Allan (2000)
The New Corporate Cultures, Reading, MA, USA: Addison Wesley

Deal, Terrence and Kennedy, Allan (1982)
Corporate Culture, The Rites and Rituals of Corporate Life, Reading, MA, USA: Addison Wesley

Deng, L. (1997)
Understanding Japanese direct investment in China (1985-93), *The American Journal of Economics and Sociology,* NY, USA: January 1997

Dyer, W. (1986)
Culture Change in Family Firms, San Francisco, CA, USA: Jossey Bass

Earley, Christopher and Mosakowski, Elaine (2000)
Creating hybrid team cultures: an empirical test of transnational team functioning. *Academy of Management Journal,* Mississippi State, February 2000

Eitemann, D. (1990)
American executives' perceptions of negotiating joint ventures with the People's Republic of China: lessons learned, *Columbia Journal of World Business,* Winter 1990

Ekonomika Press (1989)
Changing the Management System of the Firm, Moscow, Russia

Elashmawi, F., Harris, P. S. and Majeed, Abdul (1994)
Multicultural Management, Kuala Lumpur, Malaysia

Elenkov, Detelin (1998)
Can American management concepts work in Russia? A cross-cultural comparative study, *California Management Review,* Berkeley, Summer 1998

Farmer, R.N. and Richman, B.M. (1965)
Comparative Management and Economic Progress, Homewood, Ill., USA: Irwin

French, J.P. and Raven, B. (1960)
The basis of social power IN Cartwright, D. and Zanders, A., (eds) *Group Dynamics: Research and Theory,* second edition, NY, USA: Harper and Row

Gilchrist J. (1963)
The Church & Economic Activity in the Middle Ages, London: Macmillan

Goffee, Rob and Jones, Gareth (1998)
The Character of a Corporation, London: Harper Collins Business

Gomes-Casserres, B. (1990)
Firm ownership preferences and host government restrictions: an integrated approach, *Journal of International Business Studies* 21 (1)

Gomes-Casserres B. (1990)
Ownership structures of foreign subsidiaries: theory and evidence, *Journal of Economic Behaviour & Organisation,* 11(1)

Hall, Edward T. (1983)
The Dance of Life, NY, USA: Doubleday

Hall, Edward T. (1981)
Beyond Culture, NY, USA: Doubleday

Hall, Wendy (1995)
Managing Cultures, New York, USA: Wiley

Hampden-Turner, C. and Trompenaars, F. (1993)
The Seven Cultures of Capitalism, London: Piatkus

Hambrick, D.C., Davison, S.C., Snell, S.A., and Snow, C.C. (1998)
When groups consist of multiple nationalities: towards a new understanding of the implications, *Organization Studies,* 19: 181-205.

Handy, Charles (1991)
The Gods of Management, London: Souvenir Press: Business Books

Harbison, F. and Myers, C. (1959)
Management in the Industrial World, NY, USA: McGraw Hill

Hermel, Philippe (1999)
Journal of International Business Studies, London: Winter 1999

Hofstede, G. (1991)
Cultures and Organisations, Maidenhead: McGraw Hill

Hofstede, G. (1980)
Culture's Consequences, London: McGraw Hill

Hughes, E.C. (1971)
The sociological eye: selected papers, Chicago, USA: Aldine-Atherton

Ibarra, H. (1992)
Homophily and differential returns: sex differences in network structure and access in an advertising firm, *Administrative Science Quarterly,* 37: 422-447

Jackson, D.N. (1994)
Jackson Personality Inventory – Revised manual, Port Heron, MI, USA: Sigma
Assessment Systems

Jaeger A.M and Kanungo R.N., (eds) (1990)
Introduction, *Management in Developing Countries,* NY, USA: Routledge

Kimann, R., Saxton, M. and Serpa, J. (1985)
*Strategy Myopia: Culture as an Invisible Barrier to Change in Gaining Control of
Corporate Culture,* San Francisco, CA, USA: Jossey Bass

Kluckhohn, Florence R. and Strodtbeck, Frederick L. (1961)
Variations in value Orientations, ILL, USA: Row Peterson

Kotter, John and Heskett, James (1992)
Corporate Culture and Performance, New York, USA: Free Press

Kwon, Jung, Wirtz, Jochen, Tan, Soo Jiuan and Kau, Ah Keng (1999)
The Seven Faces of Singporeans: a typology of their aspirations and
life satisfaction, *Asia Pacific Journal of Management,* Volume 16

Lau, D. C. and Murnighan, J. K. (1998)
Demographic diversity and faultlines: the compositional dynamics of organizational
groups, *Academy of Management Review,* 23: 325-340

Leeds C. (1994)
*Pragmatic and Holistic Approaches to Management Development in Newly Emerging
Countries,* EIASM Workshop, Henley, Oxon.: Henley Management College

Lessem, R. and Neubauer, F. (1994)
European Management Systems, Maidenhead: McGraw Hill

McGregor, Douglas (1960)
The Human Side of Enterprise, NY, USA: McGraw Hill

McClelland, D.C. (1961)
The Achieving Society, Princeton, NJ, USA: Van Nostrand Rheinhold

McGrath, R.G., Macmillan, L.C., Yang, E.A. and Tsai W. (1992)
Does culture endure or is it malleable? *Journal of Business Venturing* 7,

Maslow, Abram H. (1968)
Towards a Psychology of Being, NY, USA: Van Nostrand Reinhold

Madonna, S., Wesley, A. and Anderson, H. (1989) and (1985)
Situational and dispositional clues that define the Machievellianism orientation, *Journal of Social Psychology, 129* (1989). Zook A., On
measurement of Machievellianism, *Psychological Reports* 57/3, 1985

Manchester W. (1968)
The Arms of Krupp, Boston, MA, USA: Little Brown & Co.

Nemeth, C.J. 1986, Differential contributions of majority and minority influence, *Psychological Review,* 91: 23-32

Nomani, F. and Rahnema, A. (1995)
Islamic Economic Systems, Kuala Lumpur, Malaysia: Business Information Press

Osland, G. and Cavusgill, S. (1996)
Performance issues in US-China Joint ventures, *California Management Review,* 38(2)

Osland, Joyce, Bird, Allen, Delano, June and Mathew Jacob (2000)
Beyond sophisticated stereotyping: cultural sense making in context, *The Academy of Management Executive,* February 2000

Ouchi, William (1984)
The M-Form Society, Reading, MASS, USA: Addison-Wesley

Ouchi, William (1990)
Keynote Address to the Western Academy of Management, New York, USA

Penaloza, Lisa and Gilly, Mary (1999)
Marketer acculturation: the changer and the changed, *Journal of Marketing;* New York, USA: July 1999

Pike, K. L. (1954)
Emic and Etic standpoints, Part 1, p.16, Glendale, CA, USA: Summer Institute of Linguistics

Porter Michael (1980)
Competitive Strategy, NY, USA: Free Press

Redding, S.G. (1993)
Cognition as an aspect of culture and its relation to management processes: an exploratory view of the Chinese case, *Journal of Management Studies,* (2), 17

Reich, R. and Magaziner, I. (1982)
Why the US needs an Industrial Policy, *Harvard Business Review,* 60 (1) 74-81

Rotter, J.B. (1966)
Generalised Expectancies for Internal Versus External Control of Reinforcement.
Psychological Monographs: General and Applied 80, Whole No. 609

Schein, Edgar (1997)
Organisational Culture and Leadership, San Francisco, CA, USA: Jossey Bass

Shaw, J., Fisher, C. and Randolph, W. (1991)
From Materialism to Accountability: the changing cultures of Ma Bell and Mother Russia, *Academy of Management Executive,* 5/1

Swain, W. (1958)
The History of Civilisation, New York, USA: Harper Bros, page 252

Tajfel, H.H. (1982)
Social identity and intergroup relations, Cambridge: Cambridge University Press

Terpstra, V. and David, K. (1985)
The Cultural Environment of International Business, second edition, Dallas, USA: South-Western Publishing

Thomas, Anisya and Mueller, Stephen (2000)
A case for comparative entrepreneurship: assessing the relevance of culture, *Journal of International Business Studies,* Second Quarter, 2000

Tönnies, Ferdinand (1957)
Community and Association, MI, USA: Michigan State University Press
Trice, Harrison and Beyer, Janice (1984)

Trompenaars, Fons and Hampden-Turner, Charles (1997)
Riding the Waves Of Culture, second edition, London: Nicholas Brealey

Turner, J.C. (1985)
Social categorization and the self-concept: a social cognitive theory of group behavior. In Berkowitz, L.L. (ed.), *Advances in Group Processes*; 77-121, Greenwich, CT, USA: JAI Press.

Weber, Max (1930)
The Protestant Ethic and the Spirit of Capitalism, London: Macmillan

Zook A. (1985)
On measurement of Machiavellianism, *Psychological Reports* 57/3

SELECTED BIBLIOGRAPHY

ABB: the Dancing Giant, Kevin Barham & Claudia Heimer, London: Pitman, 1988

American Culture, ed. Anders Breidlid *et al.*, London: Routledge, 1996

Breaking Through Culture Shock, Elisabeth Marx, London: Nicholas Brealey, 1999

Chinese Management, Shen Seow Wah, Selangor, Malaysia: MPH, 1995

Communicating Across Cultures, Maureen Guirdham, London: Macmillan, 1999

Comparative Management, ed. Raghu Nath, Cambridge, MA, USA,: Ballinger Publishing Co., 1988

Cross-cultural Management, Terence Jackson, Oxford: Butterworth Heinemann, 1995

Culture's Consequences, second edition, Geert Hofstede, London: Sage Publications, 2001

Doing Business With the Japanese, John Abecasis, Phillips, London: Kogan Page, 1992

European Business Cultures, Robert Crance (ed.) Maidenhead: Prentice Hall, 2000

Guide du comportement dans les affaires internationales, Edward & Mildred Hall, Sevil, 1990

A History of India, Hermann Kulke & Dietmar Rothermund, London: Routledge, 1986

Home, Sweet Tokyo, Rick Kennedy, Tokyo, Japan: Kodansha International, 1988

Le Management Interculturel, Franck Gauthey & Dominique Xardel, Paris, France: Presses Universitaires de France, 1988

Malaysian Development, Martin Rudner, Ottawa, Canada: Carleton University Press, 1994

Management – Asian Context, Joseph Putti, Singapore: McGraw Hill, 1991

SELECTED BIBLIOGRAPHY

Managing Across Borders, Christopher Bartlett and Sumantra Ghoshal, Harvard, MA, USA: Century, 1992

Managing Across Cultures, Pat Joynt & Malcolm Warner, eds, London: Thomson, 1996

Managing People Across Europe, eds Terry Garrison and David Rees, Oxford: Butterworth Heinemann, 1994

Moving the Mountain, Abel Aganbegyan, London: Bantam Press, 1989

Multicultural Management, Farid Elashmawi, Philip Harris & Abdul Majeed, Kuala Lumpur, Malaysia, 1994

Organisational Culture & Leadership, second edition, Edgar Schein, London: Sage Publications, 1996

Organisational Culture, Andrew Brown, Harlow: Pitman, 1998

Perestroika – Managing the Economy of the Firm, Economica, Moscow, Russian Federation, 1989

Politics, Economy & Society in Contemporary China, Bill Burgger & Stephen Reglar, London: Macmillan, 1994

Russia 2010, Daniel Yergin & Thane Gustafson, London: Brealey, 1994

Steeltown USSR, Stephen Kotkin, CA, USA: University of California Press, 1991

The Character of a Corporation, Rob Goffee & Gareth Jones, London: Harper Collins, 1998

The East in the West, Jack Goody, Cambridge: Cambridge University Press, 1996

The Global HR Manager, eds Pat Joynt and Bob Morton, London: Institute of Personnel Development, 1999

The Management of a Multicultural Workforce, M.Tayeb, London: Sage Publications, 1996

The New Corporate Cultures, Terrence Deal and Allan Kennedy, NY, USA: Texere, 2000

The New Taipans, Claudia Cragg, London: Arrow, 1996

The State We're In, Will Hutton, London: Vintage, 1995

When Cultures Collide, Richard Lewis, London: Nicholas Brealey, 2000

CASE STUDIES

THE IZMASH SYNDROME

Questions:

Explain the tensions that affect nations' arms industries when they move to dismantle part of their defence systems.

Explain what this means for their business cultures.

Can Izmash and other leading world arms makers adjust easily to the new world?

■ Changing times

One of the most impressive infantry weapons in recent times has been the Kalashnikov assault rifle. The original AK-47 was designed in 1947 by the much-decorated Mikhail Kalashnikov and, since then, whole series of rifles based on the original product have been manufactured by Izmash, a major arms producer located in the Russian city of Izhevsk. This city was, in Soviet times, a major centre of arms manufacturing. For example, a sister plant to Izmash was the Izhevsk Mechanical Plant where Tokarev and Makarov pistols were made.

Since its launch Izmash had achieved spectacular global sales success with the AK-47 – some 50m units no less. The product had become, in the words of Izmash's chief engineer, Viktor Selezov *not just a symbol of our city, but of our country.* (1) In the mid-1990s it was made under licence in factories from Poland to China and cherished by regular troops, guerrillas and terrorists alike for its all-terrain performance and rugged manufacture.

A major anxiety for many of Izmash's 70,000 employees at the start of 1995 was the possibility of redundancy. The changing nature of military spending since the ending of the Cold War had meant a reduction in demand for Kalashnikov rifles. Indeed, since the start of the 1990s, the Russian military had reduced their orders by 75 percent. Worse was clearly likely, if not inescapable.

Nor did the future of Izmash's car division – which made the ageing Moskvitch and Kombi cars – look particularly attractive. Hence the critical question for the company's directors: "What to do about Izmash's product mix?"

■ The West

Russia was not alone in having to come to terms with the reduction in arms spending brought about by the welcome arrival of an end to military super-power rivalry. There was, similarly, much anxiety in America, in France and in Britain over the likely fate of their defence industries.

Already, the first signs of strategic reaction to the crisis were evident. The USA's leading defence technologists, Lockheed and Martin Marietta, announced in 1994 that they were to merge. The deal, worth in excess of $10 billion, would allow both companies (it was said) to consolidate rationally to cope with USA's shrinking defence spending. The new company, Lockheed Martin, would have a workforce of 170,000 employees and an annual turnover of $23 billion. The merger has not been without pain since, previously, the two companies were deadly rivals for the Pentagon's dollars.

In France, the seriousness of the situation was also well-recognised. As Alain Gomez, president of the country's largest arms maker, Thomson SA, said in an interview in December 1994: (2)

*The critical things that have occurred are the ending of the Cold War...
and the contraction of defence budgets... But there is also the formidable
development of technology itself to reckon with. This has pushed up the
costs of programmes, in spite of productivity gains. And then there's the
issue of the extraordinary complexity of customer requirements. This is
growing and growing... What we are facing now, in terms of company
survival, is a process of natural selection... What makes it worse is that
the Americans have left their home base. In the mid 1980s exports
amounted to 5 percent of turnover: now, it's 25 percent. And the US
government is heavily backing company activities with an imperialistic
'USA Inc.' attitude in defence and aerospace that is like the 'Japan Inc.'
approach of the Japanese government and manufacturers in the civil
electronics field. Where the Americans enjoy a competitive advantage is
in a totally-protected home market for defence and aerospace which
makes up 40 percent of the world market.*

Under such circumstances the correct strategy for Thomson was, he declared, on the one hand to seek maximum productivity and optimal organisation for the company and its subsidiaries, and, on the other, to create a sensible series of alliances and joint ventures with erstwhile competitors. Such lessons were not lost on Russian producers, or so it was thought.

The British government shared the views expressed by Alain Gomez. It reckoned that:

- The stronger defence contractors – GEC (radar), British Aerospace (aircraft wing technology) and BAe-Sema (ship command and control systems) could take over their weaker competitors;
- Future weapons programmes should be based on the creation of a single European platform, i.e., a design shared by a number of countries which would produce economies of scale in design and manufacture;
- British firms should seek alliances and even mergers with other European companies with a leading edge technology which British companies did not possess, e.g., French capabilities in air-to-air missile manufacture.

■ The Vishegrad Countries

The problems of reduced defence spending which were giving headaches to Izmash's managers also heavily affected their former colleagues in front-line members of the erstwhile Warsaw Pact – Poland, the Czech and Slovak republics. And deeply so, as Exhibit 1 indicates below. The response of their firms to the challenge was said, by the Economist, to have been one of *chaotic adaptation.*

The arms industry is in deep recession world-wide. The Stockholm International Peace Research Institute calculates that world trade in tanks, artillery, aircraft and other large items, which had been worth $48 billion in 1987, contracted to only $22 billion last year (1993)... East European industry has been hit harder than most. True, Western defence contractors have been pampered by the standards of the rest of the economy, but they understand the vagaries of the market and have found it easier to contract and adapt...

The collapse of the Soviet Union was the first shock to the industry. Arms production in communist Eastern Europe had neither been geared to domestic defence requirements nor, by definition, operated according to market principles. Except for the Soviet Union itself, no country was self-sufficient in arms production. Under the Warsaw Pact, certain countries were detailed to produce certain items – Bulgaria made computers, Czechoslovakia specialised in jet trainers... With the dissolution of the Warsaw Pact, this arms bazaar broke up. Domestic defence budgets were slashed and exports to such countries as Iraq, Syria and Libya fell.

EXHIBIT C1.1: HARD TIMES (3)

What, in fact, had they done? The key response had been to begin collaboration wherever possible with Western firms. One subject for technological co-operation was the T-72 tank, a core piece of Warsaw Pact armament. Slovak manufacturers had been collaborating with Sabca (Belgium), GEC-Marconi (Britain) and two French companies to produce an up-dated version – the T-72 M2. The Czechs for their part were working with the French company, Sagem. All of these deals involved powerful cross-cultural lessons.

In each case what was involved was filling the basic arms platform of the tank with more advanced equipment. This would produce, it was hoped, a tank as good as Western models but at half the price. *The theory*, stated the *Economist, is simple. Labour is cheap and the region has solid military designs which can be modernised using technology from the West. To break into Western markets, it makes sense to convert.* (4)

■ Back to Russia

The strategy most used by Vishegrad and Russian companies, however, had been diversification – as in the case of the Slovakian company Detva, once famous for its armoured personnel carriers. In 1995 it was now seeking to sell its new line of fork lift trucks in Western markets, a task made extremely difficult by an absence of a sales-and-service network.

The Kirov plant in St Petersburg was another diversifier. This was the home of the T-80 tank. Although this tank, and its counterpart the T-84, were being upgraded, management at the plant had found demand to be too low to sustain the employment of its exceptionally skilled workforce at full stretch. They had similarly sought to diversify, in this case into plastic body jeeps aimed at the consumer market. The problem they ran into was one of image. The new Kirov product did not figure as well in the eyes of the newly rich *biznessmeni* as some foreign alternatives, like the Cherokee or the Land Cruiser.

Another company which had the same difficulty, though in a different product sector, was Tantal, a defence electronics producer in Saratov. They switched one production line to VCRs only to find, to their surprise, that Russian VCRs (and TVs) were often more expensive and poorer in quality than those sold by some Japanese firms.

The challenge faced by the Kirovs, the Tantals and the Izmashes in Russia was severe. Not only was there the internal question of buying new equipment and re-training workers to produce the new products, but there was also the external one of whether or not banks were prepared and able to finance the conversion, if companies could not. And that issue was linked to the amount of access enjoyed by superior – and possibly cheaper – imported products to the Russian market place. What was needed was a workable adjustment strategy (with adequate resources) and, within it, a sound conception of marketing realities. And a workforce willing to accept a loss of prestige status and their high-level terms of employment as arms producers.

This was why Izmash was now in an interesting position. A few years ago the plant enjoyed tremendous sales success (in Egypt and Libya) with its Izhevsk motorcycle. This was a rugged, high-performance yet inexpensive, off-the-road machine with a liquid-cooled engine. Engineers at the plant were now keen for the newly established Marketing Department to carry out some sort of market study – to see whether it could sell well in Western markets.

REFERENCES

(1) Live by the AK-47, die by the AK-47, Peter Galuszka, *Business Week*, 7/11/1994

(2) Les industries françaises de l'armement ne pourront échapper aux restructurations, Alain Gomez, *Le Monde*, 8/12/1994

(3) Biting the Bullet, *The Economist*, 22/10/1994

(4) As (3)

THE 1994 MEXICAN DEVALUATION

Questions:

Why did Mexico get enthusiastic about its future prospects in 1993?

What inspired Mexican businessmen (and the government) to go for growth?

What was the logic behind global investors backing Mexico (and then backing off)?

What impact would such investment gyrations have on the Mexican people?

What meaning does the case have for the business cultures of newly industrialising countries?

On the 20th December 1994, the newly-elected President of Mexico had to take urgent action to deal with a crisis situation that few had foreseen. In the face of a sudden stock market crash and dangerously dwindling foreign currency reserves, he devalued the peso by 29 percent. This led quickly to a large-scale world-wide currency turmoil. To try to halt a major crisis in world finance, a Mexican bail-out package had to be put together by the USA, IMF and World Bank.

Businessmen like Miguel Alfageme – commercial director of a USA car dealership in Mexico city – were simply baffled at the onset of the crisis. And he was not alone. *It's difficult to understand what has happened* he declared. *One minute they told us we were a rich country. Now they say we are poor again.* (1)

Mexico's debt problems were, in fact, not recent in origin. Bankers and finance ministers, who had attended the IMF meeting back in 1982 in Toronto, were worried at the time about Mexico's mounting indebtedness and how the country would deal with it. They had good reason for this worry because the debt moratorium idea Mexico came up with at the time – a simple refusal to repay its obligations – then sparked off a chain reaction of debt defaults round the globe. What was particularly problematic about the 1982 crisis was the extent to which American banks had been overly prepared to lend large sums of money without, in hindsight, adequate security. In order to stabilise the situation in which its neighbour found itself, the USA put together a safety net known as the Brady Plan. But that was 1982.

Over the period 1985-1994 it seemed to many observers that Mexico was gradually was getting its economic problems under control. The programme of free-market reforms implemented by the previous president, Carlos Salinas de Gortari, from 1988 to 1994 had been seen as a very powerful economic stimulant. The Bush and Clinton administrations in the USA also regarded it as a sound platform on which to plan for the North American Free Trade Area (NAFTA). President Salinas had worked hard for this trade deal which promised his countrymen higher-paying jobs and better employment prospects.

Mexicans began to feel that they had *turned the corner* and their culture reflected a spirit of optimism.

The Mexican devaluation of 29 percent came only two weeks after the Pan-American trade summit held in Miami where Mexico had been described by the USA as a symbol of economic growth and political stability. Some supporters were beginning to revise their views on President Clinton's much-trumpeted "win-win" NAFTA strategy now as a result, since the crisis had wiped out the USA merchandise trade surplus with Mexico. Given NAFTA and the current debt crisis, Mexico's troubles were American troubles in a way that few could have foreseen a year before.

EXHIBIT C2.1: JAM TOMORROW?

It is noteworthy that a significant element in the Salinas' programme had been the privatisation of Mexico's banks. It was these banks that had responded to the growing mood of post-NAFTA confidence in the country by loosening credit. One result was a sharp rise in the demand for personal and business term loans and for credit cards, which the banks were only too pleased to accommodate. This led, in turn, and over time, to a surge in Mexico's imports of USA-made consumer goods – *large* and *flashy* cars in particular. Thus, the county's rising economic growth and its seeming prosperity were based, in good measure, on a round of debt-financed spending.

El Presidente had inherited what amounted to an enormous nightmare, since there was another, more intractable, side to Mexico's problems beyond that of rapidly rising debt. This was the existence of a *global financial bubble*. It consisted of the massive amounts of money investors had placed in the stock markets around the world in the early 1990s. These funds were being shifted around the open trading world in a speedy, non-stop search for high returns. The rise in mobile investment money had had the effect of raising the value of Third World stock markets, with their supposedly exciting economic prospects, from $400 billion to $2.1 trillion in the five years up to 1994.

If the business culture of any emerging market now showed signs of not instantly living up to the performance expectations of the international investor, the *hot money* was withdrawn just as quickly as it was funnelled in, through the instant sale of shares or bonds once eagerly bought.

The Times' commentator Anatole Kaletsky pulled no punches in describing the phenomenon:

The fundamental problem was an international flow of money that had long since gone beyond the bounds of normal financial prudence and was being sustained by a combination of herd instinct, short-sightedness and economic ignorance. Brazil may not have a big current account deficit like Mexico, Malaysia may be better managers, but all have had their financial markets distorted by the same global mania for emerging market investment. Regardless of the relative soundness of their economic fundamentals, all will have to suffer from the bust that inevitably follows an unsustainable financial boom. (2)

One feature in the *financial bubble* was the substantial investment by international financiers in Mexican bonds, called Tesebonos. These were dollar-denominated, short-term treasury bills issued by the government. They were highly popular in 1994 and hot money flooded in, as it had done for stocks and shares.

As we have seen, the *bubble* burst on the 20th December 1994 when investors saw that Mexico *couldn't deliver*. The newly-installed President had no choice but to act to clean up his country's finances following the stock market collapse.

As in 1982, the USA stepped in to create a safety net. This time, however, there was even more urgency. Not only was the problem bigger, but the NAFTA deal linking the USA, Mexico and Canada as free trade partners had just been ratified by Congress. Hence, the political credibility of the USA was at stake. It was in the interests of all concerned to keep trade flowing between the two countries.

The starting point for the rescue was President Zedillo's own *austerity plan*. This is detailed in Table C2.1 page 210. As will be noted, the plan was highly deflationary and politically, therefore, difficult to implement in Mexico, where poverty really means poverty. Consequently, it was vital to reassure the international financial community that the Salinas era of Mexico's over-indulgence was over and that austerity would work. Finance Secretary Guillermo Ortiz publicly underlined his view that the Zedillo plan was just what was needed and was also highly pragmatic. (3)

- Tight price and wage controls.
- Major cuts in the 1995 budget and measures to reduce the current account deficit. The reduction would amount to $5 billion and $14 billion respectively.
- Peso stabilisation fund of $18 billion, incorporated in the US-IMF bail-out.
- Increase in pace and extent of privatisation, but not to include the national electricity generating company – Comision Federal de Electricidad – and Pemex, the Mexican state-run oil company.

TABLE C2.1: ZEDILLO'S RESCUE PLAN OF JANUARY 1995

The USA-led rescue package was also a bitter pill for the proud Mexican people to swallow especially as the US demanded that Mexico's annual oil output, valued at $7 billion, would serve as collateral for the $20 billion slice of the aid it was providing.

Much *Yankee-go-Home* antagonism was expressed over this move by die-hard Mexican nationalists, since the country had taken control of oil production (from the USA) in the 1920s and it was a symbol of their independence.

By mid-March 1995, the social picture in Mexico was stark. The peso had lost half its value since the December devaluation. Consumer and commercial interest rates were around 65 percent, with a credit card rate of 100 percent. Defaults on bank loans were rising as Mexicans found they could not repay them. The Mexican car industry had lost 40 percent of its sales in only two months and the ruling Institutional Revolutionary Party was forecasting the worst recession in the twentieth century. Indeed, two of Mexico's largest banks – Banamex and Serfin – had had to cut their payrolls by 40 percent just in order to survive.

No wonder Miguel Alfageme was perplexed.

REFERENCES

(1) Mexican Dream of Riches Shattered by Peso's Collapse, David Adams, *The Times*, 13/1/1995

(2) Why Mexico may have done the world a good turn, Anatole Kaletsky, *The Times*, 2/2/1995

(3) A Talk with Mexico's finance chief, *Business Week*, 23/1/1995

MEXICO 2000:
THE END OF THE SEXENIO CURSE?

Questions:

What light does the case shed on Mexico's business culture?

Will it easily adjust to the changes the new president will bring in?

Has the Sexenio curse been laid to rest?

■ The Sexenio Curse

The six-year term of office of a Mexican president is called a *sexenio*. What is popularly known as the curse of the sexenio refers to a peculiar economic phenomenon that seems to afflict the country every time it changes its president – currency devaluation. Certainly, there has been a quite remarkable coincidence between presidential elections and the country's currency devaluations, all caused by economic crashes, in 1976, 1982, 1987 and 1994. It certainly happened with a vengeance when Ernesto Zedillo took over in December 1994.

2000 was a presidential election year in Mexico and the big issue was whether the curse would strike the country again, once the election had been held. It was an exciting time with a close contest in prospect between Francisco Labastida Ochoa of the Institutional Revolutionary Party (PRI), rulers of Mexico for the past 71 years, and Vicente Fox. Fox was leader of the National Action Party, a former Coca Cola executive and rancher, as well as the mastermind behind what his party called the Alliance For Change movement.

Most external observers and not a few Mexicans could see little difference between the contestants. So, the actual run-up to the election became dominated by the theme of *alternancia* (the idea that, in a democracy, political parties should alternate in government) and by much plain speaking, at least on Fox's part. Given that he was neither a general, a lawyer nor an economist, he represented for the voters a major potential break in Mexico's leadership tradition. This was further underlined when he proclaimed to the electorate that he was the only presidential contender who had ever milked a cow and when, for good measure, he referred to his opponent as "a cissy" and "a transvestite". His electorate were, he said, the *jodidos* – all those who had been "screwed" by previous administrations. (1)

So was the curse likely to strike? Not according to the official forecasts. They were rosy if not upbeat – economic growth was up (five percent for 2000 expected), the currency was strong and unemployment was down and stood at 2.5 percent. Annual inflation was running at just under ten percent, foreign cash reserves were high and debt repayments in 2000 low. The current budget deficit was under one percent.

Just the mixture to induce popular optimism?

Hardly, according to ex-bank manager Felipe Tecuanhuehue. "There is sure to be a crisis, because every time the government changes hands, it provokes uncertainty. After the last one, in which I lost my job, lots of my friends, had to redo their whole life plans". (2) Nor was there any denying that the aftermath of 1994 had left a bitter taste. Mexican output shrank by over six percent in 1995, both as a result of the recession and the Zedillo austerity plan, and although the economy had recovered since, government statistics indicated that real wages had fallen by 19 percent over the *sexenio*. World Bank estimates also showed that that 43 percent of Mexicans lived on less than $2 per day.

Catalina Aguilar, who worked for a publisher in Mexico City, wasn't optimistic, either. *There just isn't any money* she said. *Ever since Salinas left the country without a peso in the till, the rich have kept on getting richer. But this sexenio, I haven't been able to do anything about it. It's six years gone to waste.* Taxi driver, Ezequiel Rodriguez was equally scathing about cheap labour in Mexico. The only one to benefit? "The USA" he reckoned – and not without reason either as 81 percent of Mexico's exports went to the United States. (3)

Others welcomed the format of the election as a product of the very necessary political liberalisation process begun by Zedillo. Some considered that the election might break the PRI stranglehold and bring more positive changes to the country – like a reduction in corruption, for example, or more entrepreneurship to the business culture. Worries about the possible re-election of the PRI candidate were said to have been behind the six percent fall in the peso that took place in the run-up to the election.

After all, it was rumoured that Ochoa's faction had been giving away free chickens, tortillas, roofing materials and even washing machines to selected influential peasant supporters. (4)

Characteristics	
Size	1,973,000 square kms
Population	99.7m
Life expectancy	72 years
GDP	$ 380.9 billion
GDP/cap	$ 3970
Principal products (1998) :	
Silver (No. 1 in world)	2,679 tons
Lead	152,000 tons
Oil	159m tons

TABLE C3.1: BASIC DATA ON MEXICO
Source: *Bilan du Monde,* edition 2000, Atlaseco, 2000

In the event, Vicente Fox won by a margin of 42.8 percent to 35.7 percent, with disproportionate support from city dwellers, men and young people (it is noteworthy that 80 percent of Mexicans are under the age of 40). For him it was a major victory in what he called *the mother of all elections* (5) and commentator James Bone reckoned it had the potential to be the Mexican equivalent of the fall of the Berlin Wall.

Beyond doubt, it brought an end to the claims of PRI election-rigging over the entire period from President Cardenas, who nationalised the oil industry in the 1930s, to President Salinas de Gortari, who sold off the state monopolies in the 1990s. It was also, perhaps significantly, the first Mexican election in which the internet had played a part; the existence of a web site called *elecciones limpias.com* (clean elections) allowed complaints about any malpractices to have much greater public visibility. (6)

Would the curse afflict a man who toppled a 71-year old "dictatorship"? Vicente Fox did not think so. *I'm accused of wanting to manage the country as if it were Coca Cola. It's not a question of that, but rather to make use of principles and philosophies that work.* (7) Among the new administration's plans would be fiscal changes allowing increased spending on education and health together with the ending of some corporate tax exemptions. There was also a project to open up the electric power and petroleum industries to outside investment.

Certainly, Vicente Fox was *speaking American* – on moves to combat corruption and drug trafficking (both endemic), to deal with poverty and social injustice (deeply rooted) and create more prosperity. Homero Aridjis, the noted poet and environmentalist spoke in hope when he said :

> *It was a different Mexico that came to the change of power. You saw at the inauguration different faces, more middle class, not the same old people. As a Mexican, I feel comfortable to have for the first time in my life a president who seems honest.* (8)

REFERENCES

(1) Fox casts himself as the people's amigo, James Bone, *The Times,* 4/7/2000

(2) Despite Growth, Mexicans fear six-year curse, John Ward Anderson, *The International Herald Tribune,* 4/7/2000

(3) As (2)

(4) As (2)

(5) As (1)

(6) Mexico's momentum, *The International Herald Tribune* editorial, 1-2/7/2000

(7) As (1)

(8) Assuming Presidency in Mexico, Fox outlines his Vision of Reforms, Kevin Sullivan & Mary Jordan, *The International Herald Tribune,* 2-3/12/2000

THE GERMAN MODEL UNDER THREAT

Questions:

What is meant by *the German Model?*

Given their *code of practice*, how difficult will it be for many German civil servants to adjust culturally to the new age?

What is the main challenge faced by the model?

How is the government trying to deal with the problem?

■ A Marriage made in Heaven?

Since the collapse of the Berlin Wall in 1989, the marriage between a rich West Germany and an uneconomic East had turned out, unfortunately and against some rosy predictions, to be less than happy. Not for nothing did Horst Koehler, State Secretary of the Finance Ministry, indicate at the January 1993 G7 meeting in Frankfurt that the German government was *very concerned* at the state of the German economy and *the social consequences of unemployment.* (1) Certainly, data was produced at the meeting showing that Germany's economic performance in 1992 was the weakest since the last recession in 1982.

It was also made plain by Helmut Schlesinger, Bundesbank president, that the independent central bank would not deviate from its good housekeeping policies, even in the face of vastly increased political pressure within Germany. In particular, the policy of a strict anti-inflationary approach to interest rates (8.6 percent in mid-January 1993) would continue.

This forthright stance on monetary policy gave the German government so little freedom for manoeuvre in this area that a fiscal (tax) route to pay for the rebuilding of East Germany became inevitable. Critics said that the Christian Democrat proposals announced mid-January 1993 amounted to the most drastic cut in German living standards in 50 years.

The package presented by Theo Waigel, the German Finance minister, indeed raised some taxes, cut welfare spending and reduced unemployment benefit. It planned for strict spending limits on government expenditure in areas ranging from shipbuilding to infant education and raised the Solidarity Tax to an unpopular level.

Business was aghast at the planned new taxes on petrol, insurance, investment income and, as from 1995, the surcharge on corporation tax. The opposition Social Democrats (SPD) and the trade unions pledged total opposition to cuts in welfare and unemployment benefit. Special opposition was focused on the one percent cut in the civil service pay-roll in 1994 and the means-testing of child allowance.

Like the rest of the *Sparparket* (savings package), the cuts in local authority spending also needed to be agreed by the 16 Länder (regional states), before they could be legislated upon federally. As most of the Länder were governed by the SPD whose party leader called the cutbacks *social atrocities*, it was unlikely that harmony among the state and federal levels would prevail. (2) For civil servants who had had secure jobs in the past these were anxious times. What was the most worrying aspect of all of it? The fact that the Kohl plan for reunifying East and West Germany was not succeeding as planned.

■ The German Civil Service System

Compared with the post-war British experience of intermittently re-shaping and re-focusing the public services, the German government administration system had shown remarkable stability. Perhaps this is not surprising. After all, in Germany every public service organisation operated within a constitutional framework in line with the Basic Law (Grundgesetz) which promotes the notion of a republican, democratic and social welfare-orientated state. Not only that, the Federal Constitutional Court (Bundesverfassungsgericht) stood as guarantor of rigid constitutional legality throughout the system – at federal, state and local level. Indeed, whilst the British seemed to perpetually tinker with the machinery of government, the Germans seemed to keep their systems intact, well-oiled and operational.

And so it was with Germany's civil servants. Section 5 of Article 33 of the Basic Law lays down that "the law of the public service shall be regulated with due regard to the traditional principles of the professional civil service". The Law itself entrusts the permanent civil servant with 'the exercise of state authority' and matters of status, service and loyalty are governed by public law. Conditions of service, legal responsibilities, form of appointment, mode of training are all stipulated in successive revisions of the Federal Civil Service Law (Bundesbeamtengesetz) of 1953 – whatever the role of the person in question as, for instance, policeman, judge, soldier, school teacher, postman, professor, train driver or administrator. The career structure grades are shown in Table 1 below. It is all highly structured.

EXAMPLES OF ROLE TITLES	NATURE OF SERVICE ROLES
Amtsgehilfe – Amtsmeister	Basic, sub-clerical
Assistant – Hauptsekretär	Clerical
Inspektor-Oberamtmann	Executive
Regierungsrat – Staatssekretär	Higher – Administrative

TABLE C4.1: ROLES IN THE GERMAN CIVIL SERVICE

Note: These grades cover all public service posts from railway guard up to permanent secretary in the federal government. They cover schoolteachers, nurses etc.

The permanent civil service in West Germany bears witness, in fact, to the remarkable potential for continuity of a bureaucratic ethos. Under the vastly different political conditions of the post-war Federal Republic, the civil service (Beamtendienst) has continued to follow paths of tradition and structure first laid down in Bismarck's Germany.

Any attempt by government to change the nature and ethos of the system was, therefore, bound to be highly problematic.

■ A Disintegrating Society?

The difficulties were plain. Helmut Kohl, the German Chancellor, was seen by many to have greatly misjudged the cost of the reunification of East and West Germany to which he had been, and still was, so firmly committed. One problem was how to meet the $100 billion a year unification bill, with public debt forecast to rise from 56 percent of GDP in 1992 to 63 percent by the end of 1995. (3) Quite another was how to get through the worst slump in a decade with such profoundly high Bundesbank interest rates. And, as if these were not enough, it was also claimed that the coalition deal on cabinet seats his party (Christian Democrats) had arranged with the Free Democrats (FDP) and the Christian Social Union (CSU) limited his freedom to switch tack on his existing approach. (4)

The answer was a corporatist solution. In late January 1993 Helmut Kohl forged (for the third time in post-war Germany) a so-called *solidarity pact* among all levels of government, trade unions, banks and industry to revive the economy and, with a bit of luck, his own government, which was due to end its federal term of office in 1994.

The problem was that the pact was being introduced under such exceptionally difficult economic circumstances. *Business Week* magazine pulled no punches in diagnosing the central problem:

Eastern wages are sky-rocketing under a lavish post-unification deal to ratchet up to Western levels as soon as 1995. But with Eastern productivity only a third of that in the West, such a jump would deal a death blow to hundreds of money-losing machinery makers. (5)

In January 1992 there had been 3m 'Ossies' (former East Germans) out of work. On top of this, many of those working in West German industry were covered by binding industry-wide contracts which, unless change occurred, did not give much flexibility in work rules.

Key element	1991	1992
Gross National Product increase (%)	3.6	0.8
Gross Domestic Product increase (%)*	3.7	1.5

* omits income from abroad. Official data

TABLE C4.2: GERMANY'S ECONOMIC PERFORMANCE

There was also the question of the revamping of Germany's cradle-to-grave social security system which Theo Waigel had proposed. According to Professor Kurt Biedenkopf, prime minister of Saxony, West Germans would have no rise in living standards in the next ten years. Björn Engholm, SPD leader, stated his view with brutal frankness. *The government wants to take an axe, not only to a branch of the social welfare system, but to the entire tree.* (6)

The pressure for change was unremitting. On the one hand, there was the need for German industry to enjoy conditions in which it could forge ahead strongly after the emergence of Germany from the 1990-3 recession. This dictated further government moves towards economic deregulation and public expenditure reduction. As we have seen, these were announced in early 1993. However, a combination of tax rises and an over-valued mark – caused by reductions in the value of the dollar – did not fit the business community's requirements in terms of stimulating domestic demand. Indeed, many business leaders claimed that German industry could develop strongly only if there were a reduction in the level of standardised sector-wide wage rises. For them a political thrust was needed to reverse aspects of Germany's corporatist system of collective bargaining in the public and service sectors. However, both of these had been much praised in the past for giving stability to Germany. (7)

But neither of these was forthcoming. In fact, in 1994, as a result there were extensive high pay settlements. Some employers worked in even greater harmony than usual with their employers' federations to effectively create pay rise harmony. Global competition was also advancing strongly in sectors where Germany had once enjoyed competitive advantage, for instance in aerospace, electrical/electronic engineering. Overall, this merely underlined the prospects for sluggish economic growth in Germany.

No wonder the economics correspondent of *The European*, Thierry Naudin, indicated that the German model was *lagging in the slow lane*.

■ Managing for Change

The difficulty in re-orienting the German machine towards greater economic productivity and a more effective economic management approach continued unabated throughout the 1990s and was still obvious in 1997. At this time Germany had the world's highest hourly wages and the shortest working week. And, as if that were not bad enough, in early 1997, the country's unemployment passed the level which had brought Hitler into power. No less than 4.5m were out of work and the total was still rising. According to the president of the Federal Labour Office "the trough should now have been reached in western Germany, but the decline in the eastern states continues". (8) Europe's *Wunderkind* economy, the product of the *Wirtschaftswunder* seemed mired not so much in distress, as in perplexity.

The taxation problem, to be sure, remained unsolved. The Bundesrat, the upper house of the German parliament, still refused to accept the full range of savings measures and tax changes that Chancellor Kohl's government was still resolutely proposing.

However, there were some signs that a culture change was on its way.

The first was the German government's unrelenting backing for EMU, despite considerable popular reservations and some apparent Bundesbank concerns and irrespective of the need for budgetary restraint that this required. Of course, some extra accounting measures were needed to allow Germany to meet the Maastricht rules for entry to the single currency zone. Some, like the revaluation of the Bundesbank gold reserves, were regarded as too creative. But this Chancellor, like Bismarck before him, was of an iron disposition on this issue.

The second was a wave of take-overs and mergers that hit the country over this period. The reason was simple enough. In an open trading world, German industrialists recognised that improving their global performance meant either less reliance on domestic production or a substantial improvement in its efficiency and effectiveness. Shareholder value, exporting German capital and corporate restructuring thus became corporate watchwords. Whilst there were 12 merger and takeover deals of more than DM1 in 1996, there were no less than 34 in 1997.

On the other hand, the German public did not seem too ready to accept the *Geiz ist gut* (greed is good) philosophy common to so many Anglo-Saxon deals of this nature. A hostile bid by Krupp for its steel competitor Thyssen in early 1997 triggered a furious public reaction which forced the parties to merge instead. The trade unions, too, were restive with such an atmosphere. After all, it was they who had pressured the government to push up East German wages on the basis of *equal pay for equal work*, a notion that had, up to now, simply put low-productivity workers in the East out of work in massive numbers.

REFERENCES

(1) Kohl Government, Bundesbank in growing rift, Anatole Kaletsky, *The Times*, 14/1/1993

(2) Das macht die Seele so kaputt, Eckhart Kauntz, *Frankfurter Allgemeine Zeitung*, 19/1/1993

(3) As (1)

(4) As (1)

(5) Kohl prods the giant and holds his breath, *Business Week*, 25/1/1993

(6) As (5)

(7) German model is lagging in the slow lane, Thierry Naudin, *The European*, 24-30/8/1995

(8) Germany's reforms fail to shake off the past, Oliver August, *The Times*, 6/10/1997

THE GERMAN MODEL CHANGES GEAR

Question:

To what extent has the German model changed gear?

■ Managing for Change

The difficulty in re-orienting the German political machine towards a more effective economic management approach and away from a culture of dependency on the state was large. Nevertheless, efforts to this end continued unabated throughout the 1990s. However, in the latter part of the decade Germany still had the world's highest hourly wages and the shortest working week. And, as if that were not bad enough, in early 1997, the country's unemployment passed the level which had brought Hitler into power. No less than 4.5m were out of work and the total was still rising. According to the president of the Federal Labour Office "the trough should now have been reached in western Germany, but the decline in the eastern states continues". (1)   Europe's *Wunderkind* economy, the product of the *Wirtschaftswunde,* seemed mired not so much in distress, as in perplexity.

The taxation problem, at the time, remained unsolved. The Bundesrat, the upper house of the German parliament, still refused to accept the full range of savings measures and tax changes that Chancellor Kohl's government was still resolutely proposing.

However, there were some signs that a culture change was on its way.

The first was the German government's unrelenting backing for EMU, despite considerable popular reservations and some apparent Bundesbank concerns, and irrespective of the need for budgetary restraint that this required. Of course, some extra accounting measures were needed to allow Germany to meet the Maastricht rules for entry to the single currency zone. Some, like the revaluation of the Bundesbank gold reserves, were regarded as too creative. But this Chancellor, like Bismarck before him, was of an iron disposition on this issue.

The second was a wave of take-overs and mergers that hit the country over this period. The reason was simple enough. In an open trading world, German industrialists recognised that improving their global performance meant either less reliance on domestic production or a substantial improvement in its efficiency and effectiveness. Shareholder value, exporting German capital and corporate restructuring thus became corporate watchwords. Whilst there were 12 merger and takeover deals of more than DM1 in 1996, there were no less than 34 in 1997.

On the other hand, the German public did not seem too ready to accept the *Geiz ist gut* (greed is good) philosophy common to so many Anglo-Saxon deals of this nature. A hostile bid by Krupp for its steel competitor Thyssen in early 1997 triggered a furious public reaction which forced the parties to merge instead. The trade unions, too, were restive with such an atmosphere. After all, it was they who had pressured the government to push up East German wages on the basis of *equal pay for equal work*, a notion that had, up to now, simply put low-productivity workers in the East out of work in massive numbers.

■ The Schroeder Government Arrives

In 1998 a left-wing SPD-Green Party government, led by Gerhard Schroeder, took over the reins of power in Germany. To deal with its inherited problems it moved slowly at first and, paradoxically, employed the same sort of stringent economic logic as had its predecessor. By 2000, however, there were unmistakable signs that change had arrived in the pattern of German business culture.

A small, but highly significant breakthrough was achieved in German shopping habits. By December 2000 a firm decision had been made to lift the 1933 Discount Act and the 1932 Free Goods Act, legislation that had severely restricted the ability of German retailers to offer discounts and special prices. In a world where *Letsbuyit.com,* a pan-European E-commerce company, which combined the power of individual buyers to push down prices, was radically extending its reach, such a level of market price regulation no longer made sense. Nor, for that matter, did the deeply-entrenched Ladenschlussgesetz (the early closing law for shops) which was similarly threatened.

Intriguingly, *Letsbuyit.com* has since disappeared as a casualty of the dot.com revolution.

In 2000 Germany changed its citizenship laws to reflect the fact that, with over seven million foreigners living there – of which 2.2m Turks – it is undeniably multicultural. The basis for citizenship shifted from ancestry to birthplace and made German the sons, daughters and grandchildren of Germany's first Gastarbeiter (guest workers).

The debate had been forced on the country by demographic pressures, the Institute for Economic Research estimate being that to fill out its thinning labour ranks Germany needs 250,000 immigrants per year.

One of the problems in this is the extent to which cultural assimilation can and will take place into what the CDU politician Friedrich Merz calls Germany's Leitkultur (mainstream culture).

EXHIBIT C5.1: CREATING A MULTICULTURAL GERMANY
Based on: German-born foreigners wonder what it takes to be a true German,
Peter Finn, *The International Herald Tribune*, 27/11/00

The big system changes that occurred were in the reform of taxes, pensions and state banks.

- **Tax reforms**

    In mid-1999, seeking recognition as a social and economic moderniser, the government steam-rollered a bold tax through both houses of parliament. It needed to, according to veteran commentator John Schmid, as all efforts to change *the labyrinthine tax system in a nation renowned for its resistance to structural economic change had failed.* (2)

    There were two principle alterations. Firstly, $25 billion in tax cuts by 2005, with a reduction in the top rate of income tax from 51 percent to 42 percent. Secondly, the elimination of the tax on the sale of corporate shareholdings. This meant that the leading German banks in particular could begin, if they chose, to sell off their immense holdings in German industry and commerce without paying a capital gains tax. The possibility of the bill had already unleashed a wave of corporate restructuring and more was clearly to follow. The result was a strong economic stimulus for the country but an increase in the uncertainty about what would happen when the pattern of stable ownership stakes in German industry by German banks came to an end.

- **Pension reforms**

The government was clearly hoping to repeat the pattern of tax policy success when it sought to cut benefits to the elderly and to actually dismantle parts of the pension system. Not surprisingly as pension payments in 1999 consumed one quarter of the federal budget, a figure which was due to rise to one third by 2004. (3) Politicians of the right and German industry supported such a move; politicians of the left and German trade unions opposed it. A key issue at stake was the continuation of the practice of paying retirees an average of 70 percent of their last pay check under conditions where, since the German social safety net now covers East as well as West, the pension sums were said to be unmanageable.

In the event the government backed down in the face of the unions' hostility and accepted a plan to reduce average pension payouts by 2030, not to 64 percent of wages (as they had sought), but to 67 percent. Michael Wolgast, senior economist at Deutsche Bank, thought this *a Pyrrhic victory which only delays the pain...One day the system will collapse.* (4)

Even so, for a Socialist government to actually pioneer such legislation – *Germany's biggest pension reform since the 1950s* (5) – was a massive feat in itself.

- **State bank reforms**

For years the big German *private* banks have complained to government about the activities of German *public* banks. These are institutions such as Landenbanken (regional state banks) and Sparkassen (local city banks) whose liabilities are guaranteed by the state and who therefore can borrow funds for rclending relatively cheaply. Indeed, the private banks took their case to the European

Commission, asserting that the state-debt guarantees were illegal as they were a form of subsidy.

The initial government reaction was to uphold the status quo on the grounds that the public banks perfomed vital local economic functions like financing regional economic development or helping small businesses. Given the legal problems in the case of North Rhine Westphalia's Westdeutsche Landesbank, Germany's fourth biggest bank in terms of assets, which was seeking in late 2000 to become private, the government was altering its stance. It was also acutely aware that the Association of German Public Banks had put forward a proposal to move from state funding to private insurance group funding over a period of ten years.

The impact of these cumulative changes to seek to free up the German model was quite spectacular. The German economy grew in 2000 at the fastest rate since unification and there were prospects that it would outpace the growth of Japan and the USA in 2001. The pain of the amalgamation of Communist East and Capitalist West was not yet a thing of the past – hardly surprising as it has cost the latter £153 billion to attempt to restore the former – but progress was certainly being made in turning the corner.

REFERENCES

(1)   Germany's reforms fail to shake off the past, Oliver August, *The Times*, 6/10/1997

(2)   Schroeder triumphs in battle over taxes, John Schmid, *The International Herald Tribune*, 15-16/7/2000

(3)   Unions force Schroeder to yield on pension cuts, John Schmid, *The International Herald Tribune*, 16-17/12/2000

(4)   As (3)

(5)   German pension reform plans clear hurdle, Ralph Atkins, *The Financial Times*, 15/11/2000

MMM

Questions:

What was MMM?

Explain why the Russian people seemed so gullible about MMM.

What was their rationale for purchasing MMM shares?

What sort of people were typical MMM investors?

What sort of character was Sergei Mavrodi?

Has Russia changed since – or does old thinking die hard?

■ Make Yourself a Fortune

It was the largest and most flamboyant advertising campaign ever screened in post-*perestroika* Russia. One of the screen heroes, a fictitious bulldozer driver called Lonya Golubkov, invests his surplus cash in the shares of a Russian company called MMM and gets rich remarkably quickly.

So well do the shares perform that Lonya is able to buy new boots and clothes for his family. He can even treat his brother to a trip to America to watch Russia in the 1994 World Cup. As they sit in a bar enjoying their holiday, the two nostalgically agree that USA beer is good but that Russian vodka is better.

The soap opera which grew around this make-money theme meant success for all involved. MMM was, according to Bakhyt Kilibayev, the creator of the advertising campaign, just the sort of investment company that would appeal to *ordinary people – people who identify with Golubkov because they are just like him.* (1) The advertising campaign cost about 10 billion roubles per day. (2)

In February 1994 MMM shares cost just 1,600 roubles (about USA 80 cents) to buy. By the beginning of July 1994 they were nudging 100,000 roubles (US$ 50). The rise in the MMM share price over the period was every bit as spectacular as the returns on investments that MMM was promising to its shareholders. For many in Russia it was the realisation of the dream that president Yeltsin had been speaking of – the creation of a nation of shareholders.

In fact, MMM, and a few other companies like Telemarket, had been the only outlets in Russia (apart from banks, that is) for cash investment by members of the public since the start of the 1990s. Whilst the vouchers which the government issued to all Russians as part of the first stage of its industry privatisation strategy could be exchanged for shares in companies, the public could not invest its cash directly in shares. Only in the second phase could investors buy shares directly with cash. This did not start until the end of July 1994.

Not that there was any shortage of cash in Russia, either. One reliable estimate is that, there was *plenty of cash* around the country to meet the industrial investment needs of Russian industry. This source reckons that there was even more cash – $40 billion – lodged abroad. (3)

Certainly, in early 1997, *The Financial Times'* John Plender put the figure of *amounts under the mattress in Russia* at $20 billion, adding that

> *In Russia, many pensioners who were unlucky enough to have left their lifetime nest egg in the hands of state saving institutions have seen them wiped out. Few trust the banks and there is a widespread fear that a bank account will attract the attention of the tax man or the mafia.* (4)

■ Anxious Times

And why not? said Lonya Golubkov as he bought his wife a fur coat with his MMM pay-off and whiled away his time checking the financial pages and wondering whether or not to buy a house in France. Notwithstanding the fact that only a few MMM investors had been lucky enough to obtain the 1300 percent return on investment initially promised when the company first started up, the company was said to have picked up ten million investors in its first six months. All of them seemed to have asked the self-same question – *Why not?* Very few appeared to have addressed with appropriate realism the question *Why?*

Worries about the company began to grow in late July 1994, once the government claimed that one of MMM's divisions owed it the equivalent of $24m in taxes and fines. However, the company's president Sergei Mavrodi, said at the time to be the seventh richest Russian, took space in no less than six leading papers to rebut the charge. Blaming all MMM's worries on an ill-advised government intervention, which he said might destroy market confidence and MMM's share price, he spoke defiantly:

> *I personally would not forecast what concrete shape the anger of the robbed people would take: a revolution, civil war or something else.* (4)

Two days later, on 28th July, even as 10,000 MMM investors were queuing up outside the company's Moscow headquarters in Warsaw Avenue to cash in their shares, MMM slashed the price back to 1,000 roubles and continued with its powerful advertising campaign. But it was not enough to restore any public or governmental faith in MMM. The company's 60 sales offices closed on 29th July amid scenes of desperation, like those outside the MMM branch in Moscow's Rileyeva St. On the fourth of August masked tax police arrested Sergei Mavrodi.

Why did MMM crash? According to the accusations made by the government two weeks before, MMM had been a simple *pyramid scheme*. Whilst the company had said it was investing its money in the currency markets, it had not. Indeed, it had been operating in such a legal vacuum that no effective control of its operations had been exercised by the government's finance ministry or tax inspectorate until relatively late in the day. True, the government had warned investors that MMM was *a gamble* (4), but it had never asserted that it had been a *scam* worthy of the most outrageously-uncontrolled market economy. Alexander Livshits (President Yeltsin's economic adviser) spoke volumes when he said:

The period of the Russian Klondike will soon be over. Russia is entering a period of stable, serious, civilised business enterprise. (5)

To be sure, it was entering this period slowly and with inflation running on average at 3.2 percent per month in 1994, having come down from already 26 percent per month in 1992.

And a scam it truly was. Those receiving "dividends" or cashing in their shares had been paid, not out of any profits that MMM had made on investments, but simply out of the money the company had received from selling more shares. In the end, of course, the pyramid was bound to collapse; those who bought shares last were certain never to be recompensed. Millions were fleeced. In its defence it must be stated that MMM had never claimed to have any *underlying* business investments. In fact, the price of the so-called shares had been set at the company's launch quite arbitrarily by Sergei Mavrodi himself.

Some failed investors, like businessman Kiril Konstantinovitch, claimed they knew what was occurring. *It had to happen*, he declared ruefully, *but I did think the game would go on a little longer and give me time to pull out. It seems I miscalculated.* (6)

Others, apparently still trusting MMM and its advertising, simply blamed the government for its *victimisation* of the company. After all, another MMM screen heroine – Marina Sergeievna, a lonely spinster – had found romance after buying her shares. But some Russian investors, according to commentator Elizabeth Anichkina, were natural victims of the system:

What post-Soviet Russia blatantly lacks are any rags-to-riches heroes whose fortunes are built on hard graft: the market stall holder who went on to build a supermarket empire... The Mavrodis hardly inspire a Protestant work ethic... The Communist ethic was a commitment to work and self-sacrifice and that is now discredited. In its wake the absolute reverse is immediately popular: getting the maximum possible with the minimum possible effort. Mavrodi, and his fellow millionaires – like German Sterligov, Artem Tarasov and Konstantin Borovoi – appear to have done it, as has the fictional Golubkov – it's the post-Soviet dream come true. (7)

■ Game, Set and Match

Masked tax police might have arrested Sergei Mavrodi and escorted him off to an undisclosed destination, but that was far from being the end of the story. The ex-head of MMM emerged from the Matrosskaya Tishina prison on the 13th October not to a lynching, as might have been expected, but to the warm congratulations of some 300 supporters. Having declared himself a candidate in a forthcoming by-election for the Russian parliament, he had been released on bail having promised to stay in Moscow. This is because Russia simply did not allow its potential MPs to languish in jail, even if they were on fraud and tax evasion charges. Not only that, there was the strong possibility of Sergei Mavrodi's achieving retrospective immunity as a duma member if he were elected. He clearly had everything to play for and the fact that many MMM investors now holding worthless paper thought him (and themselves) the victim of a government-inspired robbery added much to his *near-legendary status as the underdog.* (8)

The gods of fortune duly favoured him. He was supported in his election attempt by Vladimir Zhirinovsky, the leader of Russia's extreme nationalist party, and had no difficulty in winning over the electorate in the Moscow suburb of Mytishchi on the 31st October 1994 by promising to spend $10m on the constituency. The previous incumbent had, in fact, met a very sorry end. He had been gunned down in a Mafia-style murder the previous April, thus causing the bye-election. Once elected, Sergei Mavrodi did indeed find, as he had thought, that he could enjoy a much-needed parliamentary immunity from prosecution. (9)

When the national savings bank failed to attract savers' roubles with high enough interest rates, people turned to dodgy... schemes like MMM. When MMM collapsed... it dragged similar schemes down with it. The only safe investment left was dollars. Now the population's demand for dollars is cited as one of the causes of the rouble's plunge on Black Tuesday (over the fortnight to the 12th October the rouble had lost half its value against the $). Others were hefty government subsidies to... agriculture and defence which had to be paid at the cost of doubling the rouble supply.

EXHIBIT C6.1: MONEY ON TAP
Source: Russians know you can't buck the market,
Victoria Clark, *The Observer*, 16/10/94

■ **Sequel**

Once elected Sergei Mavrodi did not bother to attend the duma or even put out any sort of political programme. (10) According to John Plender, writing in early 1997,

> *his story speaks volumes about the easy-money atmosphere and heightened expectations of gain in modern Russia where the greenback has replaced the party card as the passport to power and influence.* (11)

Sergei's Mavrodi's wife was also very happy to take a leaf out of her husband's book when she sought election to the duma in a parliamentary by-election in 1997 in Tula, a his toric city 160 kilometres south of Moscow. Fortunately, or unfortunately, she failed in her attempt, having been forced to withdraw her candidacy at the last minute accused of having paid *agitators* to recruit voters. (12)

In fact, the lessons of the MMM affair were not hard to learn for many Russians.

Flemings, the Scottish fund management group, sensing a good emerging market opportunity in early 1998, forged a partnership with Guta bank, one of the more progressive Russian banks with the aim of launching the Fleming Guta Fund. Mark Jarvis, head of Flemings' Russian office, was a man of undeniable optimism with the $20 billion of Russian *mattress money* firmly in his sights. He declared:

In Brazil there is $60 per person in private pension funds. In Russia it is just 50 cents per person. Even if mutual funds here can attract five $ per person that implies ten times growth. (13)

Not only was his optimism misplaced, if the evidence of the eminent lack of success of the 23 domestic mutual funds launched over the previous two years was anything to go by. The Russian people were clearly still unwilling to part with their cash. But his timing was seriously off, as within six months, Russia was in catastrophic financial trouble. In fact, in August 1998, following the financial troubles afflicting Asia, the rouble lost two-thirds of its value and the market capitalisation of the country's 50 biggest companies had fallen to under $35 million, less than the value of Vodafone, the UK telecomms group. (10)

Having been bitten successively by hyperinflation, bank failures, fraudulent pyramid schemes like MMM and now currency instability, post-*perestroika* Russians kept their hands tightly on purses and wallets.

By 2000, however, the Russian economy had improved – chiefly because of a rise in the oil price and the ending of the Yeltsin regime – and a new system to try to protect the rights of shareholders was in place. Called the Investors Protection Association (IPA), it aimed at beefing up the Russian legal framework to stop violations of rights such as fraudulent bankruptcies, failure to comply with rules on disclosure, asset stripping moves and transfer of assets to friendly companies.

A new approach to shareholder protection, with rules for proper western-style corporate governance, would be, you might think, very welcome and bid goodbye to the MMM syndrome. But the head of the IPA, Dmitry Vassiliev, had been previously the chairman of Russia's Federal Securities Commission, where his campaign *to jail the perpetrators of pyramid schemes like MMM had provoked threats of violence*, was facing a difficult challenge. The past lack of legal framework and the economic shortcomings of the Yeltsin regime, had led to a situation where seven so-called oligarchs (key banking and industry tycoons like Boris Berezovsky and Mikhail Potanin etc.) had seized control of most of the big industry in Russia that had been privatised. In Vassiliev's view, a*s for the oligarchs, they hate me. They don't understand that it is impossible to have a market economy with only seven big guys. We need equal rules for all shareholders in Russia. And that's what they don't want.* (14)

REFERENCES

(1) Panic grips Russian investors, Peter Conradi, *The European*, 29/7-4/8/1994

(2) Russian financial scandal forces government to act, David Hearst, *The Guardian*, 29/7/1994

(3) Safe Russian markets can't be built in a day, *Business Week*, 15/8/1994

(4) Pyramid Power, John Plender, *The Financial Times*, 28/1/1997

(5) Russian 'pyramid' scam caves in, Helen Womack, *The Independent*, 30/7/1994

(6) Scam ends Russian Klondike, Marcus Warren, *The Daily Telegraph*, 29/7/1994

(7) As (6)

(8) As (6)

(9) Russian mystery moneyman is an unlikely people's hero, Elizabeth Anichkina, *The European*, 5-11/8/1994

(10) Rocky rouble shoots skywards as MMM mastermind walks free, *The Independent*, 14/10/1994

(11) As (4)

(12) Chess champ and ex-KGB chief fight for poll checkmate, John Thornhill, *The Financial Times*, 10/2/1997

(13) Rated on a par with the Ivory Coast: Russia, John Thornhill, *The Financial Times*, 1/8/1998

(14) Shareholders for a civil society unite, John Plender, *The Financial Times*, 3/8/2000

THE BERLIN CLIMATE CONGRESS OF 1995

Questions:

Why do different nations have different approaches to reducing environmental pollution? What does this tell you about their values?

Why is France so keen to cut back on gas emissions, yet so adamant about continuing with its updating of its nuclear capacity?

Explain the USA position.

■ The French dilemma

The French government faced a dilemma of considerable magnitude in early 1995. The problem was the pressure from its military to resume live testing of France's nuclear weapons. Specifically, navy chiefs wanted to perfect the firing mechanism and check the load capacity of France's newest nuclear device, the M5 submarine-launched missile.

The dilemma was caused by two factors.

The first was the 1993 decision by France's President Mitterand to suspend the country's nuclear testing programme and to state publicly that as long as he was in office, they would not be resumed. Of course, the ending of his Presidential term in 1995 brought the issue again into focus. More importantly, however, it was the question of international objections which France had to deal with.

The USA, France and Russia had taken up identical positions on halting nuclear testing in the early 1990s and had not wavered since. By contrast China and the UK had continued with their programmes. Not that France had always remained in step with the others. In fact, in the 1960s General de Gaulle had carried on with France's series of tests in the Sahara and in Polynesia, whilst the USA and the USSR were observing a two-year moratorium.

The challenge for the French military in this situation was increased by their knowledge that the number of Soviet and USA nuclear weapon tests had each exceeded their own by a margin of at least 4:1. It was also increased by the amount of public hostility, both domestic and international, against anything that increased the possibility of use of nuclear weapons.

The second factor was the position taken by France at two international conferences on the issue of improving the global environment: the Rio Congress Earth Summit in 1990 and the Berlin Climate Congress of 1995. France was highly supportive of any move to clean up the world.

It was now evident, however, that France's position on combating the *green-house effect*, the theme of these two Congresses, was diametrically opposed to its position on nuclear testing. To critics, a strange and unrealistic value combination.

In Rio, France had pledged, as had all the other 177 participants, that it would carry out an inventory of gas emissions which had the effect of warming the earth (see Table C7.1 below). At Berlin her representatives conferred with delegates from the 166 countries which had ratified the Rio accord to further underline her commitment to action. France had also pressed its views on oil-producing countries as well as China, which was strongly opposed to the convention. The aim of the Congress was to test how willing states were to increase their individual contributions to cutting back the rise in global warming. The aim of some leading countries, like France, was quite specific: to cut back gas emissions in such a way that the level in the year 2000 would not exceed that registered in 1990.

Unpublished research by the US Environmental Protection Agency indicated that, possibly due to the global warming effect, there had been a steady loss of population of some cold-water fish in its rivers. Fish such as brown trout and salmon are known to be especially susceptible to minor changes in water temperatures.

EXHIBIT C7.1: FISH IN DANGER

It was not a simple debating matter, however, at least in terms of principle. There was widespread disagreement on the nature and causes of global warming. Clearly, France aimed to set a good example to all.

When it came to issues of practical substance, however, the differences in attitudes among participants were even more marked. There were big disputes in terms of the effects on the global ecology from countries who were at different stages of their economic development. The views of poor and rich countries were markedly different.

Highly-developed industrialised countries, which were heavy users of carbon-based fuels, claimed to have recognised their problems and asserted that, since the 1980s, they had made ample progress to curb emissions. Those countries who were in the developmental phase of industrial growth were either economically poorly-placed (Brazil) or unwilling (China) to bear the burden involved.

China alone was very much a case in point since the country was thought to be responsible, because of her heavy coal usage for electricity generation, to be responsible for ten percent of all the emission of CO_2 into the earth's atmosphere. And many experts also thought that level of coal usage by China could well triple by 2020. (1) In the view of many impartial observers, this boded ill for the entire world.

Country	Carbon Dioxide Emissions (Tonnes/Inhabitant)	Energy use (Gigajoules per Inhabitant)
West Germany prior to unification	11.6	184
France	6.9	164
Japan	8.9	145
USA	20.8	317
China	2.2	25
World average	4.1	63

TABLE C7:1 WHO WAS WHO IN GLOBAL WARMING IN 1991
Source: *Frankfurter Allgemeine Zeitung,* 28/3/95

Examples of the way in which different national approaches varied are given by the cases of the USA and Germany. In the former, under the provisions of the USA Clean Air Act, it was quite possible for polluters to continue legally to pollute simply by buying *rights*.

These *rights* were tax benefits obtained by those who had taken action to cut pollution themselves. Such rights were, in fact, on sale on the Chicago market and constituted a form of insurance. The legislation was intended to support the principle that the *polluter should pay* – either directly or by foregoing the tax advantage in the rights gained by non-polluters.

Germany, in part due to its high concern for nature and in part due to its geographical location within Europe, was vitally concerned with limiting pollution. Not only had it committed itself to reducing 30 percent of its carbon dioxide emissions between 1987 and 2005, but there was even public discussion of a carbon tax.

Thus Chancellor Kohl, began the Congress with a ringing challenge to participants to produce legal and binding commitments to achieve the Congress goal. This was not seen as a problem by France. Indeed, its delegation, led by minister Michel Barnier, had been mandated to seek not just a stabilisation of nations' emissions by 2000, but an actual reduction. (2)

The French *dirigiste* position ran counter to that of the permissive British stance and also to that of the International Chamber of Commerce (ICC) which argued against any hasty move. (3) Perhaps this should not be surprising as the head of the ICC's Delegation to the Congress was, in fact, Clement Malin, Texaco's VP of International Relations.

Carbon Dioxide Emissions in Germany			
By energy users (tonnes) – 1987		By causes of emission (%) – 1990	
Oil	349	Energy production	43
Gas	120	Industry	16.7
Coal	600	Transport & Traffic	15.7
		Household	19.2
		Other	5.4
TOTAL	**1069**	**TOTAL**	**100**

TABLE C7.2: CAUSES OF CARBON DIOXIDE POLLUTION IN GERMANY
Source: *Frankfurter Allgemeine Zeitung, 28/3/95*

On the sixth of April 1995, as the Congress drew to a close, delegates decided to support a study into what was called *joint implementation*. This would allow rich Western polluters to offset their continuing levels of pollution by covering the costs of developing energy and efficiency schemes in the emerging world. The principle was exactly the one endorsed in the USA's Clean Air Act. Critics said this all added up to *a strategy of no action* on global warming.

And, within six months of France's support for *a strategy of positive action* on global warming, she was preparing to run the gauntlet of world opinion by carrying out a series of nuclear tests at the Muraroa atoll in French Polynesia in the South Pacific. These were duly carried out in late 1995. The big question was *why*?

REFERENCES

(1) L'effet de serre oppose riches et pauvres, Roger Caris, *Le Figaro*, 10/4/1995

(2) As (1)

(3) As (1)

THE WORLD CLIMATE CHANGE
CONFERENCE OF 2000

Questions:

Explain why nations continue to hold such different opinions as to the right course of action of global warning.

How strongly held are these opinions?

Why did John Prescott and Dominique Voynet cross swords?

■ Crossing swords

The World Climate Change Conference held in November 2000 finished with a bang, rather than a whimper as its predecessor, the Berlin Congress of 1995, had done. The marathon 12-day attempt to get world leaders to agree on a programme to actually reduce greenhouse gas emissions broke up on the 25th in what commentator David Harrison called *ignominious and embarrassing circumstances.* (1) It did not even come close to meeting the requirements of the Kyoto Protocol, the greenhouse gas treaty signed by all leading countries in 1997.

To many of its hostile critics, the USA seemed not to have changed its position on greenhouse gases from that which had caused such dissension in Berlin. The strategy it was advocating at the Hague now consisted of:

- leaving a certain amount of farmland fallow, i.e., not cultivating it; and
- planting more fast-growing, energy-absorbent plants, like elephant grass, from which a diesel substitute (bio-diesel) could be made; and
- protecting existing forests against felling.

The result of all three measures would be a USA pollution saving of 324 million metric tonnes of carbon dioxide on the current level – 600 million metric tonnes. But the USA was evidently protecting its farmers and, perhaps more importantly, its *gas-guzzling* car drivers. Perhaps not surprising in a presidential election year.

The European Union countries, by contrast, had already drawn up a series of wide-ranging measures to deal with what they saw as the real causes of the problem. These covered increasing energy efficiency for cars and homes and pollution-reduction schemes for power utilities, e.g., getting them to switch to ecology-friendly power types such as wind power, rather than continuing to emphasise coal and gas.

There was no disguising the fact that these two world powers were at loggerheads over the issue. Perhaps even worse, from the EU viewpoint, the USA was also advocating, along with Australia, Canada and Japan, a plan called the Clean Development Mechanism under which

- they should be permitted to plant massive new forests *in the developing world* (sinks) and, thereby, reduce their own obligation to curb *domestic* emissions; and

- possibly replace old pollution, absorption-poor forests with new types of pollution, absorption-rich trees.

According to Kalee Kreider of the highly vocal National Environmental Trust, this amounted to an *accounting con trick* which America was using *to get off the hook.* (2) She had a point since the USA was insisting that it meet its obligations under the Kyoto Accord – a reduction of greenhouse gas emissions by seven percent by 2010, *almost entirely outside the USA.*

Yet another point at issue was emissions trading between countries. The Kyoto protocol mirrored the American system in allowing those countries which have gained *points* for good behaviour (i.e., reducing emissions) to sell their points to others guilty of bad behaviour, thus reducing their own liability to pay. Because Russian industry had suffered a massive decline since 1990 (and, therefore, involuntarily reduced pollution levels) they had *points* to sell. The USA was wanting to buy. Result – a huge international outcry.

Emotions were clearly running high. So incensed was one protester over the USA plan for *sinks,* that she hurled a cream pie at America's chief negotiator, Frank Loy. After all, the USA did account for 36 percent of all the emissions from developed countries. And when an exasperated John Prescott, Britain's deputy prime minister, actually created a compromise *sinks* deal that he thought the EU and the USA would agree on, he found it rejected out of hand by the French. They accused Britain of *giving in to their USA friends.* John Prescott countered by accusing the French Environment Minister, Dominique Voynet of *getting cold feet* and *wrecking the green accord* and storming out of the meeting. (3) By any standards it was an unusual diplomatic squabble.

The next meetings of the Global Warming *roadshow* were scheduled for Bonn and Marrakech in 2001. They were bound to be interesting affairs as it was already known that the incoming US president, George W. Bush, thought that *global warming was a myth.* (4)

Not only did he think this, but in March 2001 he announced that meeting the Kyoto Protocol was not in the USA's interests. In effect, and much to the consternation of the European Union Members, he was ripping up the agreement.

REFERENCES

(1) Prescott is humiliated on climate, David Harrison, *The Sunday Telegraph*, 26/11/2000

(2) As (1)

(3) French wrecked green accord, Prescott says, Nick Nuttall, *The Times* 27/11/2000

(4) As (3)

WAWASAN 2020

Questions:

What is Wawasan 2020? What does it tell you about Malaysia's business culture?

Why are the Asia Pacific countries not so keen on free trade as the USA?

Which problems stand in the way of the likely long-run success of APEC and ASEM?

■ APEC

On the 27th November 1995 the annual meeting of the Pacific Rim Forum took place in Bangkok. This brought together more than 500 policy makers and business leaders from all over the region to discuss key economic development issues. On the agenda at this meeting were two key topics:

- a reassessment by Professor Paul Krugman of Stanford University of the widely-held view that Asia would be the next centre of the world economy; and
- a discussion of the results of the Asia-Pacific Economic Co-operation (APEC) summit that had taken place in Osaka, Japan the week before.

The first was something of an anti-climax. In Prof Klugman's view, it would not. The region's growth was simply unsustainably high. The second was much more intriguing.

APEC (Asia Pacific Economic Cooperation), an institution dating from 1989, is an official trade conference involving all the Pacific Rim trade partners. It is heavily promoted by the USA as a means of examining ways to promote *open regionalism*, i.e., trade specifically between Asia and America. From its establishment, its leaders had pledged to do away with all obstacles to regional trade and investment in member countries by 2020 and to open up various sectors of their economies to foreign ownership. Steps already taken by members towards reaching these goals were announced on the 19th November 1995 at the Osaka meeting.

However, whilst the USA had been heavily in favour of all aspects of free trade, Japan, China and South Korea had not shared president Clinton's enthusiasm for it. Also, Malaysia's leader Dr Mahathir Mohamad had again warned of the need for Asia to avoid allowing itself to be dominated by *outsiders*. Hence, the US was not pleased with the final Osaka communiqué in which APEC members promised to achieve trade liberalisation *steadily and progressively*. (1)

Without doubt, one factor which was causing problems was obvious imbalances in economic muscle. APEC contained rich *superpowers* such as the USA and Japan. It contained four first-generation *dragon economies* – Hong Kong, S. Korea, Singapore and Taiwan – and four developing *tiger economies*, too. These were Chile, Indonesia, Malaysia and Thailand. China, the biggest potential economy of all, was a powerful country waiting for its chance. If rated on a GDP/capita basis it was, however, comparatively poor. If rated on total GDP, it was among the world leaders.

> History will show that Malaysia actually saved last month's APEC meeting from... a breakdown. What was the problem? The trouble started in... Bogor in 1994. There the heads of government agreed to set targets for free and open trade by 2020. But how can any leader commit himself to set definite targets to open national markets, regardless of one's own national interests. There Malaysia alone dared to be different and expressed its opposition to the fixed time-frame.
>
> Then came the Osaka meeting. How could China, Japan, which have rice as their staple food, allow their rice production and trade to be open to competition from far more efficient producers? This is where Malaysia's insistence on the inclusion of the phrase "non-binding" won the day.

EXHIBIT C9.1: BEST WAY FORWARD?
Source: APEC – Lessons Learnt at Osaka, Tan Sri Ramon Navaratnam,
The New Straits Times, 2/12/95

Protectionism was another distinguishing feature which worried some nations. Japan, for instance, was totally hostile to opening up its still heavily-protected farm sector, whilst the USA was wholly opposed to Japan's keeping it so.

The Osaka end-product seemed a long way from the vision that had inspired the opening meeting of APEC in Seattle in 1989. It was equally distant from the free trade declaration of 1994 made by the members at APEC's Bogor summit in Indonesia where Asian members had wanted a *slowly-softly* approach to trade liberalisation and were against the USA's hard line on reciprocity in the removal of barriers. With this in mind, the pundits reckoned Osaka had been *a qualified failure.* (2)

What are the lessons for the US and its non-Asian supporters?

Firstly, they should not try to dominate us... It is easier to do so in the North of Asia where there are many strong cultural and ethnic bonds and a great deal of gratitude to the US...

Secondly, to be more sensitive to Asian culture. The "Dragons", "Tigers" and the developing countries are diverse and determined not to be dominated by alien prescriptions. It is better to work together with us rather than talk down to us. Do not try to lead Asians by the nose, especially when it is for your own benefit...

Thirdly, please keep your own house in order first before telling others what is good for their economies. After all, poor economic performances, untenable budgets and balance of payments deficits... are not good examples to emulate.

EXHIBIT C9. 2: DO NOT TRY TO BOSS US ABOUT, PLEASE
Source: APEC-lessons learnt at Osaka, Tan Sri Ramon Navaratnam,
The New Straits Times, 2/12/95

■ Malaysia: A Leading Tiger

In political terms, the publication of the official book *Malaysia Incorporated,* in September 1995 was an important event. Firstly, the book indicated the extent to which the development of Malaysia over the last decade had been modelled on the highly successful concept of *Japan Inc*, a concept seen in Malaysia as the basis for that country's post-war achievements. The idea was one of the closest possible collaboration between the Japanese private sector and the government.

Such a notion was seen by the international media, said Dr Mahathir Mohamad (or Dr M. as he was widely known), as *unethical and unhealthy*. But he reckoned it had been the best way to proceed with Malaysia's economic development and noted that *the policy has proven to be beneficial to all individuals and corporate citizens in the country.* (3) In proof of which, he cited the real GDP growth rate that the country had achieved over the previous seven years – a dramatic yearly average growth of eight per cent. Of course, public-private sector co-operation was only one element in the success. Another was *continued tax reforms as well as selective fiscal incentives to promote productive investments in new areas.* (4)

Despite faith in the Malaysia Inc model, however, all in Malaysia in the mid-1990s was not plain sailing. True, the country had transformed itself into an industrial power, having moved strongly up the value chain from its post-war colonial position as a commodity producer (palm oil, rubber, tin, tea) and little else to being a world class manufacturer of many industrial components and finished goods. True, foreign direct investment had flooded in to build up the country's infrastructure, as well as its industry. Now, however, imports were rising faster than exports, inflation was on the rise and skilled workers were getting scarcer. On top of this, the increase in wage costs had forced some movement of labour-intensive operations out of the country to cheaper locations.

Dr Mahathir himself did not share worries about the overheating of the Malaysian economy, however. It was a case of *Full Steam Ahead.* As he said to a December meeting of the National Economic Forum, Malaysia's Wawasan 2020 (or Vision 2020) was all-important. He declared:

Merely slowing growth is not the answer, since many countries with slow growth have also been faced with balance of payment deficits. The ultimate objective that we should aim for is a Malaysia that is a fully developed country by the year 2020. (5)

Indeed, as commentator Edward Gargan pointed out, Wawasan 2020 was an ever-present fact of life in mid 1990s Malaysia. It was *emblazoned on billboards, the sides of buses and in countless slick pamphlets.* Nor could anyone deny the real pace of progress in this dynamic country. Everywhere there was building and roadmaking. The new rail systems, connecting Kuala Lumpur and Port Klang, the major new airport and the Pergau hydro-electric dam, were all examples of progress. And, towering above all in Malaysia's capital city, the world's two tallest buildings were quickly taking shape. Hence, few inside the Malaysian government could, or would, share the First Boston Bank's view that it was time to be *strongly negative on Malaysian equities.* (6)

There is a growing perception that Malaysia is an area ripe for expansion. Its people are becoming more wealthy and it is politically stable. Riding along on a growing economy and fuelled by one of the world's most ambitious privatisation programmes, the stock exchange at Kuala Lumpur has expanded rapidly in recent years and is the biggest in Southeast Asia. Although activity is not as frenetic as in the heady days of 1993 and the economic fundamentals picture is not all rosy, local brokers feel the market has matured and steady growth is forecast.

EXHIBIT C9.3: JAM TODAY AND TOMORROW
Source: Malaysia set for growth, *The European*, 24-30/8/95

In fact, more was on offer. According to deputy prime minister Anwar Ibrahim, Malaysia had every intention of not just remaining one of Asia's largest stock markets but of wholly outpacing Singapore as the *premier financial center in the region*. (7) The plan was to open its long-protected capital markets, to expand derivative trading, to invite in foreign fund management operations and to underpin all of this with the appropriate regulatory infrastructure.

Again, this approach was predicated on the *Malaysia Incorporated* concept. To achieve its purposes, the government held in-depth annual dialogues with the leaders of the private sector to ensure that government policies were fine-tuned to business needs. Business success meant government success and vice versa.

■ And so to ASEM

At the start of March 1996, Asian and European leaders met together in Bangkok for a pioneering get-together of their own. The Europeans were anxious to begin to create the sort of linkage that had been established within the APEC framework. Everybody who was anybody was at the inaugural ASEM (Asia-Europe Meeting) of 26 European leaders and leading statesmen from South-East Asia, China, Japan and South Korea. But no one was expecting a specific output from the summit as, for instance, along the lines of the Bogor commitment by APEC members.

There was, nonetheless, a powerful set of agendas on both sides. The Europeans were keenly interested in raising their investments in Asia-Pacific. Having recently concentrated their efforts on building up the European Union and Central Europe, the EU's direct investment in this region had gone down in percentage terms – from 5.1 percent of all foreign direct investment (FDI) in 1990 to 2.8 percent in 1993. The Asia-Pacific side was equally keen to attract European FDI, firstly, because it would help to counter-balance the US influence in the region and, secondly, because it could contribute much to infrastructural development (the Mekong delta project, for example). Both sides were equally keen to improve access to each other's market-places.

For some in Europe the event is mere schmoozing. there is no real agenda and not much to expect by way of formal agreements... However, Europe will have been forced to consider exactly what sort of relationship it wants with a region that is rapidly becoming pivotal... Yet there are hurdles... One is a European lack of understanding of Asia's laid-back style. This focuses on informal contacts between leaders with no negotiation, no head-on confrontation over difficult issues and the sketchiest of pre-set agendas. While the process is as important as substance to Asians, the Europeans like hard-nosed talking with more tangible results.

EXHIBIT C9.4: A CLASH OF STYLES
Source: Door open to wider Europe-Asia links, Peter Montagnon
and Ted Bardacke, *The Financial Times*, 26/2/96

ASEM had its question marks however, as Exhibit 4 above, shows. Perhaps the most contentious was the attitude of some of the Europeans to the vexed question of human rights in some Asian countries. Apart from specific matters of concern to particular countries, a general anxiety was shared by some mainland EU members (who feared, not without good reason, they were losing some of their global competitiveness because of high pay and social security costs) about the comparatively-low labour costs typical in some parts of Asia. Naturally, in their minds, the issue of low pay was connected with that of an absence of employment rights, which would be seen as unthinkable back home.

On topics connected with this subject there was no shortage of data. For example, the International Labour Organisation's report of February 1996 entitled *International Labour Migration of Asian Women* and the United Nations Development Programme's *1995 Human Development Report.* Both of these illustrated inequalities of treatment of Asian women in work and in power structures. Low-cost child labour in certain parts of Asia was also a matter of great concern. (8)

However, EU members were keen not to raise such potentially divisive questions. Perhaps not surprisingly in view of pointed comments by the Indonesian foreign minister, Ali Alatas, He said:

For the first ASEM dialogue to be successful, controversial and non-relevant issues should not be brought up. I can think of at least ten issues to seriously embarrass the Europeans but we're not bringing them up. (9)

Hence the ASEM ended happily, with Jacques Santer, EU Commission president, pointing out that almost 40 percent of EU imports of manufactured goods would soon be duty-free and that, within a decade, its tariffs on other products would have fallen by a third. The EU was thus showing its commitment to open regionalism. *The EU* he declared *is open-minded and outward-looking. So let me underline that Asia is welcome in Europe – as partners, traders, investors and friends.* (10)

REFERENCES

(1) Free trade disarray puts damper on hopes for Asia-Pacific summit, Kevin Rafferty, *The Guardian*, 16/11/1995

(2) Asia-Pacific region takes big steps to end trade barriers, Peregrine Hodgson, *The Times*, 17/11/1995

(3) Factors behind strong growth, Vijayan Menon, *The New Straits Times*, 1/12/1995

(4) As (3)

(5) Malaysia's economy: will boom turn to bust?, Edward Gargan, *The International Herald Tribune*, 3-4/2/1996

(6) As (5)

(7) As (5)

(8) Malaysia lures brokers, Kevin Murphy, *The International Herald Tribune*, 19-20/8/1995

(9) Asia warns EU on human rights, Ted Bardacke, *The Financial Times*, 7/12/1996

(10) Bangkok summit redefines links, Michael Richardson, *The International Herald Tribune*, 2-3/3/1996

THE CASE OF THE LOOSE CANNON

Questions:

Why did Dr Mahathir react as he did to the situation facing Malaysia?

How justifiable are his views?

■ Economic Crisis in Asia Pacific

Many people say that I often shoot from the hip declared Malaysia's Prime Minister Mahathir bin Mohamad. *Some say I'm a loose cannon. Perhaps they are right.* (1) Coming at the end of a month which had seen a 30 percent fall in the value of the Malaysia ringgit, a massive decline in the value of the country's stock market and a well-publicised public spat between him and the leading international financial investor, George Soros, such a statement certainly needs investigation.

In fact, the nature and causes of Malaysia's problems in 1997 were common to all countries in the Asia Pacific region, even including Japan and Hong Kong. What had happened was that economies such as those of Thailand, the Philippines and Indonesia had developed at a substantially higher rate in the previous 20 years than any part of the developed world. Their growth was primarily export-led and concentrated in particular industries such as electronics, high-tech manufacture and tourism in which such countries initially had substantial competitive advantage, e.g., in unit labour cost.

Economic development led to increasing prosperity in the Association of South East Asia Nations (ASEAN) trade bloc region as a whole and to a mood of optimism. This encouraged large-scale infrastructure projects, like road/rail networks, dams and forest clearance. Such nations sought, and are still seeking, to further build up their economic bases and make them industrially strong – to move, in a word, from being developing to developed countries. To ensure stability, a necessity if they were to attract foreign direct investment, countries like Malaysia, Thailand and Hong Kong (prior to the hand-over to China) pegged their currencies to the USA $.

As in the case of Mexico in 1994, the Asia Pacific Rim thus became a *Mecca* for domestic and international investment capital, increasingly for use in office building and hotels. Credit came to be so freely available that speculators took excessive advantage of it and built to glut levels. With money supply (domestic credit and imported capital) rising more rapidly than GDP growth (the ability of the economy to create rising wealth), something had to give. And, in 1997, it was the value of the Thai baht. This currency was exposed as being heavily over-valued and, once the country had severed its linkage with the USA $ on July the second, the baht was even more savagely attacked by foreign exchange speculators as well as by international investors.

Thailand was Malaysia's neighbour. Like other members of the ASEAN trade bloc, had been seeking to transform itself into a leading centre for high-tech manufacturing. But, even by the end of 1996, it was becoming increasingly obvious that the eight percent plus growth rate trend of the ten years to 1994 was totally at an end and that the Thai economy was, in effect, experiencing a slump. Industrialists like Texas Instruments were shifting their factories to cheaper locations (such as Vietnam), large amounts of brand-new office blocks were left without tenants. Those with money were increasingly spending it on high-cost imported goods, many of which were, in terms of the country's long-term growth pattern, uneconomic luxuries. Speculators started to sell the currency, pessimism grew and the value of shares fell dramatically. As the shares were, in many cases, collateral for corporate loans, the ability of companies to repay them diminished and the credit worthiness of major banks became suspect. By the sixth of August the government had had to close down half the country's banking network. Eventually there was panic on the markets, to the point that the IMF was called upon to intervene and stabilise the situation. Whereupon, the speculators moved in force to other targets – like Malaysia.

■ Spotlight on Malaysia

The onslaught on Malaysia's currency and stock market in 1997 was such that it left banks and construction companies reeling. Under these circumstances, major corporates instinctively turned to the Prime Minister with an urgent request for the government to prop up their share values. One such was Renong, an octopus-like conglomerate with 17 subsidiaries in banking, construction and telecommunications. With over $1 billion in yearly sales, this chaebol-type company stood at the very heart of the Malaysian economy. Not only was the company now highly over-leveraged (too heavily-dependent on borrowed money), but the collapse in its share value was damaging all other companies and banks with which it traded and those in whom it had investments. Political pressure by members of Dr Mahathir's party, the United Malays National Organisation (UMNO), on the government machine rose dramatically over the period from April to September. After all, they felt obligated because it was the government itself that had built up Renong to its giant status from 1988 onwards.

Eventually, on the 24th of August, Dr Mahathir did intervene with an edict outlawing the short-selling of stocks and shares. The intention was to provide relief to Malaysian companies against speculators who deliberately sold their stocks in a falling (*bear*) market in the hope of buying them back more cheaply and who, thereby, forced market prices downwards. To make this happen, he spoke of a 60 billion ringgit share-support fund to buy back shares at premium prices from locals and at market rates from outsiders.

Given the broader base of the Malaysian economy and the lower level of foreign debt carried by most of its manufacturing sector, it was thought by the government that this action would stabilise matters. But it was not to be. The sheer weight of international speculative money and Malaysia's inability to ring-fence itself in the open global trading world of international finance were simply too much. And once foreign fund holders, particularly USA and British pension funds, realised that they could not so easily dispose of their stock because of the new rule, international sentiment worsened further. By 29th August the ringgit was at a 26-year low.

This was, however, not the only action that the Prime Minister had taken to try to ward off the attacks. Intensely proud of the turnaround his government had achieved in the country's economy since independence and of its ambitious *Wawasan*, or Vision 2020, plan for the future, he had turned up the heat in the situation by attacking the speculators themselves for what they were doing. They were *rogue traders* and *international criminals*. One, in particular, was singled out for blame: George Soros.

■ Powerful sentiments

The bitterness felt when Dr Mahathir had to bow to economic reality and remove the curbs on short selling and so restore faith in the share market could not be concealed. George Soros was labelled *a moron* and someone who was robbing the poor to give to the rich. (2) The Prime Minister even saw hints of an anti-Muslim conspiracy in what had happened. (3) Having been the country's leader for sixteen years and brought it a respectable security, he was now faced with immense loss of face. As he pointed out:

I am quite sure that the western press will be clapping and say that south-east Asian brownies cannot manage their economies. They will celebrate in jubilation. (4)

Notwithstanding the arguments in favour of freedom in the international financial market place and the sometimes beneficial nature of currency devaluation, Dr Mahathir maintained his stance. Speculators were *racists... not happy to see us prosper* (5), the borderless world of finance was *a jungle of ferocious beasts* (6), and the IMF, far from helping countries that had fallen on hard times, was only interested in saying *I told you so*. In fact, it was clear that the Prime Minister regarded the forces ranged against him as a sort of latter-day economic colonialism trying to do Malaysia down.

Not only, however, did the government have to retract the share-support plan, the notion of forcing Malaysian pension funds to spend £12b on buying shares having found no support, but it also had to cut back on some treasured infrastructure projects and slow down on others. There were indications that the mighty Bakun dam development was caught up in this.

The official view was that the crisis had set the country back ten years. Indeed, to reach the sort of developed country status, demanded within the Wawasan framework, would take a virtually unattainable seven percent average annual growth rate from 1998 through to 2020. Worse, this was the result, according to Dr Mahathir, not of normal international business pressures, but of *a manipulated economic crisis.* No wonder Dr Mahathir reckoned that currency dealing, other than that specifically required for trade financing, was *unnecessary, unproductive and immoral.* (7)

George Soros' riposte to Dr Mahathir's outbursts was characteristic of a man who was one of the world's most powerful investors. Speaking in Hong Kong on the 21st September, on the eve of an IMF/World Bank meeting preoccupied with the upheavals in the Asia Pacific region, he declared:

Interfering with the convertibility of capital... is a recipe for disaster. The Malaysian Prime Minister is a menace to his own country. (8)

REFERENCES

(1) Malaysia leader sees hidden Jewish agenda, Thomas Fuller, *The International Herald Tribune*, 11-12/10/1997

(2) Malaysia lets demons enter its doors again, Nick Cumming, *The Guardian*, 5/9/1997

(3) Mahathir denies rumours he will quit, James Kynge, *The Financial Times*, 7/10/1997

(4) As (3)

(5) As (2)

(6) Soros criticises Malaysian PM, John Ridding and James Kynge, *The Financial Times*, 22/9/97

(7) As (6)

(8) As (6)

TIME ENGINEERING

Question:

Discuss the problems of restructuring Time Engineering in the light of your view of Malaysia's business culture.

■ Time in Trouble

In mid-2000 Time Engineering, the giant Malaysian telecommunications company, was in great difficulty. Almost in receivership, it owed no less than £870m to its creditors, all of whom were pressing for an urgent restructuring plan. On the 12th July it was due to present such a plan. Early indications were that it would consist of the purchase of a 30 percent stake by Khazanah, Malaysia's state investment company and a possible link-up with a foreign partner.

Quite apart from the specifics of this business rescue attempt, Time Engineering was interesting to external analysts as a symbol of the extent to which

- Malaysia was able and willing to restructure companies that had taken on board *mountains of domestic debt* in the growth years of the mid-1990s, a process which some commentators saw as far too slow; (1) – and

- there had been any change whatsoever in the cosy relationship between government and business in that country. Traditionally, this amounted to a business culture *in which politicians and tycoons conspire together to protect companies from having to realise losses, sack workers or cede control to outside professional management.* (2)

The situation of Time Engineering was especially problematic in both areas because it was the largest subsidiary of the country's flagship Renong group and because its debt crisis was occurring at a time when the stock market was depressed.

Any failure to come to a deal with creditors would further undermine the Malaysian market, but any artificial agreement, with Time Engineering shares being simply shuffled around without strategic change and redundancies, would be equally bad. Lai Tak Heong, analyst at SG Securities, added a further complexity by saying that Malaysia simply was not able to copy Japan's style of capitalism which had allowed for the slow restructuring of industry. *We can't have Japanese culture*, he reckoned *because we don't have Japan's wealth behind us.* (3)

So, the big issue was not whether Time Engineering could be saved – but how.

■ Dr Mahathir's perspectives

Malaysia's prime minister, Dr Mahathir Mohammad, strongly supported the modernisation programme – and the corporate restructurings – that the country was pursuing. The situtation was, however, not of the country's choosing. It had been forced on the country, he said, by the impact of the speculative attack that had been mounted against all countries in the region in 1998 by international financiers. Malaysia had suffered unfairly because, although it did not have excessive foreign borrowings like other ASEAN countries, it was lumped together with them.

But the restructuring process was not to be undertaken without a great deal of care, he said. Indeed, in his view, it should not involve selling off parts of certain firms to foreigners. *Otherwise, he said, we would be merely workers for foreign companies.* (4) Nor should the rules of the international money game remain so one-sided. As things stood, Malaysia and other developing countries were obliged to have transparent financial regimes, but there was no regulation of speculators. *Countries that are rich and do not feel they are at risk,* he considered, *feel everything is OK and they are making a lot of money.* (5)

The subject of money was certainly a big issue in the potential restructuring of Time Engineering – or, more specifically, the Islamic attitude to the funding of capital. This is because the strict principles of Sharia law severely constrain the investments that Muslims can make. Islamic funds traditionally could not invest in non-Islamic banks or other financial services that charged interest, since charging interest was seen as usury and branded as sinful. They would also have nothing to do with companies which made or marketed alcohol, pork or pornography. Hotels and gambling companies were avoided as were highly-leveraged companies (i.e., those with high debt-to-equity ratios).

Times do change, as Laurent Chapuis, head of Islamic equities as the Geneva-based Pictet and Cie, one of Switzerland's largest private banks, indicated:

Whilst stock market investments were taboo areas for most devout Muslims until the early 1990s, an equity culture has since been growing fast among Muslim investors who have realised that they miss out on investment opportunities under strict Sharia laws. Many are moving out of strict Muslim accounts into international equities. (6)

It must be admitted, also, that Time Engineering's problems were occurring against a political backcloth which was not as reassuring as that which had applied when Dr Mahathir's visionary plan for transforming Malaysia – WAWASAN 2020 – had been launched. For a start, there had been a major recent shift in Malaysian politics over the trial and imprisonment of Anwar Ibrahim, the deputy prime minister, on charges of sodomy and corruption. Political activism was on the march and the Malaysian leader was said to be cracking down on opponents with *a new ruthlessness.* (7) Secondly, Dr Mahathir himself was due to quit politics in three years' time. Thirdly, his WAWASAN attempts to instil in the bumiputra – the indigenous Malay population – an entrepreneurial spirit (along with a redistribution of wealth) were simply not bearing fruit. He claimed:

It's a problem of having to change the culture of the people. To them, money is a mere convenience that they carry in their pocket. They don't look upon money as capital. You have to change their mindset. I have found that people in communist countries are just like that, too. (8)

This had done little to reduce the tenseness of the relationship between the bumiputra and the Chinese and Indians, whose wealth and entrepreneurship led them to dominate the Malaysian economy, when the Asian crisis of 1998 struck.

The question of the extent to which Islamic fundamentalists were opposed to the sort of technological development needed by the

Malaysian modernisation programme was also a prime issue for Dr Mahathir. In his opening address to the Organisation of the Islamic Conference (OIC) in Kuala Lumpur in June 2000, the 74-year old leader declared:

> *By failing to develop the Muslim countries...we are committing even greater sins from which our personal devotion to the rituals of our faith will not absolve us. In the end, we will become like banana republics where the managers of the plantations in the countries are more powerful than the presidents in them. At that stage, we will no longer be independent.* (9)

REFERENCES

(1) Time may spur Malaysia's shake-up, Sheila McNulty and Peter Montagnon, *The Financial Times*, 12/7/2000

(2) As (1)

(3) As (1)

(4) Mahathir's last stand, William Dawkins, Richard Lambert and Peter Montagnon, *The Financial Times*, 6/10/2000

(5) As (4)

(6) Private banking 2000, Elif Kaban, *The Financial Times*, 7/7/2000

(7) Crackdown in Malaysia, *The International Herald Tribune*, 9/1/2001

(8) As (4)

(9) Mahathir urges Muslims to embrace technology, Sheila McNulty, *The Financial Times*, 28/6/2000

THE AGRICULTURAL COMMISSION OF NORTH KOREA

Questions:

Describe life in North Korea.

What sort of report would the Agricultural Commission take home?

How should America deal with North Korea?

■ Sic transit tyrannus

In 1994 North Korea's *Great Leader*, Kim Il-sung, died, leaving behind him what appeared to be a legacy of little value. His son, Kim Jong-il, was elected general secretary of the Korean Workers' Party, the country's most powerful post, on the eighth of October 1997 as a replacement. He now led an administration that had to deal without delay with the threat of mass starvation and a collapsing economy. The period between the two events was one in which, on the one hand, Mr Kim was able to stick to Confucian convention in mourning his father, and on the other, the problems of the country mounted inexorably.

Underlying the immediate difficulties was the fact that Kim Il-sung had ruled North Korea with an iron hand since 1948. Under his leadership the country had looked more like a feudal monarchy than the communist state it was represented to be. The critical issue now was whether the new "Dear Leader" would follow the path of reform or would seek to maintain faith with the stonewalling ways of his father.

There were indications of change. The North Korean government signed a landmark deal with the USA within four months of Kim Il-sung's death which involved Pyongyang's abandoning its suspected nuclear weapons programme in exchange for £3 billion worth of nuclear reactors. Then there were talks:

- with the USA and Japan about the possibility of foreign direct investment and technology transfer
- with the World Bank and the Asian Development Bank on funding and the potential establishment of free trade zones at Nampo and Rajin-Sobang.

But it was difficult to establish precisely whether significant economic change could occur in such a totalitarian framework without commensurate political change. And the two North Korean diplomats who defected to the USA in 1997 did not help their country's situation much. In fact, they indicated that economic reform was not at the top of the country's agenda. By contrast, they turned out to be of inestimable help to the Americans in the USA internal debate on:

- whether current peace talks – to replace the armistice of 1953 and bring a final end to the bloody Korean peninsula conflict – could actually be brought to any sort of conclusion;
- what could be done to control the country's hyper-militarised 23m strong population, when and if it were, in fact, de-regimented.

■ Visitors for a hungry land

Barbara Crosette, writing in the *International Herald Tribune*, called them *visitors from a hungry land*. (1) They were in fact the delegates in a party of agriculturists sent by the Agricultural Commission of North Korea to tour the USA. Their invitation had come not from the administration but from a USA agricultural consultant of Korean descent, Pilju Kim Joo. The plenty they saw on their USA tour must have contrasted sharply with the utter destitution they left behind in their own country. The USA could not have been seen by them as anything other than a model of agricultural success, even though based on the principle of private farming.

A medical team from the World Vision charity visited five of North Korea's 12 provincial care establishments for orphans in mid 1997. These are all state-run, as were the country's factories and farms. Over 80 per cent of children under the age of two showed some signs of malnutrition. Older children were found to be "thin and stunted".

EXHIBIT C12.1: MALNUTRITION SIGNS IN NORTH KOREA
Source: North Korea faces mass starvation, Andrew Higgins, *The Guardian*, 12/8/97

In their homeland there had been two consecutive years of mass flooding interspersed by a summer-long drought. If coupled with the country's isolation from the rest of the world and a totalitarian approach to agriculture management that had in recent years reduced an already unproductive state-run farming system to chaos, it is not surprising that forecasts were being made of a 70 percent crop loss in 1997. Indeed, the fact that there was irrefutable evidence of widespread malnutrition (Exhibit C12.1 above) made talk of mass starvation realistic. The reason why the outside world did not see more of the developing tragedy was, according to Walt Santatiwat, Asia director of the World Vision charity, that it amounted to an *invisible famine* (2), due to Pyongyang's tight restrictions on travel and photography.

Despite the grain shipment help that the USA and South Korea was giving, the director of the Swiss government's foreign aid programme saw in it *a silent catastrophe of enormous proportions*, not seen since the famines of Ethiopia and Somalia. (3)

■ Down with the imperialists

In such a context, it is perhaps surprising to find the official communist party newspaper *Nodong Sinmun* reckoning that North Korea could, through its own efforts, *pull through any storm*. Echoing the reality of North Korea's siege economy, it recommended that citizens should be ready *to become human bombs and make a suicidal attack to defend the headquarters of the communist revolution.* (4) Whatever else, the North Koreans do not beat about the bushes when considering their enemies, the capitalist imperialists!

As if on cue, the country's arms negotiators broke off peace talks with the USA and South Koreans on the seventh of August 1997. The cause was disagreement on the topics the talks should address, one of which was the future of the 37,000 American troops still stationed in the heavily-militarised South. This was backed up later by North Korea's assertion that the USA was using economic sanctions and aid as a way of pressurising Pyongyang and by the North Koreans' withdrawal from separate talks to further slow-down the proliferation of nuclear missiles. In fact, they were alleging USA *blackmail*.

America, anxious to stop North Korea from selling its missiles to (so-called) *rogue states* like Iran, was again in a quandary. Just how would it deal with this secretive and unpredictable police state, one of the world's last, if not most entrenched, communist nations?

REFERENCES

(1) North Koreans seek famine's antidote, Barbara Crosette, *The International Herald Tribune*, 30-31/8/1997

(2) North Korea faces mass starvation, Andrew Higgins, *The Guardian*, 12/8/1997

(3) As (2)

(4) Korea talks open as food crisis in North deepens, John Gittings, *The Guardian*, 5/8/1997

FAMILY REUNIONS:
PYONGYANG AND SEOUL GET TOGETHER

Questions:

What does a Communist regime stand for?

What is business life like in North Korea?

Does Kim Il-Sung have much choice? Just how difficult would it be to change North Korea's culture profile?

■ Friends indeed?

In early December 2000, South Korea's president, Kim Dae-Jung, accepted the Nobel Peace prize at Oslo's City Hall. In his speech, he spoke movingly of two of the key episodes in his life:

- the fact that he had been sentenced to death by South Korea's former military rulers in 1980; and
- the accord he had struck with his North Korean counterpart, Kim Jong-Il, the authoritarian leader of Communist North Korea. This breakthrough agreement had led, in 2000, to two emotional cross-border meetings of families who had been kept apart since the Korean War of 1950-3.

The president had been awarded the prestigious prize for his *sunshine policy* of seeking closer ties between the two long-divided peoples. It was an award he would like to have shared, he said, with Kim Jong-Il.

The world had certainly moved on in a miraculous way since the death of Kim Jong-Il's aged father, Kim Il-Sung, who had been renowned for his implacable hatred of America and S. Korea and the democracy and market economy which, in varying degress, they both stood for. It was also curious in view of the nature of the still-isolated Pyongyang regime, an entrenched, embattled and poverty-stricken totalitarian country.

Why the shift? There was no doubt in the mind of commentator Lynne O'Donnell during a visit to Pyongyang in 2000. The reason was *a complete breakdown in the country's industrial base* as part of the knock-on effect of the collapse of North Korea's leading trade partner, the USSR. The legacy she found was one of famine, starvation and disease. China, its previously staunch ally, was apparently unable to help with the country's problem of industrial collapse. Across the city, she wrote:

people trudge from daybreak to sundown with a proletarian resignation...Above them the sky is clear and blue and unpolluted...Once the sun goes down, the city is enveloped by complete darkness as there is no power...The bulk of North Korea's 22 million people face starvation... but not the swaggering élite of the ruling Workers' Party. (1)

From her perspective, the nation's governing philosophy of self-reliance

– constantly paraded through propagandist martial music, choreographed rituals, gestures and songs – lay exposed as *a hollow mask*. But change seemed to be in the air.

USA Secretary of State, Madeleine Albright, made a visit in October 2000 to Pyongyang. Its published purpose was to discuss the possibility of North Korea's curbing what the USA called its *rogue-state* programme of developing and selling to others its Taepodong missile. But it was really about just establishing a dialogue with the outside world. As Kim himself pointed out, *I don't think the three hours of discussions we had were enough to break the silence of 50 years*. (2)

Certainly there is no absence of theorising to suggest that North Korea was pursuing its own self-interest in *cosying-up* to its partner. Aid from the South is needed, it was said, to spur a form of Chinese-style economic reform, which could be achieved without antagonising the Chinese. After all, went the argument, the latter are already strongly embracing free market changes and a failure to follow suit would be ruin for the North Korean economy.

But could it be that the leaders both recognised that the time was ripe to solve their own versions of the *Korean Dilemma*?

When he met with 50 senior South Korean media figures in August 2000, Kim Jong-il portrayed himself in a way that was at variance with the well-publicised *Dear Leader* persona needed for domestic consumption. In a three-hour meeting, wrote commentator John Gittings, he

> *delivered authoritative views on beef, wine, sexual inequality and his personal horse-riding and sleeping habits and spoke of Korean history without a trace of ideology.*

His leadership style was *confident* and he showed himself to be a proud nationalist, stating that *the smaller the nation, the stronger it must be to keep its pride*. It must have been an exciting breakthrough for the members of Kim's audience, rich and powerful executives coming from a rich and powerful country. It was as if, said Gittings, *the real Mr Kim stands up*. (3)

As for Kim Dae-Jung, he had long sought engagement with North Korea.

His pleasure at the ground-breaking deal agreed after his June 2000 visit to Pyongyang, as well as the detailed negotiations on the family reunions that took place in the resort area of Mount Kumgang in North Korea, was evident to all. Not only would *the loud-speaker war* that that been maintained for 15 years across the disputed border between the two countries cease, but two meetings of divided families would take place in August and December 2000.

To many observers it was a small but significant step in a hopeful direction and one which deserved the Oslo award. But, according to the more cautious *International Herald Tribune's* leader writer, the rapprochement strategy

> *raises the prospect of one of the world's most brutal regimes extracting a bailout from the South – and from other industrial democracies the North has been courting.* (4)

And there was no question of any change to the military approach the country had long pursued. A message from the Workers' Party published in North Korea's three leading newspapers on New Year's Day 2001 spoke of the central task for the coming year as:

> *Economic development to consolidate the existing economic infrastructure... conducting a forceful campaign for refashioning the national economy as a whole with up-to date technology... whilst strengthening the military capability.* (5)

REFERENCES

(1) Koreans starve but the Workers' Party gets fatter, Lynne O'Donnell, *The Sunday Telegraph*, 26/11/2000

(2) North Korea hints at deal, Doug Struck & Steven Mufson, *The International Herald Tribune*, 25/10/2000

(3) The real Mr Kim Stands Up, John Gittings, *The Guardian*, 15/8/2000

(4) Dilemma in Korea, *The International Herald Tribune* editorial, 17-18/6/2000

(5) North Koreans told to tighten their belts, *The International Herald Tribune*, 2/1/2001

REFORMING THE BANKING
SYSTEM OF JAPAN INC.

Questions:

Why, after so many years of financial rectitude, did the Japanese go on a credit binge from 1983 – 93?

What was involved?

What impression does the case give about the relationship between Japanese government, industry and the banking system?

Why has the reform process from 1993 - 2001 been so difficult?

■ See What Happens When Credit Gets Too Easy

By any stretch of the imagination, it was a bad business. The central problem was that, over the period 1983 to 1993, there had been a massive rise in lending by Japanese banks and non-bank financial institutions which had not been matched subsequently by an equal ability or desire on the part of borrowers to repay. Everyone – the public, the corporations, the banks, the prestigious "Big Seven" housing loan corporations (the *jusen)* and the government – was embroiled in the débâcle. It was a political as well as an economic embarrassment to a country renowned for its tight financial approach. Table C14.1 below, shows the scale of the difficulty in 1996.

Element	Japan	USA
Ratio of outstanding consumer credit to household disposable income in 1993 (%)	23.7	17.7
Annual average rate of growth of outstanding consumer loans over the period 1983-93 (%)	12.9	5.6
No. of bankruptcies in 1994 by comparison with those in 1989 (times)	4	N/A
Consumer cash loans as a % of the total consumer credit market	60.0	N/A

TABLE C14.1: CONSUMER INDEBTEDNESS IN JAPAN
Source: Japanese drown in a sea of easy credit, Michiyo Nakamoto,
The Financial Times, 13/2/96

What had occurred over the period 1983-89 to cause this problem was that, as Japan's prosperity had increased, consumer attitudes to debt had gradually relaxed. A growing consumer willingness in the mid 1980's to take out a loan, whether for capital items (house, car etc.) or merely for consumption (a night out, for example), had then been further stimulated. This had been done firstly, by the Japanese government's deregulation of the financial system and, secondly, by the rising eagerness of the lenders to fulfil their sacred mission of lending money.

The first created more competition to lend within the system, the second increased the pressure on the system to lend. The classic risk-return standards of both consumers and bankers slipped and the result was a *credit binge*, and, from 1990, when recession began to bite, a lot of distress. Take the typical case of Tokyo businessman Takehiko Ishihara. He declared:

I started out about ten years ago with just one credit card... By the time I knew I was in trouble, I had 19 and I was Y10m in debt... From around 1990, I had to borrow money simply to repay my debts. (1)

Perhaps this situation is not surprising if one bears in mind that several finance companies had even introduced automated teller machines which issued *on the spot* credit cards to those in need of immediate relief.

The *bad business* was, of course, the way in which the borrowing boom and the recession that hit Japan in the early 1990s had combined to leave Japanese banks with a huge bad debts problem. It amounted in November 1995 to Y13.5 trillion, a staggering sum. Five leading banks – Fuji, Sakura, Sumitomo, Sanwa and Dai-ichi Kangyo – accounted for 63 percent. Daiwa, a top-ten player with high ambitions, was involved to the tune of Y857 billion, for example. (2) Fortunately, the banks seemed to have succeeded in re-structuring over 50 percent of the outstanding indebtedness but they were, nevertheless, still left with a financial migraine.

An important element in the bad loan equation was the Y4.4 trillion owed by the *jusen* (housing corporations). Their suppliers of credit were the agricultural co-operatives and the banks, in the ratio of 1.5:1. The jusen had lent, and had been lent by their suppliers in their turn, substantial sums in the property development boom market of the 1980s only to find, when the downturn came, that borrowers were unable to service the loans and that the capital values of the properties against which the loans were secured had fallen.

The bad debt problem had, in its turn, focused heavy attention on the Japanese Ministry of Finance (MoF) since it was held accountable for policing the sector. Specifically, it was criticised for having sanctioned the lending relationships between the banks and the jusen and the jusen and property developers, as well as the loans themselves. Now such a degree of corporatism had turned everything sour.

The MoF has justly been described as *the single most powerful institution in Japan and architect of the country's development from post-war poverty to economic superpower.* (3) Its immense control, exercised by so-called *administrative guidance* over key areas of the economy (taxation, banking and finance, state assets and the budget), was legendary. Now it stood accused of having known of the problem of non-performing loans since 1991 and having taken no action to reduce either their number or size.

Japan's banking and real estate crisis gets messier by the minute and it is not at all clear that the Ministry of Finance's latest measures to deal with it will work any better than those of the past. One part of the problem that the MoF is finding it increasingly difficult to keep under its security blanket is the role corrupt officials and criminal gangs have played in laying waste to Japanese banks.

Toshio Yamaguchi, a former labor minister and deputy leader of the opposition New Frontier Party, has finally been arrested. That was after parliament removed his immunity to breach of trust charges that arose from last year's scandal surrounding the collapse of two large credit unions. He is alleged to have used his influence to obtain multimillion dollar loans for his family from the Tokyo Kyowa and Anzen credit associations.

EXHIBIT C14.1: A QUESTION OF CRIME
Source: Japan's Cozy Crooks & Banks, Michael Gonzalez,
The Wall Street Journal, Europe, 20/12/95

In the eyes of the public the MoF was to blame for the government's dilemma of how to solve the jusen crisis. On top of this, however, there were three extra problems that needed attention. Two were economic. The fact was that international bankers, fearing difficulties ahead with a possible banking crisis, had again begun to demand a small amount of extra interest on loans they were making to Japanese banks *(the Japan premium)*. This was increasing the cost of operations by putting up the cost of capital. Secondly, any attempt to sell off properties (to realise capital to pay off the loans) would simply depress property prices still further and be counter-productive.

The third problem was related to the extent to which the *yakuza* – Japan's crime syndicates – were rumoured to be involved in many aspects of the property loans crisis, to the point where this sector was considered by some to be *mafia-controlled*. (4) As investigations in 1996 and 1997 showed, both banks and brokers (like Nomura, Yamaichi etc.) had been heavily penetrated. Dai Ichi Kangyo was one bank to be given signal treatment for its lapses.

■ A Government in Trouble?

Public hostility towards the MoF was also aimed at the government itself. After all, the state of the Japanese economy in the early 1990s had been poor and the indicators in mid-1995 were still far from encouraging. Unemployment was officially stated as three percent (but widely acknowledged to be six percent), property prices had fallen from their peak in 1989 by almost 60 percent, over which period the yen had risen by 20 percent. 15 percent of all households were suffering from negative equity. As seasoned commentator Joanna Pitman pointed out, *the additional household wealth accumulated during the bubble years (i.e., when Japan's economy was booming in the mid-1980s) has all but been wiped out.* (5) Indeed, at the end of the bubble period, the Nikkei stock average had touched 40,000. As of November 1995, however, it was fluctuating between 18,000 and 19,000. To compound the *feel bad factor*, Makoto Kobayashi, vice minister of Japan's Economic Planning Agency, conceded in early December 1995 that the government's 2.8 percent target for GDP growth for the year ending 31st March 1996 would now not be achieved. *We're not sure that consumption will accelerate, because unemployment remains a concern* he said. The figure for the year looked like being one percent.

The growth rate was especially disappointing because of the manner in which the government had applied successive stimulus packages to the economy since 1992. These added up to no less than Y66 trillion. Also worrisome, in view of low interest rates, was the downward trend in

Japanese corporate capital investment within Japan.

It was in this context that the Japanese government were being told by the Federation of Bankers' Associations of Japan that, if the MoF required the banks to bear a disproportionate share of the costs of baling out the *jusen*, they would seek what was unthinkable in Japan: the *legal liquidation* (i.e., bankrupting) of the companies. The agricultural co-operatives had argued that, even though they themselves had been the biggest lenders to the jusen, the banks had in fact a greater responsibility because the jusen were owned by the banks. Catastrophe loomed. As can be imagined, much interest was focused on the publication in early December of the Bank of Japan's quarterly corporate survey, the *tankan*. What would its mood be? And, more importantly, what would the government do about the jusen crisis?

■ A Shock to the System

In the event, the news that most seized the public's attention in early December was the resignation of the Japanese prime minister, Tomiichi Murayama. As leader of the Social Democratic Party (SDP), he had been part of a coalition government in which the largest party, and the least left-wing, was the Liberal Democratic Party (LDP). This was headed by Ryutaro Hashimoto.

On the eleventh of January 1996 Mr Hashimoto was elected prime minister. In the eyes of most commentators, this strengthened the grip of the right-wing in Japanese politics, with both the government and the opposition New Frontier Party being led by Conservatives.

This was an interesting flashback to the situation before the general election of 1993, when Japan had been ruled continuously for 38 years by the LDP and when Ichiro Ozawa, the opposition leader, had himself been within the LDP ranks. Mr Ozawa had broken with the LDP over what was known as *the normal country debate* (*futsu no kuni*). At the heart of this was Mr Ozawa's backing for his promotion of the notion of strong leadership coupled with national self-reliance. This had proved a popular stance and had resulted in the squeezing of the Socialists between two powerful parties whose ideologies are contrasted in Exhibit C14.2 below.

> Mr Hashimoto... is a tough talker whose popularity soared when he successfully fought off American demands in trade talks last year... but his instincts lie with the status quo... He is unlikely to risk the ire of powerful bureaucrats, let alone the retailers and farmers who form the backbone of traditional LDP support, by championing the support Japan needs... He would settle for growth without real political change, relying mainly on classic Keynsian pump-priming... Mr Ozawa is the author of... Blueprint for a New Japan... He wants Japan to become a low-tax, laissez-faire economy, open to competition; and also a democracy in which consumers and voters are king.

EXHIBIT C14.2: MATTERS IDEOLOGICAL
Source: *The Times* editorial, 15/1/96

A key first task for Ryutaro Hashimoto was to handle the shock waves that had been caused by the eventual decision by the outgoing government on how to handle the jusen problem. In the event, they made up their minds to use Y685 billion of taxpayer's money (Y10,000 for each tax payer) to liquidate them.

Whilst, at least, the position of the financial community would not be damaged by this move (as it would have been had the banks gone ahead with their plan), it caused public outrage and was one of the reasons why Tomiichi Murayama had felt the need to step down. Intriguingly, there were those who thought Ryutaro Hashimoto somewhat vulnerable, not least *because, as the finance minister between 1989 and 1991, he should have reined in the runaway housing corporations but failed to do so.* (6) At all events, by late 1997 the Prime Minister was having to live with a Nikkei level of under 17,000.

■ Worse before better?

In October 1997 the Japan premium suddenly surged. The blame was put on the increasing visibility of the country's bad debt problem, caused by the collapse of the asset bubble, and the increasing difficulty of measuring its size. Despite the fact that Hokkaido Takushoka, a "city" bank was allowed to fail, the government pledge that it would protect the largest banks was still disbelieved. Until, that is, the Bank of Japan stepped in to *nationalise* (i.e., take into state ownership) the failing Nippon Credit bank in November 1998.

The turn-around came, however, in autumn 1998 with:

- demands by the government's Financial Supervisory Agency that there should be far stricter standards of disclosure on bad loans;
- a new government pledge of a further Y 450 billion of public funds to be injected into the capital base of Japanese banks. This would help to write off bad loans (42 percent), nationalise weaker banks (30 percent) and protect bank depositors (28 percent). This put the total injection of government aid to the banks in 1997 and 1998 at over Y1 trillion;
- the unleashing of a wave of bank restructuring – a *Big Bang* – sanctioned by government and involving the creation of bank groups (for the strongest banks) and nationalisation (for the weakest). The strongest banks were encouraged to declare publicly that they would apply for public funds.

It was clear that the Japanese government meant business. But would it all work? As analyst Gillian Tett pointed out:

Cutting costs alone is unlikely to boost profits, since most Japanese banks are surprisingly lean. Compared with Citicorp's 97,000 employees, Japan's top ten commercial banks employ 124,000 to manage six times the assets of the US bank. The problem appears to lie in a weak revenue base (i.e., turnover) and very low margins, which are about one-tenth of their US rivals'. (7)

It seemed that it would. Starting in January 1999, there began a large-scale wave of bank mergers and alliances among private pension providers – like the Mitsubishi and Sumitomo keiretsu – eager to take advantage of the liberalisation of the pension market as part of Big Bang expected in 2000. So, by late 2000, the ten commercial banks of 1998 were located inside four commercial groups: Sumitomo-Sakura, Dai-ichi Kangyo-Fuji-Industrial bank of Japan, Sanwa-Tokai and the bank of Tokyo Mitsubishi. The rigid categorisation of bank businesses which had kept competition in the financial services sector to a minimum was a thing of the past, as was the practice of not allowing new entrants into the industry. The result – *a slow move was under way from the bank lending that had dominated post-war Japan towards financing from the capital markets.* (8)

But this progress was not enough and the bad debt problem had not gone away. On September 2000, it was estimated that the entire financial system, after ten years of turmoil, still had bad debts of Y100bn. (9)

The country elected its eighth prime minister in eight years in mid-April 2001 against a background of continuing economic malaise. The Nikkei average stood at one-third of its value at the height of the bubble in the late 1980's. *The Times* editorial writer put the issue succinctly when he wrote that Japan was suffering from *systems fatigue.* (10) Indeed, the new prime minister Junichiro Koizumi still had to face up to the effects of the *bad business* by writing off no less than the equivalent of $109 bn of public and private debt!

REFERENCES

(1) Japanese drown in a sea of credit, Michiyo Nakamoto, *The Financial Times*, 13/2/1996

(2) Les banques japonaises revelent la totalité de leurs créances douteuses, Babette Stern, *Le Monde*, 26-27/11/1995

(3) Angry Japanese home in on big loan scandal, Peregrine Hodson, *The Times*, 23/2/1996

(4) As (3)

(5) Central bank and its governor are being blamed for the dire state of the economy, Joanna Pitman, *The Times*, 20/6/1995

(6) Tokyo Swords, *The Times* editorial, 15/1/1996

(7) A second lease of life, Gillian Tett, *The Financial Times,* 18/3/1999

(8) Japan: Is there half a problem or half a solution? Gillian Tett, *The Financial Times*, 19/9/2000

(9) As (8)

(10) *The Times,* editorial 18/05/2001

BREMER VULKAN

Questions:

What is the German Model all about?

To what extent is Bremer Vulkan an example of corporatism gone wrong?

■ Biting the Bullet

Four million people or eleven percent of the working population were without work in Germany in February 1996. The fact that unemployment had just passed this barrier provoked a flood of hostile comment about the rationalisation and productivity drives then taking place in German business. According to a national business survey the month before, moves like this, if continued, would eliminate a further half a million jobs during the year. It was a time of great anxiety and nowhere more so than in the town of Bremen, headquarters of Europe's biggest shipbuilder Bremer Vulkan.

The government's response was to issue its Alliance for Jobs plan (*Bündnis für Arbeit*). This was a comprehensive ten-point scheme designed, it said, to bring down the existing level to two million by the end of the century. *Ludicrous*, said many government critics, among them Count Otto von Lamsdorf, the Social Democrat MP. He claimed that Germany was on a trackway, not to reducing unemployment, but to actually increasing it to five million. (1)

On the other hand, there were signs that there were major changes afoot in German commerce and industry aimed at improving the country's competitiveness, a necessary ingredient in any move to cut joblessness. Perhaps the most revolutionary of these was the way in which companies, such as Daimler Benz, Hoechst or Germany's fourth largest company Veba, were being driven to take on board the concept of shareholder value seriously. As Ulrich Hartmann, Veba's chief executive, pointed out in the firm's 1995 annual report:

Satisfying the shareholders is the best way to make sure that other stakeholders are served as well. It does no good when all the jobs are at sick companies. Our commitment is to create value for you, our shareholders. (2)

According to big business supporters of the concept, there were two key imperatives driving such a change forward, namely the failure of traditional German corporatism and the difficulty of raising adequate equity capital for future expansion. The first was a model of decision-making based on co-operation between shareholders, managers and workers. Its critics attacked it as being unresponsive to the threat posed by the more open trading world created by the Uruguay GATT accord in

---

Germany isn't going to the dogs quite yet. It remains an extremely rich country. Four decades of post-war prosperity have enabled households to squirrel away an astonishing four trillion marks ($ 2.7 trillion) in savings, and the vast majority of ordinary Germans enjoy a standard of living much envied by most of their European neighbours. But, for the first time since the Weimar Republic (1919-33), there is growing angst among educated white-collar workers and managers.

This German middle-class squeeze is taking a toll on the economy. People... are dipping into their savings more than they have in over ten years. Families are hit the hardest. In just over ten percent both parents are unemployed and living on the dole. German families with children are more likely to reflect the traditional structure-husband as breadwinner and wife as home maker – than in many other North European countries.

EXHIBIT C15.1: GERMANY UNDER STRESS
Source: German families feel the squeeze, Matt Marshall,
The Wall Street Journal Europe, 9-10/2/96

1994 and by the rising impact of the rapid growth of manufacturing capacity in comparatively low labour cost areas of the world. Failure to adapt Germany's approach would, they said, simply lead at best to sluggish growth. More unemployment was unavoidable. According to them, the German system was just too cosy for a new, harsher world. As Exhibit C15.1 above, shows, such fears were not misplaced.

■ **Capitalism with a Human Face ?**

The second, and equally significant, driver for change was the growing need for German companies to source their capital requirements in the international market-place, since the amount and nature of the funds required was beyond Germany's capacity to supply. Ulrich Hartmann again:

There is no German or French or American capital market any more. It is

a global capital market and we all have to play by the same rule. (3)

This was meaning, in its turn, an increasing change in the ownership of major German firms, traditionally under majority German control, as well as changes in their traditionally secretive approach to financial disclosure. In mid-1995 nearly half the stock of the pharmaceutical giants Bayer, Schering and Hoechst was now owned, for example, by non-Germans. Voting rights, however, did not necessarily equate with the volume of stock ownership.

Others were by no means so sure about the wisdom of dropping the time-served German model of *capitalism with a human face*. Leaner, more powerful, more aggressive companies might certainly result from the new ways of doing things, but the danger was that workers could become increasingly disregarded and marginalised. Hence, supporters of the traditional approach were much heartened by the talks that took place among the government, employers and trade unions in mid February 1996.

Hailing the result as a contribution to *the humanisation of work*, government minister Norbert Blüm was delighted that his plan to provide part-time jobs for some of those originally opting to take early retirement at age 55 had been accepted. The previous early retirement scheme had, in fact, had brought state pension and unemployment funds to crisis point.

To be sure, the new scheme would still need subsidies from the Federal Labour Office. However, any downside would be compensated for by the fact that employers would have to fill every freed-up full time job (vacated by those taking early retirement, that is) with an apprentice or unemployed person. The German government considered that the plan would still allow Germany to meet the Maastricht criterion for Economic and Monetary Union (EMU) by 1999, by which each aspirant country's budget deficit could not exceed three percent of GDP.

■ A Trade Union View

One German trade union which recognised that change was unavoidable was the white collar union, DAG. In mid-February 1996, it took a momentous decision to change its approach to wage bargaining. Hitherto, it had moved in lockstep with other unions in negotiating universal pay and conditions contracts which applied to all firms in an industry, big and small alike. Now it would permit individualism. In so doing they were rejecting the traditional viewpoint of the DGB (the German Labour Federation) and its leading members. Their argument had long been that lack of union solidarity placed greater bargaining power in the hands of the employers and was to be avoided at all costs. This, too, had in the past been the DAG watchword. But DAG members were now aware of the ramifications of the blanket pay and conditions deal that IG Metall Germany's largest union had struck with employers in 1995. DAG stated that this deal was directly responsible for the mass lay-offs which were then taking place in the German metal industry.

DAG broke ranks, therefore, by allowing a situation in which the workers' council (Betriebsamt) which could negotiate wages and conditions locally, providing that DAG was the main union. In DAG's view their stance could only give relief to those companies who were hard-pressed and would help preserve their members' jobs.

■ Trouble in the Shipyard

One German company that was, by any standards, hard-pressed was the country's largest ship-builder, Bremer Vulkan. The news that the company was having liquidity problems broke first in the press on the sixth of September 1995. By the eleventh, an emergency meeting of the firm's supervisory board had met at the Bremen headquarters and chairman Friedrich Hennemann had resigned, amid talk that the company's losses for 1995 would amount to Dm one billion.

Friedrich Hennemann had become chairman of Vulkan in 1987. He had immediately brought in a strategy designed to build a widely diversified industrial group, whilst seeking to maintain the economies of scale enjoyed by the company – Germany's largest ship-builder. To this end, he had acquired such companies as Atlas Elektronik and Dorries Scharmann, a mechanical engineering firm. In the early 1990s he then bought from the

Treuhandanstalt, the privatisation agency set up to sell companies in what had formerly been East Germany, three shipyards on the Baltic coast. These were the Flender Werft AG in Lübeck, the Volkswerft in Stralsund and the MTW Schiffswerft in Wismar. As can be imagined, the cost of up-dating their technology and working practices, and of improving their quality was massive, even if the government financing initially available (paid for in part of the Solidarity Tax or Solidaritätzuschlag) had been liberal. For the record, revenue transfers in DM equivalents from West to East had risen from $97 billion in 1991 to $135 billion in 1995. Indeed, in 1995 some 40 percent of East German GDP was accounted for by subsidies.

As a result of Friedrich Hennemann's powerful conglomeration-and-growth strategy, Bremer Vulkan now had a total workforce of 23,000. It had also become more important economically and politically within Germany as it was now, in fact, the largest ship-building concern in Europe.

According to Johannes Ludwig, under-secretary at the Federal Economics Ministry, the idea was to ease the shift of an economy from... a socialised, communist command system to a so-called market economy. But that was not easy and in the previous five years, one third of the jobs in East Germany were lost. Moreover, there is no end in sight. A nationwide economic slump and a surge in unemployment in the East mean that the six new German states are as dependent as ever before on Western support – a phenomenon that had sparked debate over whether the subsidies are hampering development of Eastern Germany or creating an economic dependency. The Bundesbank warned last year of a 'subsidy mentality' taking root in the East, suggesting that, for the health of the German economy... subsidies should be limited to what was absolutely necessary.

EXHIBIT C15.2: EAST IS EAST AND WEST IS WEST
Source: Do Bonn subsidies help or hinder the East?, Rick Atkinson,
The International Herald Tribune, 23/2/96

■ Shipbuilding Economics

The three main challenges that remained despite the successes were, however, clearly visible; the high level of subsidies world-wide that were given by individual governments to their own ship-builders; the low prices at which ships were being sold in the international market-place; and the amount of competition for the ship-buyer's dollars.

- The Organisation for Economic Co-operation and Development (OECD) had tried to deal with the first problem by trying to set up an international convention to deal with excessive subsidies. This had commanded much respect and an international agreement was due to be signed in mid-1996. However, countries accounting for over one fifth of new tonnage had refused to sign it.
- So far as the second challenge was concerned, China and Poland were heavily out-pricing traditional producers and Italy and Finland were benefiting from currencies which had recently been devalued. By 1999 South Korea had taken over poll position as the world's cheapest supplier.
- In terms of the third, no ship-builder was willing to quit the market, however bad the conditions, and no country would want to persuade its producers to do so, unless forced.

The talk of losses at Bremer Vulkan was indeed true, but it was only part of a complicated story. Another element of it was the tight political and financial relationship that had existed between the city of Bremen and its chief employer. Not only had Friedrich Hennemann been a state secretary in the SPD-controlled (i.e., Socialist) Bremen government during the 1980s, but the city had in the past acted as the company's debt guarantor and was continuing to do so to the tune of £300m.

Another strand was the fact that Bremen was not only the smallest of West Germany's federal states, it was also West Germany's unemployment blackspot with a February 1996 level of 13.6 percent. Finally, the close relationship that Bremer Vulkan had enjoyed with its banks (Commerzbank, Dresdner, Bremer Landesbank) in the past needs to be considered.

■ The Plot Thickens

It was on the 14th of December 1995 that Bremer Vulkan's supervisory board, with its shareholder and workforce representation fully in agreement, decided to appoint new executives to try to rescue the company from a rapidly worsening situation. They were Udo Wagner, a director of ABB, and Hero Brahms, formerly with the Treuhandanstalt. The former was to be chairman of the board of directors, the latter chairman of the supervisory board. The board of directors had the duty of reporting on its success, or failure, to the supervisory board. Sadly, they were unable to halt the downward drift in Bremer Vulkan's share price. This fell from DM45 in September 1995 to DM15.75 on 21st February 1996, before trading in it was stopped. Indeed, they were unable to control events at all.

■ Things get worse

The directors recognised quite quickly, in fact, that the company's 1995 losses had, in fact, amounted to DM one billion, that it was now haemorrhaging cash and that it owed the banks the massive sum of DM 1.4 billion. Bankruptcy loomed. A second, and politically fraught, issue to deal with was a serious accusation by the European Union's Competition Commissioner, Karel van Miert, that Bremer Vulkan had misused state-backed funds, earmarked and authorised specifically for the up-grading of the East German yards it had acquired, on its mainstream business.

The inevitable outcome of all these financial pressures and political uncertainties was a decision on the 21st of February for Bremer Vulkan to seek court protection from its creditors. Such a move would allow the company a breathing space to come to some agreement with its creditors. (4)

Despite the company's DM ten billion order backlog and the direct action taken by the Bremen workforce to try to safeguard their jobs, a deal was, however, thought unlikely. Indeed, Johannes Ludwig reckoned that anyone who thought the company could be saved as an entity was *living in cloud-cuckoo land*. Much more likely was a break-up, as Exhibit C15.3 page 296 indicates.

Filing for protection has left the banks with a stark choice. Under any settlement they will be asked to forgo a big proportion of their loans, probably 40 percent. With most of these loans secured by the government or secured on individual ships, letting Bremer go bust may be more attractive. The banks might do a deal if Bremer promised a radical restructuring and focused on its modernised East German shipyards. But that idea would run into heavy opposition from the Bremen government, which wants to preserve local jobs. Nor has the suspicion that the group misused huge sums of state aid won it many friends in Bonn or Brussels. The shares are probably worthless.

EXHIBIT C15.3: THE COLD LIGHT OF DAY
Source: Lex, *The Financial Times*, 22/2/96

So what had gone wrong? Wolfgang Dettmer, deputy head of the Workers' Council at Bremer Vulkan Werft, had no doubts about where to place the blame. It was the failure of the company's supervisory board to stand up to Friedrich Hennemann. It had not had *enough authority* he said. (5) This was a point echoed by Hero Brahms who, as mentioned, had been a Treuhand board member before his appointment to Bremer Vulkan. He commented:

We were under huge political pressure to sell to Hennemann. He wanted the entire East German shipping sector. (6)

Nearer to home, of course, was the enormous cash drain of financing the production of Bremer Vulkan's loss-making cruise liners (7) and simultaneously rationalising and modernising all the yards.

■ Epitaph

Was this the end of the road for the once-proud Bremer Vulkan? Not quite. By the end of February 1996 the company's creditors had produced an infusion of funds which was adequate to keep operations moving ahead for two months and to secure the payment of the workforce's wages for a further three months. At all events, Gunther Rexrodt, the federal economics minister, felt somewhat relieved. He said:

The government can't guarantee it, but it looks as though we've won a bit of time for structural and conceptual changes at Vulkan. (8)

The investigation into the possibility of Bremer Vulkan Verbund AG's illegal diversion of money intended for its East German shipyards into its West German operations was not the only one. When Friedrich Hennemann resigned from his post in November 1995, the Bremen State prosecutor's office began investigating him and his business affairs.

The company had declared bankruptcy on the first of May 1996 after having failed to gain support for a rescue. On the 18th June the police raided 29 company offices in Bremen, Wismar and Stralsund to investigate claims made by the successor organisation to the Treuhandanstalt (the polysyllabic Bundesanstalt für Vereinigungsbedingte Sonderaufgaben) that former managers had siphoned off at least 716 million marks of the aid that had been provided to the company. Friedrich Hennemann was firmly in the frame.

The final epitaph for the company was, however, written in on the 15th August 1997. The brief headline *Der Vulkan ist endgültig erloschen* (The volcano is finally extinct) in *Die Welt* (9) marked the end of 104 proud years of shipbuilding in Bremen with the closure of the Vegesack yard and the placing of Bremer Vulkan shares in the archive of the state of Bremen.

■ The Wismar Yard

It was here, and at Lubeck and Stralsund, that Friedrich Hennemann sought to build up the ship-building base of the comnpany and to capitalise on aid from the EU and Bremen state. What had happened to MTW Schiffswerft?

In 1998 this was purchased by Aker, a Norwegian shipbuilder from the receivers of Bremer Vulkan. Its chairman, Oswald Muller, had lived through the ten-year revolution that stretched from Communist rule, through the Treuhandanstalt sale to Bremer Vulkan to the Aker acquisition. Hence, he had experienced the failures of central planning (raw Russian steel of the wrong quality and sizes, for example) as well as the perils of life under free entreprise (corporate downsizing and company liquidation) as well as its attractions (Dm 600 billion for yard refurbishment). It had clearly been an exciting experience and at least the company was not now expected to create all the services it needed for its employees, from kindergartens to housing. Interviewed in late 1999, he explained:

> *This shipyard will always have a future, just as eastern Germany has a future. Now our tasks are clear: to cut costs to innovate and to concentrate on those ships that are not built in South Korea or Japan, such as ferries and cable layers.* (10)

But, it wasn't easy. The Kvaerner shipyard in Rostock, with some of the world's most up-to-date facilities, had just been *fined* by the European Union £26.5m for breaking the terms of the aid it had received. It had managed to drive up productivity and offset falling prices by reducing the number of jobs by 80 percent but its rising competiveness had not paid off as it thought. The European Union aid had been made available on the strict condition that Kvaerner would not exceed strict capacity limits, set to safeguard other European yards. *The Rostock yard had become the victim of its own success by exceeding its capacity limit – and now it had to pay. The Kvaerner response had been to put the yard up for sale.*

As for this part of eastern Germany, analyst Ralph Atkins reckoned it was a *bastion* of the Party of Democratic Socialism – successor to East Germany's Communists. (11)

REFERENCES

(1)   Jobless crisis grips shipyard city, *The Guardian*, 1/3/1996

(2)   Germany's Veba shows controversial trend on shareholder value, Greg Steinmetz, *The Wall Street Journal, Europe*, 8-9/3/1996

(3)   As (2)

(4)   Shipyard stalls creditors, Michael Kallenbach, *The Times*, 22/2/1996

(5)   How to sink a shipbuilder, Judy Dempsey, *The Financial Times*, 1/3/1996

(6)   As (5)

(7)   Creditors throw Vulkan a cash lifeline, Ian Traynor, *The Guardian*, 28/2/1996

(8)   As (7)

(9)   Der Vulkan is endgûltig erloschen, *Die Welt*, 16/8/1997

(10) Germany's shipyards see old certainties disappear with the Wall, Ralph Atkins, *The Financial Times*, 5/11/1999

(11) As (10)

DAEWOO

Questions:

What sort of company is a chaebol?

How do chaebols and their home country, Korea, manage their affairs?

Just how attractive to Korean chaebols is Britain as a place to invest and why?

Why did Daewoo fail?

■ Banging the Drum

Gillian Shepherd, Britain's Education and Employment Secretary, had no doubts about Britain's opt-outs from the European Union's Maastricht treaty. The one she was most concerned with, the opt-out from the Social Chapter, seemed to have brought nothing but good in its wake. *Britain* she declared *is getting back to work. We have growing numbers of successful companies and rising numbers of people in work.* (1) The Social Chapter was, of course, an element in the Maastricht treaty which reflected human resource management practices common in mainland Europe but, up to now, less common in the UK. It seemed that it was this difference that was making Britain a better place for foreign companies, like Daewoo, to invest in.

At the time Britain, with its unregulated and heavily de-unionised labour market, was undeniably out-performing its continental neighbours by a large margin in the field where it really mattered – reducing unemployment and job creation. Attracting inbound direct foreign investment was, it seemed, Britain's forte. Its relatively low pay rates and manageable employers' social security costs, as well as the productivity and flexible working patterns of its workforce, made it a natural home for inbound investment. Especially as it was the case that a British base allowed such investors unlimited access to the lucrative continental European market-place, through Britain's EU membership. Korean companies such as Daewoo found Britain a highly attractive springboard.

Of course, not everyone was enamoured of the British approach. France and Germany wanted their system of worker consultation to apply, as provided for within the Maastricht treaty. France even had an interest in seeing its approach to minimum pay widely accepted. Britain's Conservative government was prepared to accept neither of these two things. Its approach really reflected a belief in what has come to be called *market fundamentalism* – a strong trust in the effectiveness and efficiency of neo-liberal economic management. Naturally, the result was an economy which was market-driven, companies that were shareholder-driven and investors who were in charge.

There was worry bout this, however, in a most unexpected quarter – the USA. Experienced American commentators such as Irwin Stelzer (2) and William Pfaff (3) informed the British public of the sense of unease that existed in a country where *cut-and-slash globalization* had apparently become the norm. This expression referred to the increase in the competitiveness of the USA economy in its global battle with rivals, producing much improved returns and higher stock prices for investors, but bringing gross job insecurity for manual workers and, for the first time, educated white-collar employees. As Exhibit C16.1 below, indicates, the resulting danger was a high level of employee demotivation and consumer anxiety.

> America's managers are the intellectual slaves of business school theorists, journalistic commentators and politicians who have in recent years promoted a highly destructive economic program based on their version of ideas formulated by David Ricardo and Adam Smith, writing about a British society and empire which bears little resemblance to today's world. American industry has been remaking itself according to fashions that have purported to be truths... The American social contract has been grievously damaged... Why should Europe imitate America? The usual answer is that it must do so to be competitive. The conventional wisdom says that everyone must downsize companies, cut wages and dismantle structures of social welfare so as to compete...

EXHIBIT C16.1: THE IMPACT OF GLOBALISATION

Source: A passing ideological fashion, William Pfaff,
The International Herald Tribune, 16-17/3/96

So far as the impact of globalisation on the European Union is concerned, it could not be denied that the ability of most Western industrial countries to protect their markets was substantially less after the signing in 1994 of the GATT trade treaty than it was before. By the same token, investors in such countries were much freer than ever before to seek the best returns internationally, rather than purely domestically, by exporting their investment money. Indeed, with technology transfer now more feasible than previously, the scene in the 1990s was well set for a massive relocation of productive resources to the best places for manufacture and distribution, especially of low – or intermediate – value-added products.

That is, of course, precisely where Britain fitted in with its splendid foreign direct investment opportunities. The negative side of the British equation was, of course, the typical assertion by critics that *downsizing has entered the corporate culture... and a company's financial virility is now measured by the stock market in terms of its most recent redundancy announcement.* (3) The plus factor, by contrast, was the way in which Britain, in the mid 1990s, was creating new jobs from inbound foreign investment. In particular, the South Koreans had arrived.

The Koreans were really warming to John Major's message that Britain was the home of the *enterprise economy.* Four leading South Korean companies regarded the country as a natural production-distribution location for accessing the whole of the EU. These firms – called *chaebol* or major business conglomerates – were Daewoo, Hyundai, LG and Samsung. Together, they dominated Korean industry. With wage costs rising fast in their home country and an inescapable need to play *the global game* in order to achieve the economies of scale that were needed in capital-intensive industries, such companies had to expand overseas. Undeniably, they were doing so with relish.

The sums of money being invested overseas by the four firms were dramatic. Some $8 billion had been shipped out of South Korea since the start of the decade. The USA, China, Thailand, Vietnam and, increasingly, Britain had been the preferred destinations. In 1995/6 about 40 percent of all South Korean investment in the EU came to Britain. Daewoo was a leader in this.

So far as Europe was concerned, one of Daewoo Corp's main interests was car manufacture. In early 1996 it was negotiating to buy Lotus, the luxury sports car manufacturer and erstwhile leading British marque, from its Italian owners. It had already invested heavily in car plants in Romania, Poland and the Czech Republic, as we shall see later. Like Samsung, however, Daewoo also had interests in consumer electronics (video recorders, televisions). Its rival Hyundai also produced cars, but like Samsung, was heavily involved in chips. Back in South Korea there was hardly anything of economic significance in which these leading chaebols were not engaged.

■ All That Glisters

The positive image presented by the chaebols' entrepreneurship overseas was unhappily tarnished by events back in South Korea. Admittedly, these had their origins in the past, but they still provided current leaders with immense headaches. The biggest problem was with two past presidents of Korea, Chun Doo Hwan and Roh Tae Woo. These two had been former army generals who had ruled South Korea over the period from 1980 to 1993. In December 1995 they were indicted for their roles in the December 1979 coup, which had brought them to power, and their alleged part in the turmoil which followed. The second biggest problem was the fact that the heads of seven of the leading South Korean companies had also been indicted, on charges of bribery. The ex-chairmen of Daewoo and Samsung figured prominently in the list of those charged.

President Roh had admitted that he had taken $650m in *backhanders* from industrialists. Interestingly, among those firms who featured in the accusations laid against him was the American company General Dynamics. It was asserted to have paid over a *kickback* to the Roh administration in return for re-deciding on its choice of McDonnell Douglas F/A fighter jets in favour of the General Dynamics F-16. (5) It was all a far cry from market fundamentalism, it appeared.

His successor as president, Kim Young Sam, the first in South Korea's history to be democratically elected, was anxious to bring in *a new political culture*, as it was called, to put a final end to Korea's period of military dictatorship. This was made possible by two factors. (6) The first had been the move to de-politicise the army, which seemed to have succeeded. The second was the advancing age of the political class which had supported the old regime. Their passing from the political scene was also loosening the ties of commitment and obedience which had bound the people to the leaders who had built the country to its present status as an industrial leader in Pacific Asia. It goes almost without saying that, from Kim's perspective, the two cultures were to be made as completely separate as was politically possible.

What this involved was, in part, re-making the chaebols. Accused of having paid over $31m to president Roh in exchange for a contract to build a naval base in Chinhae, Kim Woo-choong, Daewoo's president, was one of those who was heavily exposed to the wind of change. Although bribery à la Roh could be said to have its origins in the authoritarian regimes which governed South Korea over the key industrialisation period 1961-87, it had also gained impetus from the *democratisation* of the system under president Roh himself.

The size of the task of remaking the chaebols, i.e., re-engineering corporate approaches, is indicated in Exhibit C16.2 below. What was at stake was, in fact, the dismantling of a highly-integrated, collectivist machine. Not only that, the sheer scale of industrial concentration in South Korea needs to be borne in mind. Thus, it is noteworthy that the leading three chaebols controlled no less than 140 of South Korea's leading companies between them.

The financial linkages between the political authorities and the industrial groups date back to the 1960s. This was the start of South Korea's economic golden age under the rod of iron of president Park Chung-hee. State interventionism meant collective decisions on the objectives to be pursued (sectors to be concentrated upon, products to be made, exports to be achieved etc.).

It also made available to the chaebols the necessary finance (bank credits and government subventions) for economic development to occur. Part of this involved a thrust towards 'national stability' funded in part by the chaebols.

EXHIBIT C16.2: COLLECTIVISM, SOUTH KOREAN STYLE
Source: L'etat et les chaebol sud-coréens devront rompre des liens
trop intimes, Philippe Pons, *Le Monde*, 18/11/95

The net result of all of this was that economic power was concentrated in South Korea in a way, and to an extent, unparalleled in any other country in the Asia-Pacific region. The top ten chaebols were responsible for 23 percent of South Korean GDP and for 60 percent of its exports. Two thirds of their capital was still in the hands of the founding families.

■ That Will be the Daewoo

Meanwhile, elsewhere in Asia and in Europe, Daewoo was acting as the exemplary entrepreneur.

So far as Asia was concerned, Daewoo in early 1996 was planning the investment of £480m on a plant to produce cars and vans at Andizan in Uzbekistan. The strategy behind this was to export to Russia, Kazakhstan, Pakistan and Iran from this geographically central base. Its joint venture partner here was Uzautoprom with whom Daewoo were sharing a 50:50 joint venture. Koudrat Parpiev, vice-chairman of the new Uz Daewoo company, brimmed over with enthusiasm for the firm's future prospects:

The right spirit is created when control isn't concentrated in the hands of one partner and South Koreans prefer equal partners... Some 1000 Uzbeks are being trained in Daewoo's plants... Vehicles of this quality are not being made anywhere else in the former Soviet Union. We're already calling the Andizan region 'Little Detroit'... The region contains 11.5 percent of the country's population, with an average age of 20... We have even greater potential when we can say we have our own engineering industry. But I admit motor manufacturing is new to us and we have lots to learn. (7)

Daewoo's confidence in Uzbekistan was similarly large. According to Daewoo's new executive managing director, Hee-Choo Chung, the country was the most stable of all the members of the former Soviet Union; it was the centre of transportation for Central Asia, keeping up the traditions of the Silk Road; it would be, within a few years, self-sufficient in oil and grain. Such factors would, he said, serve as the basis for the new industries – automobiles, electronics, telecommunications – which would transform Uzbekistan into an industrial country. (8)

Poland was the centre of Daewoo's automobile interests in Europe. Here it had agreed to invest $1.12 billion in Poland's Fabryka Samochodow Osobowych SA (FSO) over a seven year period, giving the company a 70 percent slice of FSO. Whilst the deal did not give Daewoo strategic control, the Polish government retaining a golden share, it did enable the company to begin production of the Tico, Nexia and Espero cars as well as the FSO Polonez. Other ownership stakes Daewoo was also seeking to arrange in early 1996 included the Austrian company Steyr-Daimler-Puch and, as mentioned, Lotus.

Daewoo's adventurous strategy had, however, revealed itself to the greatest extent in its marketing of cars in Britain. Its aggressive approach was neither to use salesmen, nor the existing network of dealers, nor to pay commission on sales of cars to any of its staff.

The net result? Daewoo, much to the consternation of competitors, claimed to have managed to shave 30 percent off the price of its cars and sold more than 13,000 in the year to March 1996. Whilst retailers complained bitterly about what the Scottish Motor Trade Association called *highly negative marketing material*, one advertisement entitled *the dealer's slice* featuring a rival's car being sliced up with an electric saw, Daewoo were unrepentant. *We have broken the mould of selling cars in Britain so it is only natural for our competitors to be concerned* said a spokesman. (9)

The concern was nothing if not justified. Daewoo Motor was in fact, a part of privately-owned Daewoo Corp. In 1995 it made its first profit for five years ($12.5m) on sales of $4.6 billion. Unlike the open British market, its home base of South Korea was one of the most protected in the world, with foreign car makers taking only a minuscule 0.5 percent market share in 1995. And this was a rise of 80 percent on 1994. As such, it outpaced the growth rate in the exports of Korean-made cars. The number shipped out in 1995 was almost one million, up 40 percent on 1994.

■ Daewoo pays the price of ambition

The story of the creation of Daewoo was also the story of the rise of South Korea. Over just three decades, Kim Woo Choong, a former shipyard worker of modest means, built through energy, guts and determination, a global giant that reached from automobiles and electronics to financial services and construction. (10)

Thus, reported *The Economist* in a downbeat August 1999 article entitled *The Death of Daewoo*. It was a sombre epitaph to a company that, over the period 1996 to 1999, had intensified its efforts to become a player on the world stage – and failed. Not for nothing had its founder called it *Great Universe*. After all, Daewoo in 1998 employed no less than 2.5m people in Korea.

What had gone wrong was that, as its profits had never been enough to fund its expansion, it had turned to loans. The bigger the expansion, the bigger the debt. Just, for that matter, like Korea. Daewoo had worked, as had the other leading family-owned chaebol (Hyundai, Samsung and LG), on the premise that the company was simply too big to fail. In this way, it disbelieved the president's declaration, delivered in a televised address on the 15th August 1999, that, under pressure from the International Monetary Fund, he was intending to reform the chaebols and that *the era of political patronage and government bailouts was over.* (11) The company felt that neither the government nor the Korean banks would *dare* to liquidate any Daewoo subsidiary because of loss of jobs.

Its record of growing indebtedness makes sad reading:

- At the end of 1997 the debt/equity ratio of the four leading chaebol was 5:1 but, whereas the others cut back on their debt during 1998, Daewoo increased its by 40 percent. During the year, the company lost $458m on sales of $51 billion but this did not stop it from adding 14 new firms to its massive tally of 275 subsidiaries;
- One of the acquisitions was Ssangyong Motors which itself lost $417m;
- The total debt of Daewoo when it collapsed in mid-1999 was $50 billion of which foreign banks accounted for almost $10 billion and 60 Korean banks, *not all of them government-owned*, for the remainder.

Daewoo had, sadly, become a loan junkie on an imperial scale. In order to save as much of the company as possible and stave off receivership, the government plan involved the sell-off of the Daewoo electronics business for $3.2 billion to an American investment group, General Motors' taking a controlling stake in Daewoo Motors and the disposal of the company's ship-building division. General Motors, it should be noted, had owned half of Daewoo Motor for 15 years until a management dispute in 1992.

But it was difficult as, in the past, *cash and loans flowed freely between Daewoo subsidiaries regardless of shareholder interests and so, if any one of the creditors calls in loans and bankrupts a Daewoo company, it could pull the whole lot down.* (12) Not only that there were widespread suspicions that, despite its protestations, the corporatist Korean government was not prepared, in late 2000, to actually proceed to action. True, Kim Woo Choong had been forced to quit as company boss but, by now, the company's debts had been revealed as $80 billion, $26 billion more than its assets, and Korea's unemployment rate had doubled since the 1997-8 Asia Pacific economic crisis. So, it was thought the government was loath to do anything to weaken the country's shaky banks, buried under a mound of non-performing loans like Daewoo's, or destabilise the economic situation further.

Ford, not General Motors was now in the frame as a possible saviour of the car division. But, on the 15th of September 2000, Ford dropped out and 25 billion dollars was wiped off the value of the Korean stock market. (13)

REFERENCES

(1) Shepherd bangs the drum overseas for jobs in Britain, Philip Bassett, *The Times*, 14/2/1996

(2) Down and out in Britain, Neasa MacErlean, *The Observer*, 17/3/1996

(3) After the economic boom, Korea grows up politically, Mary Jordan, *The International Herald Tribune*, 8/12/1995

(4) As (2)

(5) Seoul inquiry turns to allegations of kickback on US F-16s, AP-AFP dispatches, *The International Herald Tribune*, 7/12/1995

(6) As (3)

(7) Daewoo brings a touch of Seoul, Unimedia, *The Times*, 19/1/1996

(8) As (7)

(9) Car dealers put the squeeze on cut-price Daewoo, Randeep Ramesh, *The Sunday Times*, 17/3/1996

(10) The Death of Daewoo, *The Economist*, 21/8/1999

(11) The Crawl of Reform, Moon Ihlwan, *Business Week*, 4/9/2000

(12) As (10)

(13) As (10)

THE CHANNEL TUNNEL
HIGH SPEED RAIL LINK

Questions:

Explain why HSRL was such a hot potato.

Do you think the Conservative government did give sweeteners to LRC?

What does the case tell you about Britain's business culture?

■ Taking for ever

The Channel Tunnel was one of the most exciting engineering achievements of the twentieth century. But, to make the whole project work as intended by speeding up the time of the London-Paris journey, high speed rail links were needed in both Britain and France. Britain's Conservative government recognised this by declaring in November 1989 that the government had a *national responsibility to ensure that a high-speed rail link is built quickly.* But it didn't and it wasn't.

The French had had no difficulty in planning to synchronise the building of the Coquelles-Paris link with their part in building the Tunnel itself. After all, building French railways and running French trains were naturally seen as matters of public sector management. The interests of the French state demand such an approach.

Not so in Britain in the 1980s. The British government simply selected the short list of Channel Tunnel builders in 1986, announced the first High Speed Rail Link (HSRL) plan in 1987 and took until 1994 for the final route to be agreed.

It was a case of bitter political arguments. These caused the southern route, proposed by Eurorail, to be dropped in favour of an alternative easterly route and the station terminal to be changed to St Pancras. To those who wanted to move things forward, it was a matter of shame that Eurostar trains could run at only 70 mph on the British side of the Channel whilst hitting a top speed of 167 mph in France.

Even on the 29th of February 1996, with the two final bidders awaiting notification of the winner of the contest to build the link, there was still anxiety about whether it would go ahead. And, if it did, whether it would succeed.

There had been three main reasons for the British problems.

The first was who pays the bill? The 68-mile HRSL was always going to be expensive. The 1992 estimate was £2.7 billion; the 1995 figure was put by

The Telegraph's commentator Andrew Griffiths at, possibly, close to £4 billion. Whatever the exact estimate, the Conservative government was not prepared to let British taxpayers pay for it. Thus, for political reasons it was necessary for the private sector to foot the bill. Hence the inclusion of the HSRL in the list of those investments that the government was wanting to be, in part, financed by the private sector under the Private Finance Initiative (see Exhibit C17.1 below).

The idea is to get the private sector to help pay for the roads, railways and hospitals that the government believes should be built in the public interest. The Private Finance Initiative means cost saving. The government can borrow money more cheaply, but private sector skills make the designing and building more efficient. Sadly, the trick of finding the right balance has eluded even the best private and public sector brains. Too much risk borne by the government means easy profits for contractors at the expense of taxpayers. Too little risk accepted by the state means projects simply do not happen.

EXHIBIT C17.1: THE PRIVATE FINANCE INITIATIVE (PFI)
Source: Rail Link under strain, Andrew Griffiths,
The Daily Telegraph, 25/11/95

Lying behind this rationale was the governmental economic strategy that had been pursued throughout the recessionary period from 1989 to 1993. This had involved lowering taxation (wherever possible) by reducing (wherever possible) the rising tide of public expenditure and the public sector borrowing it entailed.

The second reason for the delay was something known as NIMBY or **Not in My Back Yard**. This was the phenomenon that had caused the endless discussion of the alternative routes, the public disputes and the heated exchanges over planning applications, all of which had made route selection such a hot political potato. However wonderful the scheme, no-one, but no-one, wanted the route to pass through, or even by, their property. To let this happen would simply cause property values to fall, both immediately (through so-called planning blight) and subsequently.

And, it should be noted, the people who were living in Kent were among the richest in Britain (per capita). With a well-paid job in the city of London, the average Kent commuter was an articulate and highly motivated *capitalist* who typically placed personal interest way above the needs of public transport. Not only that, the countryside in Kent was exceptionally beautiful and building the HSRL through it was a socially unattractive concept.

In this, the Kentish British, living in a highly-populated, well-heeled part of the country, were totally different from the French residing in the Pas de Calais region. For the latter, the Channel Tunnel and the link to Paris brought work and prosperity to an area of France where land prices were low and unemployment high. Lille, in particular, scored very highly as a result as a railway network hub and as a centre for inbound commercial investment.

For those who lived in Kent, the HSRL was all about the chance that *your* house price might fall. So, in this part of Britain, the prospect was viewed with immense distaste by those about to suffer. And, for the majority, these were Conservative Party supporters.

The third major reason for the delay was the fact that the *government said it could not legally pay for the HSRL.* Lord Parkinson, transport secretary in 1990, had stated categorically that it would be illegal for the government to provide money for the Channel Tunnel rail link.

At the time this was true, since the 1987 Channel Tunnel Act stated specifically that no government subsidies could be paid to the publicly-owned British Rail for such a purpose. So, unless and until British Rail could be privatised, the government could not help and, of course, if the railways *were* privatised, the government would not need to help! In the event, British Rail *was* privatised by 1997.

Paradoxically, the talk in private railway circles then focussed on *just how large subsidies would have to be to encourage the winning bidder to do the HSRL work.*

What the government was known to be offering to bidders was a 999-year monopoly to build and operate the link which was scheduled to open in 2002. What was not known and was, at all events, difficult to value, was the level of subsidy the government would provide.

■ The Great Day Dawned (or so we thought)

On March the first 1996 it was announced that London & Continental Railways (LCR) had won the contract to build the HSRL. It would be the biggest railway engineering project since Victorian times and would allow Eurostar trains to travel at 167 mph on both sides of the Channel instead of, as now, only the French side. This would allow 30 minutes to be shaved off the London-Paris journey time of three hours. Whilst, arguably, a temporary nightmare for affected citizens in Kent, it was stated that the project would directly create 5,000 jobs and indirectly some 50,000. It would involve two new stations (Stratford and Ebbsfleet) and allow greater trunk route access to the Continent (for example Birmingham-Paris in 210 minutes). It would regenerate the Thames Gateway area.

L&C planned also to take over and run the loss-making Eurostar service, a prospect seen as highly attractive by Richard Branson, head of the Virgin Group, a key shareholder in the London and Continental Consortium.

So far as subsidies were concerned, Labour's shadow transport secretary Clare Short, reckoned that the government was giving away assets worth £5.7 billion. The chief of these were the lucrative development area including St. Pancras and Waterloo stations (valued at £3 billion) and the Eurostar service run by the government's European Passenger Services organisation (valued at £1.2 billion). In return London & Continental were prepared to fund the project to the tune of £1.6 billion.

The Labour opposition, having failed to halt the government's railway privatisation plans, now appeared wholly hostile to the HSRL move. In the words of the party's transport spokeswoman, Glenda Jackson, it was *the biggest sweetener since Hansel and Gretel were allowed access to the gingerbread cottage.* (1) Of course, the government rejected Labour's view that this was the *mother of all sweeteners* and indicated that they were, in fact, providing only £1.4 billion for the venture.

■ So What's the Snag?

In fact, there were two snags (or opportunities, if you are an optimist).

The first was Eurostar, the London-Paris train service, itself. Far from being a financial success to date, as initially predicted, it had turned out to be an expensive failure. True, it had suffered from technical problems at launch and marketing problems since and, true, it had been introduced a year late. But since then it had been managing by itself to lose money at what commentator Jonathan Prynn called *an extraordinary rate.* (2) It had thus come to require a subsidy from the British government in 1996 which had amounted to £200m.

The main reason, however, was the extent of the company's indebtedness. It should be noted that, for political reasons, both the rail service and the Channel Tunnel itself had had to be financed privately and the weight of debt had become a millstone around the whole endeavour. At the time of signing the Channel Tunnel Treaty, the-then Conservative prime minister (Margaret Thatcher) had refused to countenance public funding of the Channel Tunnel and the-then French president (Francois Mitterand) had agreed.

There was also an initial unhappy combination of too many empty seats and too high fees paid to Railtrack for the use of rail lines on the British side. Naturally, the government's expectation was that the London and Continental Railways (LCR) consortium, with the known skills of its members in transportation and tourism (Virgin Group and National Express, for example), would be able to turn the service around. Certainly, LCR had set themselves a target of making Eurostar break even within two years.

The Channel Tunnel itself was the biggest of all the problems. The worst fears of commentators were realised on the 14th of September 1995 when Eurotunnel suspended interest payments on its £8 billion debt. The action would save the company £2m per day, it was said, but it also put it technically in default of its loan agreements. The banks had no option but to begin a re-negotiation of Eurotunnel's debt schedule. After all, they were owed a mountainous amount of money.

On the tenth of March 1996 it became known that the 35 Japanese banks, the largest single group in the Eurotunnel loan syndicate of 225 banks, had started off-loading Eurotunnel debt at a face value of 33p in the pound, making it the most distressed debt in the secondary debt market. This action had been taken in advance of the restructuring proposals which were to be put forward by the mediators (*mandataires ad hoc*) appointed by the French.

Hence, the HSRL was nothing if not a massive gamble. LCR were, however, ecstatic over their victory in the hard-fought bidding contest. As for the government, transport secretary Sir George Young congratulated LCR and said that the project represented *excellent value for the nation, a historic day for transport in Britain and a triumph for PFI.* (3)

■ More Angst

As it turned out, Sir George Young's optimism was far from well-founded. By late 1997 the HSRL project was, depending on one's viewpoint, either deep in crisis or on the brink of collapse. Certainly, the intentions of the LCR consortium had not been matched by reality.

For a start, the tragic Tunnel fire in November 1996 had adversely affected the operation of the Eurostar train service. Although LCR, under the terms of the deal, was *to inherit the service free of debt*, the fact that it was still not achieving the right level of revenue meant that a stock market flotation was still impossible. Secondly, the start-up of tunnelling operations and engineering work for the Link had been very slow and spasmodic. Thirdly, the viability of the Link was intertwined with the speed with which Railtrack (the owner and operator of Britain's rail network) could restore the infrastructure feeding in to the Link – especially the strategically important but severely run-down West Coast main line route between London and Glasgow. This last project was valued at £1.5 billion in itself. So, private sector money was needed on a grand scale.

Hence the LCR consortium were finding it difficult to get investors to put up the £2 billion that was needed to match the British government's conditional contribution of £1.4 billion. The word *conditional* is important because it had been agreed by all parties that public money would only be forthcoming after all the private sector funds had been used.

This was why, in late 1997, Railtrack and LCR were said to be having urgent discussions as to the way forward. The Labour government that took over from the Conservatives in mid-1997 had let it be known that they were not prepared to intervene to change the deal originally struck but, in the event, they were.

■ The real dawn comes (we hope)

In June 1998 the Labour government gave the go-ahead for the HSRL at a total cost of £5.8 billion, with the government underwriting the private financing of £3.8 billion of this sum. The link was to be built in two stages, with the first being the stage between the Channel Tunnel and Fawkham Junction in North Kent. LCR were the promoters. John Prescott, Britain's deputy prime minister, began the project by digging a ceremonial silver spade into the bank of the Medway river in October 1998.

Railtrack had committed itself to buying this part of the link for £1.5 billion and the second stage for £1.8 billion. The company, naturally enough, was wanting to ensure that it was getting the best possible price for Eurostar's use of the track to maximise the pay-back on its investment.

Thus, by the end of 2000, six years after the completion of the Channel Tunnel, construction of the HSRL was underway, the financing of the HSRL firmly in place and hopes were high that it would be completed, as John Prescott had stipulated by 2007. Then, high speed trains would travel at the same speed on their journey from London to Paris – and from Paris to London.

REFERENCES

(1)   Favourite wins Channel link competition, Charles Batchelor, *The Financial Times*, 1/3/1996

(2)   As (1)

(3)   As (1)

GOING BANANAS

Question:

Review the business culture issues are at stake in this case. Who, if anyone, is in the right?

■ The WTO Ruling

This is a classic example of industrialised agriculture within a free market causing enormous damage to tiny, very poor farms in developing countries. (1)

This was the powerful view of John Corrie, Member of the European parliament (MEP). He was supporting a resolution condemning the World Trade Organisation (WTO) for its negative position on the import and sale of bananas in the European Union.

It was a matter of great importance to many of the parliament's members because the WTO's pronouncement in late September 1997 almost certainly meant either a change to, or even an ending of, the long-standing system of EU aid to small-scale banana growers in Africa and the Caribbean. This, in its turn, would involve some European countries' virtually turning their backs on what had been former colonies and were now often simply poor developing nations. It was a matter of differences in the business culture of Europe and the USA.

The substance of the problem was that, the WTO, on grounds of promoting free trade, had ruled that the EU's preferential aid system breached trading rules by discriminating against the USA and four Latin American countries. Therefore, said the WTO, it must stop. Despite a call by the EU's Agriculture Commissioner, Franz Fischler, that the WTO should be reformed to make it more accountable, his Trade Commissioner colleague, Sir Leon Brittan, insisted that the WTO ruling must be upheld.

Nevertheless, given that the EU countries imported almost four million tonnes of bananas every year and that only ten per cent of this was made up of Caribbean products, members of the EU parliament felt the ruling unfair, to say the least.

In the debate on the WTO ruling, for example, MEP Giacomo Santini went out of his way to indicate that growers in Latin American countries received far less of the ultimate retail selling price than did those enjoying the EU scheme. Hence, changing the system would not benefit the former and would gravely disadvantage the latter.

Another MEP, Glennys Kinnock, saw *a hidden agenda* behind the WTO moves. (Bates, 1997) The complaint put before the WTO originated with Carl Lindner, chairman of Chiquita, a major trader in bananas, which already enjoyed a 70 percent share of the EU market, and which had supported the last USA Democratic Party presidential campaign with a $500,000 donation. (2) So, for her, it was *a case of an American multinational trying to get its own back.* The three largest USA fruit companies – Dole, Chiquita and Del Monte – control about 66 percent of the world banana market, compared with the Caribbean growers' three percent, she said.

For MEPs in general, there was no problem with the principle of free trade. But it was clear that the EU-supported producers would need time to adjust to global competition and that a strict interpretation of free trade could mean their collapse. So, the resolution voted for by John Corrie sought to assist banana growers in ACP (African and Caribbean countries) by alternative methods. It was vital for them because, as Marshall Hall, Jamaica'a banana trade supremo, declared:

This is a matter of life and death for us. We seem to have fallen foul of a standard American way of doing business. (3)

Not all the MEPs agreed, however, and the resolution was carried only by 286-124. Among those supporting USA and Latin American exports – so called *dollar bananas* – was Germany. It had never enjoyed the colonial linkages of, say, France and Britain in the West Indies. On top of which, German people wanted to buy the bananas of their choice and enjoy cheaper prices. (4)

■ Round 2: The Banana War Hots Up

On the third of March 1999 the USA finally lost patience with the EU's banana stance and threatened to impose swingeing duties on 15 luxury products imported from Europe, like Italian sheep cheese, German coffee makers and French handbags. The annual value of the trade amounted to $520m and the move was regarded as a reprisal for the EU's continuing intransigence. (5)

Britain, as America's leading supporter in Europe, felt especially aggrieved, as its cashmere industry had been singled out as one of those to be subjected to punitive sanctions and called in the USA ambassador, Philip Lader, to register its disapproval about the move. He retorted that it was *Europe's turn to take its lumps and play by the rules.*

The decision followed hard on the ruling by the WTO's arbitration panel that the EU's banana regime was inconsistent with WTO principles and was damaging the USA economy. America had complained for years about the situation and had received no less than three rulings in its favour, the first in 1994.

But the action was seen as not just "illegal and inflammatory" – the EU view – but also as potentially very damaging indeed to world trade relations. It wasn't just, as Peter Riddell put it, a case of two countries – USA and Britain – *divided by a single fruit,* but of a danger of the eruption of a severe bout of protectionism which could lead to a US-EU trade war. (6) And, as *The Wall Street Journal* itself indicated:

> *With the world economy still wobbling after almost two years of crisis, the last thing anyone needs is America leading the charge toward the same kind of protectionist chain reaction that started with the Smoot-Hawley tariffs in the early 1930s. This severely curtailed world trade, contributed importantly to the Depression and, ultimately, World War II.... This is just how trade wars get rolling...It is a dangerous game of chicken for the world's two leading economic powers. (7)*

The final ruling by the WTO atbitration panel was delivered on the sixth of April. A 160-page report spelled out that aspects of the EU's preferential import regime for Caribbean bananas was indeed illegal and it awarded damages of $191m, but not $520m, to the USA. Sir Leon Brittan, the EU trade commissioner said that the USA retaliation, even if on goods amounting to a value of $191m, remained illegal.

The producers on the island of St Lucia spoke for all their fellow Caribbean growers when they bewailed the fact that their *green gold* was now losing out to *dollar bananas.* (8) According to Rupert Gajadar, ex-chairman of the St Lucia Banana Growers' Association:

Who will care if, as a result of this policy, we lose our houses, our children die from disease or are going to be uneducated? I think we have a strong moral case; I just wonder who is going to listen to it? So long as the banana boat keeps coming in, we still have our livelihoods.

Could the growers become more efficient in order to compete? *Of course we have to become more efficient and we are doing so,* says grower Albert Leonce, *but I employ eight people. How am I ever supposed to compete with Chiquita?* (9)

The point was well made. Most plantations on St Lucia were small and employed from five to 20 people; in colonial times the island's people had lived seven times under British rule and seven times under French. Banana pickers earned about 35 eastern Caribbean dollars per day (say £8); banana growing represented seven percent of the island's GDP.

It was not until November 1999 that the European Commission proposed a plan to EU governments to overhaul the banana regime. It stated that it would phase out the existing approach over six years and replace it with a tariff system that would open up the market to other competitors. The Commission spokesman recognised that there were no easy solutions to the problem and that it had poisoned relations among the USA, European countries and the banana-producing countries themselves. He hoped that the plan would fit USA requirements and lead to a speedy lifting of trade sanctions.

It did not. The USA position, as stated in October 2000, was that sanctions would only be lifted when the EU's approach complied with WTO open trade rules or when the company which had originally brought suit in the matter – Chiquita – retracted the suit. This put Carl Lindner, *top banana* at Chiquita, in a very interesting position. Even more so, as, according to the USA Center for Responsive Politics, he and his family had given $786,000 in hard and soft political donations in the first 18 months of this electoral cycle. (10)

■ Round Three

On the 25th January 2001 Chiquita Brands International brought the period of uncertainty to an end by re-launching its lawsuit againt the European Union. It claimed damages of £360m on the grounds that, since 1993, it had lost more than $1 billion in profits due to the EU's banana approach and that this had been a contributory factor in driving the company to the verge of filing for bankruptcy.

Their asssertion was that the EU's changes to their banana regime in 1997 and 1999 still left a system that was incompatible with WTO rules. Chiquita was feeling very bitter over the eight-year banana war, as well as the fact that, in Europe, it was selling its bananas in euros yet buying them in South America in dollars and that, since the launch of the euro in 1999, the currency had depreciated by over 20 percent against the dollar. They were also confident they were in the right. *When we talk to people in Washington about this* declared Steven Warshaw, Chiquita's CEO, *we are talking about the law, we are talking about morality and whether our side is right and just.* (11)

Fortunately, for all involved, the eight-year-old dispute came to an end on the eleventh of April, 2001 when the EU agreed to change its rules on banana imports to suit the USA's requirements. Caribbean growers would still be protected under the deal, with an albeit reduced market share.

REFERENCES

(1)   Anger at banana ruling, *EP News*, September 1997

(2)   Europe slips up on banana laws, Stephen Bates, *The Guardian*, 25/9/1997

(3)   As (2)

(4)   As (2)

(5)   American reprisal over bananas hits small European companies, *The International Herald Tribune*, 6-7/3/1999

(6)   Two countries divided by a single fruit, Peter Riddell, *The Times*, 5/3/1999

(7)   The Smoot-Banana Tariffs, *The Wall St Journal, Europe* editorial, 5-6/3/1999

(8)   Green gold loses out to dollar bananas, Gary Young, *The Guardian*, 20/4/1999

(9)   As (8)

(10) Banana Republic, *The Washington Post* editorial, 31/10/2000

(11) US group sues European Union over banana war, David Lister, *The Times*, 26/1/2001

IRAN: THE SOUTH PARS GAS FIELD

Questions:

Sketch out the relationships among the main players in the case.

What do you make of these relationships?

■ The best deal on the Middle East block?

By any standards it was a superb deal. In late 1997 a powerful oil exploration consortium, led by France's Total Oil giant and including Russia's Gazprom and Malaysia's Petronas, agreed with the Iranian government to develop one of the country's largest gas fields. The timing of the accord was right; there was an international consensus in the late 1990s that a global shortage of oil was on the horizon. Iran's export revenues in the twenty-first century would be strengthened by the move, a hugely attractive prospect to the country. Hence, Iran was pleased as the South Pars gas field was known to be the biggest in the world. As for the French Prime Minister, Lionel Jospin, he was elated at the prospect of an increase in France's trade with such a powerful partner. *Personally*, he said, *I rejoice in it.* (1)

The value of the deal was substantial – $2 billion – but it would only increase Iran's output incrementally. So far as oil alone was concerned, in 1997 this country was producing on average 3.6m barrels per day. For Total, however, it meant a very significant breakthrough in a part of the world where the prospects were good. It was, in fact, one of 60 companies which were only waiting for the trade embargo imposed on Iran's neighbour, Iraq, to be lifted in order to sign up to exploit this country's reserves. These were the second largest in the world, after Saudi Arabia's, and Iraq was much in need of foreign direct investment. The embargo was, it will be recalled, imposed by the United Nations after Iraq's defeat in the 1991 Gulf War.

■ But, seen from a different angle

On the third of October 1997, the USA government ordered its aircraft carrier Nimitz to break off from its scheduled operations in Asia Pacific waters and to sail directly to the Gulf. The purpose was to back up USA warnings to Iran not to repeat air attacks it had carried out in eastern Iraq in the previous week. These raids were aimed, not at Iraq per se, but at a left-wing group called the Mojahedin Khalq (People's Holy Warriors) who were opposed to the Islamic state in Iran and fomenting trouble for it from their bases in the border region between Iraq and Iran. The reaction of Iraq to the incursion into their air space had been to launch their own Russian-built MiG 21 and MiG 23 fighters and to successfully repel the Iranians.

This was a matter of the greatest importance to both countries because the 1990 peace agreement, which both had signed to end a bitter eight-year war between them, had left a residue of continuing tensions. The fact that the Mojahedin Khalq had rebelled against the strict Islamic fundamentalist regime, set up under the Ayatollah Khomeini after Iran's 1979 Revolution, and had carried out border raids with Iraq's support was one aggravation. So also, at the other end of the scale, was the aid supplied by Iran to enemies of the *feudal* Saddam Hussein regime in Iraq – rebel Shi'ites and Marsh Arabs – in the strategically important Shatt al'Arab waterway region.

What with each side helping the other's rebels and then launching air attacks, the USA was hard pressed to carry out the mission set in the aftermath of the Gulf War: to maintain a "no fly" zone in southern Iraq. Notably, the province of Kut, home to substantial numbers of insurgent Shi'ites, was within this zone. The overall USA purpose was, of course, to seek to achieve its Gulf War aim of unseating Iraq's leader and containing the threat of further eruption of conflict.

Thus, the strategy followed by the USA was one of "dual containment" of both Iran and Iraq and involved maintaining a military presence and an array of trade sanctions against both countries, which was becoming more and more problematic for all concerned.

■ Introducing Alfonse D'Amato

Thierry Demarest, Total SA's chairman, did not enjoy the afterglow of striking a successful deal for very long. Within a week, a storm of criticism blew up which threatened to push the USA and the European Union into a trade war.

The problem was that the oil deal breached the USA's Iran-Libya Sanctions Act (ILSA), a piece of legislation which called for penalties on any foreign companies investing over $20m in these two countries' power sectors. This Act put the USA in the exposed position of being a sort of *world trade policeman* and capable of being attacked for advancing its own trade and political interests over those of others, as in this case, France. Of course, the USA defence of this law lay in the assertion that investments in these two countries simply aided international terrorism which America was pledged to curb.

So hostile was USA senator Alphonse d'Amato to the Total success that he called for sanctions against the company. He was ILSA's author and felt strongly about the issue. So did France. Its approach to Iran was one of reinstating through "constructive political dialogue" the type of successful bi-lateral trade relationship it had had with Iran before the Shah had been deposed from his *peacock throne.*

Whilst the USA administration was pressing its point of view and debating the correct course of action to uphold the law, the European Union's political machine was backing the Total position. France, also, had everything to gain through stalwart defence. Foreign Ministry spokesman Jacques Rummelhardt summed up matters by saying:

France hopes that the American administration will weigh very carefully the consequences of an application of the ILSA law. It would constitute a serious precedent in international trade. (2)

From the politico-economic point of view it was certainly an embroiled situation, a possible international trade dispute between the USA and the EU over what was to the French a piece of global trade orthodoxy, and to the Americans a major breach in a key domestic anti-terrorism rule. And, as if that were not enough, there was a cultural dimension to it. *The Guardian's* Ian Black put it neatly when he wrote that this could all turn out to be only the latest instalment in the old and long-running story of *America's obsession with truculent men in turbans.* (3)

■ The Millennium Instalment

The deal that was struck on the 27th of July 2000 between Iran and ENI of Italy was even bigger than that in 1997. Valued at $3.8 billion, the agreement flew in the face of continuing USA attempts, under ILSA, to limit foreign investment in Iran's oil and gas sector and was hugely welcomed by Iran, which depended on energy for most government revenue and hard currency earnings. ENI's chief executive, Vittorio Mincato, could hardly hide his delight when he declared:

The USA legislation is a joke. The only thing it has succeeded in doing is preventing American companies from investing in Iran. (4)

He was also satisfied with the *buy-back* form of the contract which allowed Iran's national Oil Company to operate the field once ENI had developed it. In this, Iran was keeping control of its own national assets, an essential feature given the heated national debate on the issue since the 1979 Islamic Revolution and hardliners' suspicions about foreign exploitation.

The USA was still not happy with the Iran situation and was now focussing on its so-called Caspian energy policy. This laid down American requirements for an east-west energy corridor linking Baku, the Azeri capital, Tiblisi and Ceyhan in Turkey through which oil and gas would flow to the West from Kazakhstan, Turkmenistan and Azerbaijan. The pipeline, costing $2.4 billion, would not pass through Iran. For its part, Iran was promoting the notion of series of pipelines to allow these countries to export to Iran at a cost of $ 420m. Said Hoseein Kazempour Ardebili, senior adviser to Iran's petroleum minister:

For each barrel of oil exported to Iran the Caspian producers would save up to $2. I do not think countries can afford to subsidise the political aims of the USA. (5)

Neverthless, the Georgians, Azeris and Turks signed up for the project, which was scheduled for completion in 2004. There were already strong indications that a potential victory of George W. Bush in the millennium presidential election in the USA would change none of American thinking on its energy security in the Middle East. And it did not.

REFERENCES

(1)   America Can Stand Up to the Rush to Help Iran, A. M. Rosenthal, *The International Herald Tribune*, 4-5/10/1997

(2)   US threatens trade war over oil deal, Paul Webster, *The Guardian*, 30/9/1997

(3)   War dance in the Gulf, Ian Black, *The Guardian*, 1/10/1997

(4)   Iran signs $3.8 billion gas deal with Eni, Robert Corzine, *The Financial Times*, 28/7/2000

(5)   US to push for Caspian-Turkey pipeline link, Mathew Jones, *The Financial Times*, 2/6/2000

THE VILVOORDE AFFAIR

Questions:

To what extent is Renault adopting *the Anglo-Saxon model*?

Why?

Was there any alternative at Vilvoorde?

■ A Difficult Year at Renault

Louis Schweitzer, chairman of Renault SA, was not understating things when he declared the 1996 year end results. It had been, he said, *a difficult year.* (1) In fact, the company had lost 5.25 billion French francs on a sales revenue of 184.08 billion FrF, the first negative result the company had posted in ten years. Naturally enough, the French government, which had just reduced its ownership stake from 52 percent to 46 percent, was disappointed at the fall-off in the sales of the heavy truck and car divisions (9.5 and 2.3 percent down on 1995, respectively) which had contributed to the losses. But, it was more concerned with the *political hot potato* it had been handed by the fact that over 70 percent of the loss was attributable to the restructuring charges associated with the closure of one of Renault's factories.

The factory in question was at Vilvoorde in Belgium. As soon as Prime Minister Alain Juppé had heard of the closure plan, he had called for an explanation – especially of the abrupt manner in which the announcement had been made. But it was evident that the right-wing government was not going to take matters further. As for the right-wing French President Jacques Chirac, his comment was *La fermeture des usines, c'est aussi, hélas, la vie (Closing factories – alas, that's life).* (2) Nevertheless, the howls of outrage which had greeted the company's action were such as to cause the government considerable concern.

Renault SA itself was sure of its ground. It was facing fierce competition in a stagnant European market. Over-production was endemic and margins tight. According to specialist analyst Prof Garel Rhys *only the most efficient manufacturers can avoid going into the red.* (3) Against this background, Renault's market shares in its home market had fallen from 29.2 percent in 1995 to 26.6 percent in 1996 and its European market share had dipped by 0.2 percent to 10.1 percent. The fall in its domestic share had occurred in spite of the fact that the Juppé government was operating a tax incentive scheme to accelerate the scrapping of old vehicles. Certainly, the Paris bourse reckoned that the closure was justified and Renault shares were marked up by 25 percent.

■ Matter Strategic

The issues that Renault needed to address most quickly were, according to Garel Rhys, over-capacity, the use of a base model or common floor-pan (which allows a variety of other types of car to be made more cheaply from it) and economies of scale. The company was facing an increasingly aggressive Volkswagen and the Japanese were aiming straight at the heart of Renault's market share. The most recent critical problem had been the failure to pull off the proposed merger with Volvo.

It is interesting to compare such views with the more up-beat picture of the way ahead presented by Louis Schweitzer. In an interview published in *Le Monde* (4) he claimed that his aim was to make the company *the most competitive car maker in Europe by the year 2000*. Among the ways of achieving this, two had significant ramifications for the company's culture. Firstly, he said, it was necessary for people to think differently about their jobs and futures. People still thought of the French state as being the owner of Renault. *They have to get this idea out of their heads* he commented. Secondly, there had to be a plan to downsize the company by approximately 3,000 people per year. This was on top of the move made in 1997 to lower by 6,000 the number employed by Renault – 141,000. This strategy of improving productivity lay behind the closure of Vilvoorde, a plant which had, in fact, been suspect in company eyes since 1994.

So, what was the problem?

The problem was that the Renault workers at Vilvoorde did not want to lose their jobs. And, so effective was their two-track strategy of direct action (causing disruption through, for example, sit-ins and protest marches) and court action, that the Vilvoorde affair achieved notoriety in some political circles in Europe as a case study in how not to deal with staff. For some it exemplified the worst excesses of the Anglo-Saxon model of the free market at work.

Louis Schweitzer's team managed to stonewall in their direct negotiations with trade union and works council (comité d'entreprise) representatives of the 3,100 Vilvoorde employees at Beauvais on the 20th March 1997. They said there would be no rescinding of the closure and they rejected the argument put to them that Vilvoorde could be saved if the company were to cut working hours in all its European factories by ten percent. Indeed, they countered by saying that Renault costs were too high precisely because of the way production was parcelled out among small units like Vilvoorde.

The court action undertaken by the resisting workers was more successful and in early March rulings were made by courts in Brussels and Paris which raised the temperature considerably. The Brussels judgement was that the company had broken the rules on worker consultation when it arbitrarily announced that the factory would close on 31st July and had to pay a fine of 15,000 francs to the works council. Whatever else, it could not close the plant until it had consulted with the unions and produced a formal plan for dealing with redundancies (*plan social*). The Paris ruling reiterated this conclusion. As can be imagined, this stiffened the resolve of those advocating direct action.

■ The politicians take a hand

One early entrant to the fray was Padraig Flynn, the European Social Affairs Commissioner. He indicated that he shared *the shock and consternation* of those on the receiving end of Renault's move. Not only had the company's management been *irresponsible* but they had also ignored two relevant European laws: the European Works Council Directive and the Collective Redundancies Directive. Ironically, it was Renault that had laid some of the groundwork for the former. If business did not explain to workers the difficult commercial decisions they faced, he said, *the core of our social consensus will be under attack*. There clearly was a need for *adequate social measures to accompany the internal market*. (5)

On the fourth of March 1997, Lionel Jospin, leader of the French Socialist opposition to the Juppé government, demanded that the government should intervene. However, as newly-installed Prime Minister, following the Socialists' poll victory in mid-1997, he was obliged to indicate to his Belgian counter-part Jean-Luc Dehaene that it was not up to the French government to decide this matter, however sympathetic he was personally to the workers' cause. And, indeed, he was sympathetic to promoting the idea of job creation (if not preservation), if his government's autumn 1997 plan to reduce the French working week from 39 to 35 hours (with no loss of pay that is) by 2000 was anything to go by. Nonetheless, the new Socialist government said it would re-examine the closure plan. As can be imagined, Lionel Jospin's Communist allies in government were restive with this minimalist stance.

■ End Game

By the end of June 1997, it was becoming apparent to all concerned that there was no alternative to closure. The negative Vilvoorde economics were insuperable. The report by the outside specialist, Danielle Kaiser-Gruber, commissioned by Louis Schweitzer to investigate, was duly presented to the Renault board (conseil d'administration) with the key findings that the notion of working time reduction was not feasible as an alternative to plant closure and that this was, in fact, unavoidable.

The company set about renegotiating the terms of redundancy with the Vilvoorde workforce, using the social plan mechanism, and achieved its aim of plant closure. But the bitterness remained. As recently as March 1997 Lionel Jospin had joined a Europe-wide protest against the company's action by car workers from Belgium, France and Spain. Now he was not intervening, French trade unions like the CGT and the CFDT said the government had broken its promises.

REFERENCES

(1) Renault posts yearly loss as workers protest job cuts, Douglas Lavin, *Wall Street Journal Europe*, 21-22/3/1997

(2) M Schweitzer confie une mission sur Renault-Vilvorde à un expert independant, Virginie Malingre, *Le Monde*, 11/6/1997

(3) Hard facts that led to Vilvoorde closure, Charles Masters, *The European*, 13-19/3/1997

(4) Renault veut être le constructeur le plus competitif en Europe a l'horizon 2000, Claire Blandin & Virginie Malingre, *Le Monde*, 22/3/1997

(5) Renault's spanner in the works, Padraig Flynn, *The European*, 13-19/3/1997

UNITED PARCELS SERVICE

Question:

Did the Teamsters actually win?

■ **Fairness in the workplace?**

United Parcels Service (UPS) is an American institution. The largest company of its kind in the USA, it deals with an average of 12m parcels per working day and employs 185,000 people. Almost all of them, drivers, handlers and sorters, are unionised and members of the International Brotherhood of Teamsters. At the start of August 1997 the company was hit by a strike with a difference. It was about what one striker in downtown Manhattan called *saving the American dream* of fairness in the work-place.

UPS' business activity has periods of frenzied peak-time work interspersed with off-peak quietness. Being caught up in a highly competitive battle with other parcel carriers, UPS had increasingly come to rely on part-time, as opposed to full-time, workers. Indeed, over the period 1992-7 a good 80 percent of the new jobs created through company growth had been part-time. So far as wages are concerned, the company paid the latter typically between $8-9 per hour as against the full-time hourly rate of $19.95.

The key complaint of the strikers was that UPS, by using the part-timers in larger volume and getting them to double up on short-time shifts, was actually displacing the full-time workers and getting much more work for much less pay. USA Bureau of Labour statistics indicated that, whereas in 1968 the percentage of part-time workers in America was 14 percent, in 1997 it was 18 percent. So the company at least could argue it was not doing anything unusual on this score. But the union held that the company was behaving as if it were part of what commentator Richard Tomkin called *faceless corporate America* sacrificing *real* jobs to the relentless pursuit of profit. Certainly Tony Vee, another Manhattan striker, had no doubts about this. The company's bottom line was, he said, *total greed*. UPS' full-time employees were extremely bitter: they wanted job security and the compensation of a good pay rise. (1)

The UPS' counterclaim that their employment policy benefitted students and housewives who were unable to take up full-time jobs did not carry much weight. Nor did their contention that the union was using the part-time work issue as a pretext to cover its dissatisfaction with other aspects of the company's plans to change the method of pension management. But, the Teamsters' campaign found favour with the American public. Polls showed an average level of support for the union of 55 percent.

The entrenched position of both sides turned the dispute into the USA's biggest in 20 years with no less than 185,000 UPS employees caught up in it. However, Minister of Labour Alexis Herman and her team of conciliators finally found a way through the dilemma in mid-August when, much to the satisfaction of President Bill Clinton, the strike ended. The result was hailed as a *great victory for all workers* by the AFL-CIO leader, John Sweeney (2) and, indeed, many would think of it as *a big win for Big Labour*, according to a *Wall Street Journal* editorial. (3)

But in the cold light of day another picture emerged. Although UPS full-time employees would receive a three percent pay rise, 15,000 would lose their jobs as a result of business lost during the strike. And the company's pension plan change would go through.

To many it looked like a Pyrrhic victory which had done little to change American business culture. Indeed, as analyst Irwin Stelzer pointed out:

Nothing in the UPS settlement can repeal the facts of economic life: globalisation provides a new labour pool on which many companies can draw, and venues to which they can flee if workers' demands become excessive. (4)

On the other hand, it had been a substantial dispute involving the USA government as mediator. And that was something American Big Business could not ignore.

REFERENCES

(1)   UPS strike to save the American dream, Richard Tomkins, *The Financial Times*, 7/8/1997

(2)   Little Big Labour, *The Wall Street Journal, Europe*, 22-23/8/1997

(3)   As (2)

(4)   Bolder Unions strike fear in boardrooms, Irwin Stelzer, *The Sunday Times*, 24/8/1997

VERIZON COMMUNICATIONS

Question:

Imagine life inside one of Verizon's call centres. Now consider the cultural issues involved in the practice of mandatory overtime in Verizon.

■ Work hard, play hard?

In September 2000, in the USA, the Labour Day weekend was a time of celebration for most American workers. It was still a case of good times for the country – rising output, growing employment prospects and rising prosperity – even after the economic *bull run* the USA had experienced during the 1990s.

But Charlene Bobel, a customer-service operator at one of Verizon Communications' high-pressure call centres, was far from happy. Indeed, along with many of her colleagues, she had just been involved in an 18-day strike over the reason for her depressed state, Verizon's practice of forcing employees to do overtime.

Like many other American companies, Verizon was finding the job market in 2000 increasingly tight and was compensating for the inability to find new workers by obliging existing staff to work longer hours. However, its staff had begun to balk at the demands being placed upon them by the company's approach to the new round-the-clock economy it was experiencing. Hence their strike.

They had won important concessions from management, it was true. The new Verizon work contract reflected cuts in *mandatory* overtime working and increases in the period of notice of extra overtime duties that had to be given to staff. It did not move away from the principle of mandatory overtime and was not out of line with the Fair Labor Standards Act of 1938. This law only obliges companies to pay hourly-paid employees extra if they work more than 40 hours a week. It does not stop companies from *demanding* extra work or from firing those who do not comply with the demand.

It is certainly not surprising that, given the late 1999-early 2000 USA unemployment rate of a miniscule four per cent, that many companies much preferred paying even double time to the cost of new hirings. Equally unsurprisingly, those who suffered most from this *disease of plenty* in the USA were hourly workers, like Charlene Bobel and her colleague Viola Figueroa. According to Robert Reich, former secretary of the USA Labor Department, "The movement toward family-friendly workplaces – with telecommuting, flexible working time and child care- has largely been a movement for professional workers". (1) Charlene and Viola did not enjoy such benefits.

Was Verizon's tight labour problem helped in any way by the fact that, according to the Bureau of Labor Statistics, the number of immigrant workers in the USA in 1999 was 15.7 million and that, of these, nearly five million were illegal? Not really, it seems, since the arrivals are divided along a range between

- much-in-demand highly-paid professionals, like computer programmers from India, with $100,000 salaries; and
- poorly-paid workers who often receive less than the USA minimum wage of $5.15 an hour and typically serve as supermarket deliverymen, gardeners and nannies. Illegal immigrants in their ranks can find themselves paid at $3 an hour and forced to work up to 80 hours per week, with the threat of being reported to the Immigration and Naturalisation Service hanging constantly over their heads. (2)

Little wonder that Charlene Bobel, with two small children to look after and a one-hour commute to work, was not pleased by the extra *demands* on her time as a full-time Verizon employee. *Sure,* she reckoned, the pay is good, but the family suffers.

REFERENCES

(1) US Workers Start to Balk at Forced Overtime, Sarah Schafer, *The International Herald Tribune*, 5/9/2000

(2) *The International Herald Tribune,* editorial, 5/9/2000

BOO.COM

Question:

Describe the culture of Boo.com through its various life stages, including its intended revival under Fashionmall. To what extent was Boo.com a business game rather than a business business?

■ Shooting stars

They became known to all in the media and the high-fashion clothing industry as the *Boo Crew* – the team who had created and run the world's biggest on-line sports fashion retailer, Boo.com. Under the inspirational leadership of Ernst Malmsten and former model Kasja Leander, who were featured together for their achievement on the front cover of *Fortune* magazine in 1999, the idea was to become the world's dominant on-line sportswear retailer.

As a UK start-up in the global business world, Boo.com had in its mind's eye the spectacular success that Amazon.com had enjoyed in the retail book market in the USA where it had well and truly upset the market leader, Barnes and Noble. The launch of the company was also buoyed up by the seemingly unstoppable rise in early 2000 of the Nasdaq and Techmark indices. And it was backed by over $135m (£90M) of finance from such investors as Bernard Arnault's LVMH luxury goods group and the Benetton family, with additional support from the USA investment banks JP Morgan and Goldman Sachs.

The wind looked thus set fair for Boo.com's success and it seemed to have much going for it. The Malmsten-Leander strategy was based on the creditable performance of their first on-line business, a bookselling operation in Sweden, called Bokus.com, which they sold in 1998 for some $30m. Their target market, the sports fashion business, was high margin and global; the customer base dynamic and discriminating.

From a modest start with a three-letter web site which cost only $3000 and a personal investment of $3m, the owners rapidly began to attract interested, high-profile investors. Their web site was highly ambitious in its 3D technology; the potential buyer could turn an on-screen image of (say) a pair of shoes or a jacket through 360 percent, zooming in and out at will, and you could even put your chosen clothes on a model to see how they looked. Nor could the launch be faulted in terms of explosiveness. Boo.com was born on the back of a massive advertising campaign in 18 countries and seven languages.

■ Growing up

Charismatic leadership was one of the key ingredients driving Boo.com forward and, in a sense, it had to be so in such a frenetic industry. Looking back over the company's career, Leander remarked, "Everything we did was high profile – we had big ambitions but we were a small private company". (1) This meant, for example, actively promoting the personalities of the owners, with first-class global travel and hotels for key Boo.com staff a must.

The company grew at an explosive rate from seven employees in November 1998 to 400 by summer 1999 at a time when, according to commentator Neil Bennett, "money seemed no object. The salary bill was enormous, there was endless air travel and the West End offices in Regent Street were *top rent*". (2) So far as technology was concerned, the innovatory web-site was supported by a separate and outsourced global ordering and delivery system called Dolphin.

The key problem that arose early on, however, was that the Boo.com web-site's zoom technology just did not work. Indeed, technical problems had delayed the launch of the company until November 1999 and, even then, the web site was extremely slow and prone to crashing. It was apparent that the owners had been too ambitious in their timing of the launch and had radically underestimated the technical complexity of the task, perhaps because the computer system used had originally been designed for an e-commerce opportunity in the car industry.

Even worse was the fact that the company's expensive public relations advisers were working hard to create a demand for Boo.com products, which the technology simply could not meet.

By mid-May 2000, however, the web-site was functioning well and sales were beginning to take off. The February figure had been in the region of $.5m and April turnover was put at $1.1m. The company was selling some 50 popular brands but did not have distribution deals with market leaders like Nike and Adidas.

Somewhat surprisingly, perhaps, the company's founders were given little help by investors in dealing with the company's growth pangs. The company lacked a non-executive chairman and, on occasion, shareholder representatives simply did not turn up for board meetings. When they did, it could still be problematic. As Leander pointed out:

"We would prepare great presentations for them and they didn't even read them. Some hardly spoke English. To run a successful business you need to have some expertise. If only we had had some grey hairs in the organisation, someone who could have guided us and given us the right contacts". (3)

It seemed to many outsiders that all the investors, the Arnaults, the Benettons and Omnia (a Lebanese investment vehicle), ever did was to provide the finance.

■ Money Counts

And provide finance they did, in five tranches amounting, so it was said, to $135m. When Boo.com collapsed in mid-May 2000, all this money had been consumed. The last despairing efforts, a plan to raise another $30m just to remain in business, came to nought. This would have meant halving staff numbers, by closing the satellite offices in Stockholm, New York, Amsterdam, Munich and Paris and by de-merging the Dolphin operation to allow it to take on other e-commerce companies' distributing activities.

Whilst the main investors (Arnault and Omnia) had been prepared to put more money in, they had made a proviso that others should follow suit and, in the event, the Benetton family's investment vehicle, 21 Investimenti, refused. As for JP Morgan, with their fee income capitalised to equal a four percent stake in the company, they had already pulled out in March.

How did Boo.com get through $135m in little more than six months? "If Dean Hawkins had been with us from the start" commented Leander "things might have been different". (4) Dean Hawkins was, in fact, a trained accountant from Adidas who took over as finance director after Patrick Hedelin, a friend of Malmsten and Leander and former banker, left at Christmas 1999. But Hawkins only stayed with the company two months. According to analyst Dominic Rushe, "Hawkins defection signed Boo.com's death warrant. Costs went out of control and investor confidence vanished". (5)

■ Finis?

On the 18th May 2000, the two young Swedes who had had a controlling stake in Boo.com gathered together their 250 young employees to tell that that the business had been placed in the hands of the liquidator. Emotions ran high as staff were thanked by a tearful Ernst Malmsten for their "incredible support". (6)

The *burnout* at Boo.com, together with a Merrill Lynch estimate that three-quarters of European internet firms would disappear over the next few years, put a further crimp in the Techmark Index. E-tailers were under the most selling pressure. Over the period February-May 2000, the Index had fallen 40 percent in value. Price Waterhouse Coopers' pronouncement that a quarter of British internet companies would run out of cash within six months did not help either.

It was not long before the autopsy began. Dr Mike Lynch, founder of Autonomy, one of the most successful global e-businesses in the late 1990s, reckoned that:

> *"There was a certain inevitability about this. The new media orthodoxies of just throwing money at something simply do not work. Investors seemed to think that the internet was magic. There was an incredible arrogance among UK start-ups that the situation here would be just like in the USA. They looked at how Amazon.com caught firms like Barnes & Noble on the hop, but they were stupid enough to imagine that the bricks and mortar players over here were not going to learn from that experience".* (7)

For commentator Neil Bennet, the collapse had all the makings of "a modern morality tale" with more than its fair share of "greed and hype". Boo.com was "a corporate cock-up" whose "plausible technocrats deserved exactly what they got". (8) This was a view echoed by Dominic Rushe, who described Boo.com as "an archetype of the dot.com era". He accused its founders of "profligacy on a biblical scale, living a life fuelled by the three Cs – champagne, caviar and Concorde". (9)

For Therese Torris, an analyst with Forrester Research, it was a more prosaic matter. She saw it as a case of a mistake by an e-commerce business in promoting a 3D technology website when "99 percent of European homes lack the bandwidth access needed". (10)

The liquidators, KPMG, were not, however, downcast by their role and indicated early on that some 30 potential buyers had already expressed an interest. The company had, after all, created a technology and fulfilment platform with high potential value and had some excellent people in its team. All interested parties needed to do to qualify to make a bid was to lodge a refundable deposit of $1m with them. But the situation was, undeniably, a mess. All Boo.com investors had lost their stakes and creditors, mainly advertising and delivery firms, were owed at least $25m. It was thought that either Kingfisher or Chello, a pan-European internet company that Boo.com had been seeking a deal with and whose finance director was, in fact, Dean Hawkins, might want to bid.

But, there was no getting away from the fact that what was needed was competence as well as cash. Brian Condon, director of Close Brothers, the investment bank, declared:

> Not all dotcoms are run by 28-year old former models. Most of them are run by experienced managers. Focussing on the burn rate (the rate at which cash is used for working capital) alone misses the point. It is investors' belief in management's ability to implement a plan that counts. Money is not in short supply. What is scarce is skilled management. (11)

■ Tailpiece

On the first of June 2000, Fashionmall.com, a Nasdaq-listed USA portal, bought from the liquidator what it called "the very heart of Boo.com". This included all the internet domain names, trade-marks, front-end contents and contents rights. Other parts of the business such as the e-commerce technology assets and associated intellectual property rights had already been bought. The total value of the acquisitions was put at $.7.5m. Fashion's CEO was elated. "We want to use Boo.com" he said "as a global fashion portal for the UK, German, Swedish, Italian, French and Spanish speaking markets". (12)

But the internet scene still remained gloomy, nevertheless. Especially worrying to hopeful high-tech start-ups was the manner in which financiers were rushing to negotiate new, and more stringent, terms. Typical of the attitude of investors was that of Martin Bodenham, CEO of Ernst & Young's Internet Incubator. This is the accountancy firm's division that supplied services, rather than capital, to start-ups in return for an ownership stake. At issue for financiers were the specifics of the entry price they would pay (i.e., the number of shares per £ of investment) and the exit strategy (protection in the event of things going wrong). The fact that the eventual capital used up by Boo.com turned out to be double the original estimate of $135m, after a revision by KPMG in August 2000, did not inspire confidence. Indeed, trade creditors alone were owed no less than $75m.

One man who was not gloomy about the fact of Boo.com's having burned through over two million dollars a week in its meteoric, no-profits career was Luke Alvarez, a senior executive with EMAP, the media group. In early June 2000, having just signed up one of the high-flying members of the Boo Crew, he commented wryly:

Boo effectively spent $135m educating 300 people on how to launch and how not to launch an internet retailing business. No one else has that experience. That lesson has a certain value in the market. (13)

Nor was Fashionmall.com at all downcast by the prospects of making a return on the assets it had acquired. Indeed, by mid-October 2000, it had already set up a web site, containing a survey and a sign-up list, which aimed to restore Boo.com to fame as "a global hotline and arbiter of the latest trends in street fashion for young adults aged 18 to 30". (14) The notion was one of

- chat rooms where someone in (say) Amsterdam could find out what's *new and hot* in (say) Chicago;
- "style editors" who would be picked from the website audience and rewarded for selecting winning fashion items. These would build to a group of 500 *global trend* products to be sold by Miss Boo, the site's digital assistant;
- a separate boutique where Boo.com partners would e-tail their products, paying their host for the privilege.

The strategy of the new head of Boo.com, Kate Buggeln, a former retailing consultant, was, she said, to create "a magazine that sells product" on the web in order to capitalise on the "immense amount of interest in Boo" that still existed, i.e., 35,000 visits per week. Where was the profit coming from this time? A mixture of low costs (ten full-time employees only), a gradual roll-out (step-by-step in Europe starting in 2001) and healthy revenue from boutique sales and advertising. Profitability and a workable business plan was the focus, not infrastructure, she declared.

But it was not to everyone's taste. One particularly sceptical analyst was Ruth Porrat, MD of Morgan Stanley Dean Witter's Technology Group. She reckoned:

> *Morbid curiosity should get them traffic – but that doesn't make a business.* (14)

REFERENCES

(1) From Boo to Bust, Dominic Rushe, *The Sunday Times*, 21/5/2000

(2) Now it's boo.gone, Neil Bennett, *The Sunday Telegraph*, 21/5/2000

(3) As (2)

(4) As (1)

(5) As (1)

(6) It all ends in tears at boo, John Cassy and Mary O'Hara, *The Guardian*, 19/5/2000

(7) As (6)

(8) As (2)

(9) As (1)

(10) As (6)

(11) As (1)

(12) Boo.com assets fall to US buyer, *The Guardian*, 2/6/2000

(13) Life After the Crash, Chris Ayles, *The Times*, 14/6/2000

(14) *The International Herald Tribune* 16/10/2000

INDEX

to chapters 1 – 8